Joy
Bliss
THIS

A teacher's journey

WILLIAM QUIGLEY

Paperback ISBN 9781946824110
Hardcover ISBN 9781946824127
Ebook ISBN 9781946824134

Editing, Interior Design, and Cover Concept:
Janet Angelo of INDIEGO PUBLISHING

Cover Design by Kura Carpenter
www.kuracarpenterdesign.com

Library of Congress Control Number: 2017962610

Publisher's Cataloging-In-Publication Data
(Prepared by The Donohue Group, Inc.)

Names: Quigley, William, 1969-
Title: Joy bliss this : a teacher's journey / William Quigley.
Description: [Florida] : IndieGo Publishing LLC, [2018]
Identifiers: ISBN 9781946824110 (paperback) | ISBN
9781946824127 (hardcover) | ISBN 9781946824134 (ebook)
Subjects: LCSH: Quigley, William, 1969---Career in education. |
Teachers--Biography. | Teaching. | BISAC: BIOGRAPHY &
AUTOBIOGRAPHY / Educators. | EDUCATION /
Professional Development. | EDUCATION / Teaching
Methods & Materials / Social Science.
Classification: LCC LB885.Q542 J69 2018 (print) | LCC
LB885.Q542 (ebook) | DDC 370.92--dc23

Published in the United States of America by
INDIEGO PUBLISHING LLC
Think Indie. Go Create. Publish.
www.indiegopublishing.com

Saint Thomas More:
"Why not be a teacher? You'd be a fine teacher, perhaps a great one."

Richard Rich:
"If I was, who would know it?"

Saint Thomas More:
"You, your pupils, your friends, God. Not a bad public that."

~ *A Man for all Seasons*, **Robert Bolt**

We are on a journey to keep an appointment with whoever we are.

~ **Gene Roddenberry**

Drive away and try to keep smiling. Get a little rock and roll on the radio and go toward all the life there is with all the courage you can muster. Be true; be brave; stand. All the rest is darkness.

~ *IT*, **Stephen King**

Dedication

To my first teachers, my parents, who taught me all the lessons that helped to make me the man and teacher I am.

To my brothers and sisters, who have always been on this journey with me, thank you for being the best.

To all the colleagues, the great teachers, the leaders, the comforters of kids, thank you for being my friends and my guides. I have seen excellence in so many, but I especially must acknowledge Linda Gass, Carter Hannah, Roseanne Ganim, Sue Cooper-Smith, and Carrie Hyacinth.

To my mentors, especially Jeanne Kurth, Elfie Israel, and Debbie Tabie, you were the standard, the excellence I sought.

To the great leaders who always encouraged excellence in me, especially Frankie St. James and Peter Bayer.

To all my friends, especially Nat, Sean, and Tracy, who were always there for me and have always pushed me to be better.

To my editor and publisher, Janet Angelo, for making my words shine, and for becoming my friend.

And to my students, all the names, the faces, the souls, the kids who have blessed my life, I am nothing unless I am your teacher. You've made my life. I've learned far more from you than I ever taught you, and I owe you more thanks, more appreciation, than language can express. When my teaching career is over and I look back on my life, I will be able to say with nothing but pure, deep, joyful pride, "I was a teacher!"

Thank you for letting me be yours.

A Note from the Author

We are our stories and the journeys we've had. We are made up of millions of moments filled with people, places, and experiences. This book is the story of all the things that have impacted my journey as a teacher and brought me from where I was to where I am. I give this account to understand where I have been, but also to help you have a better understanding of what I know to be true about kids, teaching, and education. I hope that in some meaningful way I can make your journey easier.

Of course my journey is not yours; you may be reading this in a different state, a different country, and probably a different era than the one during which I honed my craft as a teacher. Though the place, the journey, and the era may be different, I hope our goal has been the same: the search for excellence. Though I do not claim to have found it, I do know that excellence is the destination, and I believe the things that have happened to me can serve as signposts to you, to help you on your journey.

A career in education was never the journey I expected to take. I never expected that the things that happened to me, both good and bad, would happen.

I never imagined the kind of teacher I would become or the kind of classroom I would have.

I always knew I would be good at conveying information, but I never expected the kids to like me.

I never expected that I would care far more about my kids as people than the subject matter I taught.

I never expected any of this, but I am glad for the journey. I am grateful for what I have learned, and I can look back at the dark places and see how they lit my path toward the man I would become.

In the end, we are our stories, and this is mine.

William Quigley

Joy *Bliss* This

My Journey

Your Journey

Work on Yourself

Work on the Class

Work on the Work

My Journey

Endings, Beginnings, and the Ends of Beginnings

T he day before winter break in 1993, a meeting took place in the office of my principal, Frankie St. James. Outside the sun was shining, a glorious winter day in South Florida. Inside, the atmosphere in the room was the opposite — cold and bleak. Attending the meeting were five people: the two teachers who had mentored me since August, the school's two assistant principals, and the principal. All five were caring and dedicated educational professionals. All were people I greatly admired. Each was an excellent example of great teaching and leadership. All of them worked tirelessly inside the classroom and in the making of a school for the best interest of kids and teachers. I had turned to these dedicated coworkers when I needed advice and guidance. Each had cared about me and helped me, and had gone out of their way to assist me on my journey.

I was not present, but I was the subject of the meeting. They were discussing whether I should be fired.

And the truth is, I should have been.

I had been in almost every way possible a complete failure as a teacher, not just failing in the ways so many new teachers do but in completely new and novel ways.

I was boring. My lessons were dull. I lectured hour after droning hour and called it teaching. Kids fell asleep in my class or worse, they acted out, and honestly, when they did, how could I blame them? I didn't have the skill or the ability to make my class the passionate and vital place it deserved to be. I was teaching block schedule classes which meant each period was nearly 90 minutes long; this coupled with no idea how to really engage and involve kids led to disaster.

I had no control, no classroom discipline. I didn't have the faintest idea how to get a group of thirteen-year-olds to listen. Though my classroom was never chaos, it was also never really in control.

As an example of my lack of control, let me introduce you to one of my students. I will call her Karen. Karen had nothing but contempt for me. My class was so boring that she made her own excitement. She talked back; she yelled things out; she asked inappropriate questions. I responded in the best way I knew how, which was to confront, respond haltingly, answer shaking with anger, turn beet red, and challenge her in front of her peers.

These daily confrontations were some of the few times the class seemed to wake from their stupor and pay attention to what was happening.

Our school had an in-school suspension program, and whenever a student acted up, we teachers sent the student to this "class." For several weeks straight I sent Karen out every single day. The ultimate example of my lack of ability to manage my class took place one day when I was going on and on about the settlement of the American West circa 1880. I had placed Karen in the back of the room and surrounded her with my very best male students. On this day, I noticed that the boys were all looking at her. I left my lectern and hurried over to where she sat. When I got there, she was sliding a pen in and out of her mouth making slurping, sucking sounds, and just as I approached, she looked at each of the boys and asked, "Okay, who's next?"

Of course I threw her out of the class.

In each of my six classes, I had students who were like Karen: they ran the class, and I had no idea how to get them to stop. What is worse, the good kids were getting cheated out of an education.

As the meeting in my principal's office progressed, all of my failures during the first half of the year were talked about openly. They hashed out each of the times and situations when administration had been alerted to my classroom failures. They were well aware of the number of times kids had been thrown out of my class. They knew all about my lack of control and how poor a job I was doing trying to control my classes.

My lack of control was only matched by the lack of quality teaching that was going on in my classroom.

There was another cloud, never mentioned, but it hung over every word spoken in the meeting that day. There had been other good reasons, since my first week of school, to wonder about my fitness as a teacher.

I am so glad those reasons weren't discussed openly with me there, because I would have simply died, died, died if they had been.

I have always been self-critical to a fault. It would have crushed me to hear my own words presented to me as an accusation, to sit through the list of my professional failures, and to hear a litany of all the mistakes I had made. It would be several years later that I would be told about the meeting at all. And even though by then I had figured out how to do the things I had so readily failed at as a new teacher, I would grow red with embarrassment at the memory of that impotent time and my inability to do this job.

I should have been fired.

Five months of futility and a nearly complete lack of success had culminated two days prior with an event that led to this meeting to discuss my fate.

I was attending the middle school Holiday/Christmas band and choir performance. I had been a band student during my middle and high school years. To this day, my favorite school memories are of my time spent in marching and symphonic band. It was exciting to be on the other side, to sit in the audience, to be a teacher of the kids performing. The performance was everything middle school band is: a few squeaks, lots of sharp and flat notes, the sounds of young voices singing sweet familiar carols, and tons of proud parents.

In one of the last pieces the highest middle school band played, they featured each of the sections of the band, and when each section came up in the song, that part of the band stood up, played several bars, and received attention, applause, and happy parent smiles from the audience. The piece played on, with each group receiving their moment, and as the flute section got ready to play, one of the musicians got her foot caught on something and with a loud crash fell back hard into her chair. There was an audible gasp from the audience. The girl (we'll call her Betty) was one of my students. Betty was like many middle school girls, self-conscious, growing into her body, very sweet, very quiet, and she turned bright red as her friends helped her up so they could play their feature piece.

Without any more disturbances, the band completed the performance, the chorus sang, and the night was filled with the sounds of Christmas.

As I mentioned earlier, the school was on a block schedule, which meant I taught eight classes but only saw four of them on any given day: one day I would see four, the next day I would see the remaining four and then the following day back to the first four and so on.

It so happened that the next day was Betty's class. It was the last time I would see her before winter break.

It was a relaxing school day, with not a lot going on, and at the end of each class, I stood up to talk to the kids. I congratulated them on getting through the first half of the school year, telling them how much I appreciated all the work they had done and how good it had been to get to know them.

When it came to the end of Betty's class, I started with my usual spiel about how the year had gone so far, but I decided at the end to deviate from my script:

"This whole school year I expected you to fall down and fail, but I guess Betty did that for you last night." The moment the words left my mouth, I wanted to take them back. I looked at the class and then at Betty expecting them to laugh, but instead they gasped, and Betty's face was turning brighter and brighter red. I gulped and started to speak again, stumbled and finished going through the usual goodbye blather that I had used in my other classes, and every time I looked over at Betty, I could see her getting more and more upset, a growing horrible look of utter and complete embarrassment suffusing her expression. As I was about to finish speaking, she stood up and ran from room. I was shocked, and I reacted by violating every rule of teaching by taking off after her. The bell had not rung, there were several minutes remaining of class time, but I left my students unsupervised and ran after her.

My classroom was in a portable at the back of the school, and as I came down the walkway from my portable, I saw Betty headed straight for the front office a few hundred feet away.

She got to the doors before me and threw them open just as the bell rang.

I entered the office lobby and looked around for her but all the visitor seats were unoccupied. I entered the swinging door that led to the back administrative offices. Room by room, office by office, I peeked in trying to find her. I can only imagine how crazed I must have looked to these people as I searched franticly for her.

As I got near the back of the building, I heard sounds of sniffling coming from the very end of the hall. I knew whose office this was, and what I heard next made my stomach drop with the worst dread I had ever felt as a teacher.

"Oh, Auntie, he was so horrible." This was followed by another wrenching sob. Something was mumbled, and then the words I had said to her in class came out of this sweet child's mouth.

I stopped dead in my tracks.

No one had to tell me how bad this was.

Until that moment, I had no idea I was teaching the principal's niece. I did not know how thin the ice I was standing on was, but I could feel this coldness creep over me, this clammy coldness of just what a terrible thing I had done. I was in much more trouble than just one stupid cruel statement.

I walked in and opened my mouth to speak and to make the best apology I could, but one look from the principal told me it would be better if I just left, so I did. I turned and walked out without a word.

That afternoon, the meeting took place.

As the group talked, it became obvious that I had to go. I had made too many mistakes, and I needed to be fired. I needed to be gone.

But I wasn't.

In the end, two things saved me. One of them was my own doing, but the other was not something I directly controlled.

As the meeting went on and all of my failures were put on the table, only one thing was said in my favor: from the moment I started teaching, I vowed to be good at it. Instinctively, I knew that to get better, I had to seek out people who could guide me, and I had done just that. At some point, I had asked everyone in that room for help. In little and big ways I had never stopped asking, pleading, imploring that I needed help figuring out how to do this job better.

I am certain that I drove my superiors crazy with my constant need for help and guidance. I had spent hours sitting with the very people in this meeting, the ones who would determine my fate as a teacher, listening to their advice, their stories, anything they were willing to share as to how they perfected their art. I went to workshops and sat there wanting to be as good as the presenters. When things went badly in my classroom, I didn't hide from people with more experience than me; on the contrary, I sought them out, anyone with advice, anyone who could point me in the right direction, anyone who would listen. I tried everything they suggested with the hope that it would work. I was open, ready to be guided and taught.

For the first five years of my teaching career, I stumbled, bumbled, failed, and flailed. I was a failure. I was in the dark, bumping around knocking down chairs and desks, and worst of all, I knocked down some kids in the process. But — and this was the one thing that saved me — I constantly asked for help, over and over and over: "Help me. I want to be better. I want to be good. I'll do whatever you suggest, just please help me."

That attitude is what helped save me from being fired that day, but in the end, it isn't what saved my teaching career. What did was when one of the two teachers who had mentored me spoke up and defended me in that meeting.

And here I will name Jeanne Kurth, because she deserves so much of the credit for me becoming the teacher I am today. I cannot sing Jeanne's praises loudly, strongly, or long enough. When I was at the lowest points of my teaching career, she put out her hand and raised me up. She fought for me, defended me, spoke for me. If it weren't for her, I would have left teaching, and I have no idea what would have become of me. A line from the movie *Titanic* does better to express what Jeanne did for me, far better than I could (with a slight pronoun change): "You see, she saved me in every way a person can be saved." And she did. From the moment I met her till this day, I owe her everything. As you will see, her saving me was not just in that fateful meeting but in others sprinkled throughout my first year of teaching. When she spoke for me, she sent the message that I was salvageable, that they needed to give me a chance. "Don't fire him," she told them, "and he will become a success."

Somehow, it was enough.

A Saint Named Leo Shows Me the Way

The ironic part of my journey is that I never aspired to be a teacher. I went to college specifically *not* to be a teacher. I thought anyone who taught for a living was wasting his or her time. Ever since I was a little kid, I had known — heck, everyone had known — that I was destined to be a lawyer, but not just any lawyer. I was going to work in law for a while to gain some experience, and then I would pull out the big guns: I would run for political office and win. Based on what the twenty-year-old me believed, I should be deciding right now whether to run for governor, the Senate, or the Presidency.

I loved to argue. I loved politics. I loved law. I loved history. I watched presidential debates the way people watch sporting events. One of the proudest days of my entire childhood was waking up early in March 1988, having turned eighteen the previous November, to vote in the presidential primary. This was the world I wanted, the adrenalin rush of politics, and all the power and status that comes with that world. I was ready to get out there and shake all kinds of dirty hands, and scratch your back if you scratched mine, as long as you gave me a leg up in politics, all for the benefit of society, of course.

Be a teacher? HAH! What a waste — a waste of an education, a waste of a life, a waste of talent. Besides, when you're a teacher, who benefits? Kids like me who didn't see the value in teaching. On top of that, I'd be poor, unknown, unimportant — the definition of everything that a well-lived American life is *not* supposed to be.

These were the reasons I told myself that I had no interest in being a teacher, but the real reason I resisted wouldn't reveal itself until I finally walked into a classroom as a college student to learn how to be a teacher.

Just as I had always known what I wanted to do with my life, I also knew from a very young age where I would go to college.

I had for years dreamed of the College of William and Mary. This was Thomas Jefferson's college, in stately Colonial Williamsburg, a place of brick, cobblestones, and ivy: the definition in my mind of what a college should look like. I researched the school and knew exactly what GPA they wanted in an incoming freshman, what SAT score I needed, and everything else that was required to get in. All throughout high school, I focused on this one college, and finally, after four years of hard dedicated work, I knew I was everything they wanted. I was so obsessed with William and Mary that when I started my senior year of high school, it was the only college I intended to apply to.

The day I sent off my college application, the future, my life, was set. I would be a William and Mary undergraduate, Ivy League for law school, and the White House sometime after that. Quigley 2008, or 2012, or 2016, or....

As I waited for William and Mary to send my acceptance letter, it never dawned on me for a moment that I wouldn't get in.

One day, while I was shrouded in certainty and going on and on about it, my mom came to speak with me about her doubts. She told me that my father and she were concerned. What if I wasn't accepted at William and Mary?

(My God, was that a possibility?) They had decided they wanted me to apply to a Florida college; they didn't care which one, but I needed to apply to a college in state. After resisting and telling her that she knew that the only college I wanted to go to was William and Mary, and that of course I was going to be accepted, I gave in.

Fine. Whatever. Who cares? I'll apply to some Florida school to make my parents happy, but it doesn't matter — I know what college I'm going to, and I know my future!

When I was a kid, there was no internet, and thus no quick and easy way to research colleges like we can do today. The only way to find out about schools and their requirements were books that described the profiles of colleges, and what they were looking for in the students they admitted.

So the next day I walked into my school's library and asked the librarian if there was a book specifically of Florida colleges and universities. She said yes, pulled it down from the shelf, and gave it to me.

When I tell my students this story, they look at me with mild fascination, curiosity, and horror. To have to look up a college in a book, and not to be able to go to their website where you can see videos of what the college looks like, email students who go there, see pictures and testimonials on tons of chat websites — to them this is just too incredible to believe.

Now, how to do this, to pick a college I would not be attending? When I researched William and Mary, I had spent hours looking through books, reading everything I could get my hands on to make sure it was the right college for me. But this just felt like a waste of time.

And so, I didn't even sit at a desk, I just put the book down and said to myself, *Whatever page I open the book to, that's the school I will apply to. Because who cares? I'm going to William and Mary. This is just to make my parents happy.*

So I did just that.

I put the book on a tabletop.

I opened the book — to the page for Saint Leo College.

Never heard of it? Me neither!

But who cares? I was going to William and Mary. This was just to make my parents happy.

I wrote down the information, and when I got home, I quickly typed a letter saying I was interested in the school. They responded with some material I didn't read, but I filled out the application without giving it much thought and mailed it to them

So I had applied to Saint Leo College. Where was it, anyway? Didn't matter. Why? William and Mary. What kind of school was it? Didn't matter. Why? William and Mary. What kind of degrees did it offer, was it public or private, how old was it, what was its history, how big was the campus, how many males attended, how many females, what were the dorms like, what traditions did they have? IT DIDN'T MATTER. Why? WILLIAM AND MARY!

To this day, I think Saint Leo knew I was applying even before I applied. It seemed to me that within a day of sending in the application, I got my acceptance letter.

But again, who cares? I was going to William and Mary. This was just to make my parents happy.

That's when the phone calls started.

Saint Leo: "Mr. Quigley, we would like to offer you a partial scholarship."

Me: "Thank you very much, but I'm going to William and Mary."

A few days later . . .

Saint Leo: "We would like to offer you a full scholarship."

Hmm . . . William and Mary, in Virginia, $30,000-plus for tuition . . . hmm.

Me: "Thank you very much, but I'm going to William and Mary."

Saint Leo: "How about room and board? We can offer you free room and board."

Hmm . . . William and Mary, in Virginia, $30,000-plus for tuition plus $15,000 for room and board every year for four years, that's $200,000 . . . hmm.

Me: "Thank you very much, but I'm going to William and Mary."

Saint Leo: "And we can give you a job on campus."

Hmm . . . William and Mary, in Virginia, $30,000-plus for tuition and $15,000 for room and board for four years, that's $200,000, and I don't live in Virginia, so I would have to travel from Florida to Virginia each semester, and of course there are books and supplies, and then of course, eventually law school . . . hmm.

And most importantly, I have four siblings, and my parents had no money to help me pay for any of it, no matter where I ended up going to school.

It was right about this time that I got the letter from William and Mary.

It had become my habit to check the mail daily. When I opened the mailbox that afternoon, my heart stopped. There it was, embossed with the beautiful emblem of the vaunted College of William and Mary. Suddenly, I was terrified. Holding it in my hand, that letter felt like a precious and fragile life-changing gift.

I dumped the other mail onto the kitchen counter and walked into my bedroom clutching the letter. I sat down on my bed and tried to work up the courage to open it. What if they said no? My whole world and four years was in my hand.

At some point, the fear, hope, and anxiety got the best of me, and I just had to open it.

The letter was written on thick, clean, crisp paper, *just the sort of paper William and Mary would use*, I thought. I took a deep breath, unfolded it, and looked at the opening sentence. I will never forget the first few words:

"Congratulations, William Quigley, you have been accepted...."

I made it, did it, got in, my dream, in my hands, it was everything, every, every, everything! All my dreams, the hopes of my life burned brightly like the pure flame of knowing every step of my own path — the man I would be, the lawyer I would become, the elections I would campaign for and win.

IT WAS EVERYTHING.

Me: "Thank you, Saint Leo, yes, I've decided to come to your college."

I put down the phone.

Why I did it was simple.

My parents had no money. I had no money. Besides, the ultimate goal had not changed. I was going to be a lawyer, so my choice of undergraduate school didn't matter. I would go to William and Mary Law School. I would take Saint Leo's money and their degree and still make my dreams come true.

But I still had no clue as to where or even really what Saint Leo College was. What if I had taken their money and made the worst possible mistake?

Turns out I had nothing to worry about. Saint Leo was exactly what I needed in a college. It was so small that it had fewer students than my high school, South Dade High. It was situated near the city of Tampa but far enough away that it felt remote and separated. It was in one of the few areas of Florida that actually has hills.

Saint Leo was also an intriguing mix of old and new. Yes, the school was only a hundred years old (during my time there it celebrated its 100th anniversary), which is not old by the rest of the country's standards, but by Florida standards, it's ancient. The school had not always been a four-year college. First it was a prep school, then a two-year college, then a four-year college, and finally a four-year university.

The very center of the school housed administrative buildings on one side and the oldest dorms on campus on the other. Between them spanned a beautiful lawn of lush green grass and ancient moss-covered oak trees where you would often find kids lounging or playing Frisbee. To the east of this central point was the student center where the school cafeteria was and then beyond that three dorm buildings. South of the dorms were the two main classroom buildings and the front entrance to the college. To the west of the school center was the old Saint Leo Church that also housed the monastery. A bridge connected the largest part of campus to two more buildings of girls-only dorms, and beyond that the nunnery and the small chapel that was used by students for Sunday services. The entire school sat along the banks of Lake Jovita and was bordered to the east and west by orange groves. Directly to the west was the city of San Antonio, and to the east was the much larger town of Dade City.

It was a sleepy and quiet place, a perfect place for someone who felt a pull to a particular place and a particular future, and who needed the time to rethink both.

Saint Leo was also a desperate place. Situated forty-five miles northeast of Tampa, a little more than an hour from Orlando, it was a forgettable stop off Interstate 75, a school searching for a reason to be. It was literally nowhere geographically, and it was going nowhere as a university.

For my entire adult life, I've had to explain where Saint Leo is located: yes, it is in Florida, and yes, I know you have never heard of it. It was a school in search of an identity. It desperately wanted to be a top-flight liberal arts college, to attract great students and to make itself grow and matter. The population of the college had dipped dramatically in the years before and during my time there. The majority of its financial support was from the satellite campuses situated on military bases throughout the world. The school had embarked on an ambitious plan to improve its standing. They had created an honors college and had aggressively put money into giving scholarships to the best-qualified students who applied. Saint Leo was trying hard to buck its well-earned reputation as a school of last resort. In the northeast, Saint Leo was considered the college you could get into when you couldn't get in anywhere else. To the locals, it was a rich preppy school for kids who weren't even sure they wanted to go to college. The school had no identity and no name recognition. Even people in the Tampa Bay area did not know of its existence.

When I visited Saint Leo in the spring of my senior year, I felt completely at home as I walked around the campus. It just felt right as my parents and I explored the school. I could see myself at this place. There was one large lecture hall at Saint Leo, and it was empty when we entered it. My father took that moment to sit me down and have a conversation with me. "You can be anything you want to be here, son. You're a tabula rasa, a blank slate. No one will know you, you will know no one, so come here and just be whoever you want to be."

It was what I needed to hear. I wanted so badly to throw off the skin of the person I had been. I had always found it uncomfortable being around kids my own age. I found the give and take, the process of making friends incredibly difficult. I had tired of being the nerd, the loner, the quiet one. I was ready to go someplace where I could start over. The great thing about places like Saint Leo is they allow you to be the proverbial big fish in the small pond.

The moment I got to Saint Leo as a brand-new freshman, I immersed myself in student life. I joined the Pre-Law Society, Campus Ministry, helped to co-create the Young Republicans, became a justice on the Student Court, and became a writer and eventually the editor of the college newspaper. I loved being involved, and most importantly, being known. That was one of the giant advantages of going to a small school. Everyone knew everyone.

I also knew my professors by name. Not only that, I went to their houses, drank with them, partied with them, got drunk with them, and more importantly, I got to know them as people. In one memorable occasion, I lay in bed and discussed sex with my Philosophy of Love professor in his bed with my girlfriend at the time, the three of us discussing love and sex and being young and free. I felt completely comfortable sitting in professors' offices learning about life even as I was learning whatever material they were teaching.

My fellow students were equally great; again, the thing about a small college is that students cling to each other. Sure, there were campus cliques, but it was completely common to be at a party with every kind of kid of every background and every interest. I had a close friend who was a frat guy, another who was one of the leading actors on campus, a third who was an amazing artist, another who was the devoutly religious leader of the Campus Ministry program. I would float from a group of artists, to a group of religious kids, to my fellow tennis players, to a mixed table.

At Saint Leo, I fell in love for the first time and had my heart broken the first time. Had my first real kiss and took the first few steps to finding what kind of emotional and sexual life I wanted. I explored and learned at Saint Leo.

I learned and grew so much in that place. I grew up there. I became a man there. I met so many great and wonderful and good people there. I had a series of passionate and caring educators. I had fun, silly fun, getting stupid drunk, being crazy, running across campus. I entered Saint Leo as an English major (it was part of the scholarship that Saint Leo gave me) but quickly changed it to pre-law, a program that has disappeared at most colleges today but then it meant taking lots of history and political science courses. I loved my classes, but more than that, I loved my professors. Most of the classes I took were taught by one of two professors: Dr. McGee and Dr. Horgan. They taught what it meant to understand social science; they gave me discipline and taught me the ways of a historian.

They showed me that history is not a series of facts or disparate events but rather a series of choices, of connections, of lessons, and if you find the thread, you can see the past, the present, and the future in a unique way.

I owe my interest in these subjects to my father. From an early age, I had been immersed in history, government, and politics. It was common at the dinner table to discuss the politics of the day or the history of a thousand years ago. I am so grateful to my father for instilling in me that passion. I'm even more grateful to the two patient and passionate educators I met at Saint Leo who helped me take that interest and understand the academic study of it.

Teaching Internship: Good, Bad, and Ugly

I had a clear idea of what I wanted for my life: college, law school, law practice, meet a girl, get married, and enter politics. There was no telling how far I would rise!

And that would have been my life had it not been for my parents.

Two times in my life, my parents intervened, and by doing so, they completely changed the direction of my life. The first happened when my mother insisted that I apply to a Florida college. This led me to Saint Leo. The second happened at the end of my sophomore year at Saint Leo, but this time, my father stepped in and changed everything.

As I prepared to return to Saint Leo for my junior year, my father expressed a concern that he and my mother had about my future. They were worried that by picking pre-law, I was setting myself up for possible problems.

The conversation began with a very simple question: "What if you don't want to become a lawyer? What if at the end of four years, you graduate with a pre-law degree, and you don't want to go to law school? What job can that get you?"

I listened with the same open mind and gave the same rational thoughtful response that I had given my mother two years before when she wanted me to apply to a Florida college.

I didn't want to do it. I knew I was going to law school. End of story. No fear. No worry. Stupid question. Stupid conversation.

My father continued. "We are just worried that you won't have skills or anything that could possibly get you a job when you finish college if you change your mind about being a lawyer."

I responded again that I knew my path and knew what I wanted. I had spent two years at Saint Leo, gotten straight As, and each political science or history class I had taken had reinforced my career goals.

My dad pulled out the ultimate argument, the parent card.

"We are helping you pay for college, you live here in the summer, and this is something we want you to do."

I had no comeback for that. He was right.

What I didn't know at the time was there was another reason my father felt so strongly about this. One of my father's greatest embarrassments and failures drove him to have this conversation with me. Years ago, he had gone to college with a specific trajectory in mind. For him it was medicine. But like so much of my father's life, it meandered away from where he wanted to go. Part of it wasn't his fault; his father died during his freshman year at Kent State, so out of necessity, he had to quit for a brief period. But the larger fault was his: he studied botany, biology, chemistry, sociology, psychology, history, and by the end of six years, he had many credits but nothing that would actually give him a degree. So he left without one. It haunted him the rest of his life. It contained and controlled his life, and prevented him from ascending in his professional life.

He was expressing this fear without naming it.

I agreed to my parents' wishes, and I went back to college with the intent to take some classes that would fulfill my father's wish but that would not interfere with my goals.

I knew from the get-go that science was out. I had always struggled with the subject. It was the only C I had gotten in high school. I had already taken the one required science credit in college and was done with the subject forever. So there went nursing, engineering, medicine, and every other career that required science classes to earn a degree.

I considered business, but the truth was I just never could see myself as a businessperson, owning or running a business or working as a manager in some cubicle world. Worse yet, I feared becoming some mid-level go-nowhere administrator, the twenty-fifth vice-president of some lame company that no one knew or cared about.

How about accounting? Unlike science, I had always been a good if unremarkable math student. I loved statistics and keeping track of things. But the thought of spending my life adding up other people's money seemed horrible to me. It wasn't that I expected to be rich. I always somehow knew that even as a lawyer, it was not likely that my life would be about riches, but if you'd asked how I felt about fame — well, that was a different story. You couldn't be an un-famous President of the United States.

So I was stymied. What to do?

And then, a conversation with a fellow member of the newspaper staff led me in the direction that would change my life. Dan told me he had taken an introduction to education class and really loved it. It had gotten him seriously thinking about being a teacher.

"Teaching?" I shot back. "No way!" I had no interest in wasting my life teaching a bunch of kids.

But then he said the thing that convinced me to take the class. He told me it was easy.

Cool! Make my dad happy.

Easy A.

I'm going to be a lawyer anyway.

So I signed up for Introduction to Education.

It's such a laughable title for a class. If there is anything any kid in college doesn't need an introduction to, it's education. We have been in the education morass for thirteen, fourteen, fifteen years. We have suffered the indignity of terrible teachers, boring classes, and mindless lessons.

Intro to Education, I've met you, and I'm not interested.

I would come to find that the way Saint Leo structured their education program was unusual for that time. Lots of people I taught with who became teachers in the 1990s, especially at large universities, spent their two years in education classes learning the theory of teaching, being taught what a teacher does and how they do it, by college professors. They taught a few lessons to other college students, but never in a real class with real kids, never in a real school with thirty little faces looking up at you. Often at other colleges, you do not get into a real classroom until the final semester of your senior year when you do your teaching internship.

This can be likened to teaching a musician how to play an instrument by explaining it to them. Imagine you're the musician, and you never actually get to play the instrument. Then, after two years, you are expected to perform a solo recital. Good luck with that!

For many education majors, it is only in their senior year, four months before graduation, standing in front of a group kids teaching a lesson for the first time, that they realize, oh my God, this is not for me. Luckily, Saint Leo did not do this, probably because of the size of the school and the philosophy of the department. Every education class, from Intro up, required the student to go into the classroom and interact with kids. Even if it was just to observe, you were in the classroom watching real teaching occur.

Even with this much exposure to the real environment of secondary education, I still wasn't completely convinced that teaching was for me.

My reasons were the same that many people give when they say they would never be a teacher: mediocre income, lack of position in the community or society, lack of importance. I believed that teaching was a job people did when they had no interest in making a larger impact on the world, and worse, it never gave them the opportunity to reach their fullest potential.

I believed all of this to be true, but that wasn't the real reason I didn't want to be a teacher. Mainly it was because the teachers I'd had from elementary through high school were unremarkable for the most part. I'm sure they tried hard, and in their way, they cared. But the vast majority of teachers were a parade of people for whom I was just another kid, just another student, just another desk filler. Most teachers seemed to come from the same school of thought: you teach by talking/lecturing, or you teach by giving kids a textbook to read and telling them to answer the questions at the end of the chapter. After some time — a few days, a week, two weeks — we would get a test, and then it would be time to move on to the next chapter. Lessons were didactic, teacher directed. It was hands-on if you consider holding a textbook, a pen, and a sheet of paper hands-on.

The teachers I had didn't seem to care about their students. I don't think this was a conscious decision; rather, this was simply what was done. My teachers wanted me to come in, sit down, shut up, do the work, and leave. At the end of the year, a teacher might know my name, my grade, and maybe remember that I was a good writer or did math well or memorized some scientific ideas or could do the right amount of sit-ups or whatever their curriculum demanded. But that was it. No idea of me. No idea of who the people in their classes were.

Teachers spend more time in any given week interacting with the kids than the kids spend with their parents. But the people who taught me didn't even know if I had parents. They didn't seem to care that I was lonely, or that a kid might have lost his mom, or that a girl was good at ballet, or that the kid in the corner was getting beaten by his dad on a regular basis.

This may sound unkind, but the main reason I didn't want to be a teacher was because of how I was treated by my teachers, which taught me the unspoken message, "Don't care about the people you spend every day with, don't make a difference, don't reach out, don't transcend the course description or the state-mandated curriculum."

Why would anyone want that for a career?

And then I entered the senior high school class I had been assigned to by my Intro to Education professor.

The teacher met me at the door, but not just me; she met each of her students. She smiled at them. She talked to them, not about the work they were doing in class but about sports, the weekend, life. And the kids smiled and were generally happy to see her. I entered the room, and the first thing I noticed was the desks were in a circle. In all my years as a student, I had never seen the desks of a classroom in anything but rows. When the class started, there were no books opened, no notes taken, no lecture given; instead, the students discussed an article the teacher had provided. The students argued. They disagreed. They spoke passionately for or against some political position. Students countered with historical facts relevant to the discussion. The teacher guided, coming back to the article, focusing the class but never telling students what to think or how to think. It was invigorating. I was supposed to be taking notes for an observation paper I was to write about what I saw. I completely forgot, taken up by the passion, the exchange, the ideas.

Not once during the class did the teacher ask the kids to take notes, and there was no bookwork; it was the students expressing their points of view and the teacher guiding the discussion, but it was all about them. The atmosphere was warm and open. From the start of class, there was this relaxed air, but as relaxed as things were, there was real, deep, thoughtful work going on. Instead of studying from the textbook, students were exploring those ideas as a group.

Wait.

School could be this?

A teacher who allows kids to think and to express their own ideas?

And the teacher cares about those kids?

Not just about their grades but about them? As people?

Wait, school could really be this?

Oh, okay — maybe this was just a special lesson, maybe for my benefit.

So I went back the next week, and of course the room was in rows. Sure, the teacher was at the door. And sure, she still seemed interested in them and ultimately in me, but I knew the truth would come out in the lesson. And just as I thought, it wasn't a discussion like the previous week. It was a debate. The class had been divided into two groups. They had spent the week researching the topic. They had worked together as a team to prepare. Each kid had to speak at least three times. They argued, attacked, discussed, and questioned. What had been only a surface-level discussion the week before had become deep, well rounded, and more reasoned.

The hour flew by.

Afterward I sat and spoke with the teacher. She explained her idea of education and how you get to know your kids, and when you do, you get them to open up. The more open they are to you, the more engaged in your class they become. She explained how she felt that real education happens when you give students a background; this is where lecture and the textbook come in handy, but you move beyond that. You go deeper, and you use all kinds of techniques to make learning matter to them.

In other words, make the learning matter; make the kids matter.

I had seen teaching from a new perspective, and it was all about making kids matter. But it also included the things I loved: arguing, debating, ideas, history, politics, and law!

One week later, I changed my major to history and secondary education.

Because of my father, I was on the path to be the teacher I never planned on being at a college I never planned on going to.

Years later, I told my father how I shared this story with my students at the beginning of each new school year, the story of how I became a teacher, and the central part he played in setting the course of my life. As I did, I could see him cringe. He hated the story, and he confessed something to me: as much as I had wanted to be a lawyer and a politician, my father had wanted it just as much. He told me that he felt like I was not using my gifts to their fullest extent, and that it was not too late for me to give up being a teacher to go to law school and become a politician. I didn't know how to react. How do you tell your father that his cringe-worthy belief is the thing that has brought you the greatest joy? Maybe I was wasting some skills (or not), though I defy a lawyer to juggle all the skills a teacher has to have, but it didn't matter. I had found my calling. I would never be President or matter much in any way outside the extent of the four walls of my classroom. And that was okay. It was better than okay. It was exactly what I wanted!

So now that I knew the direction of my life, I had to figure out what that meant. What kind of teacher would I be? How would I get there?

I began my education classes. They were helpful in giving me a foundation, but they were like learning how to play a sport by having someone explain it to you instead of doing it yourself. We learned a lot of education theory, and much of it was incredibly helpful to understanding kids, but it wasn't always practical. We spent very little time learning about how to create a classroom, but one part of the Intro to Education class stood out in this regard. The book described four basic types of classrooms, and though two of the four types are long lost to my memory, two stood out. I remember one vividly because it is what I believe a classroom should be, and it was what I wanted for my classroom.

The other was the authoritative teacher, which I dismissed as unfeasible and the opposite of what a classroom should be. In this paradigm, the teacher is the head of the class, the leader, judge, jury, and executioner of every aspect of the classroom. Rules are rigid and strictly enforced. A student's job is to fit within the classroom structure that the teacher creates. Students have little freedom. Often the teacher follows a strict pedagogy of lectures, notes, and the use of a textbook.

The other kind of classroom is the democratic one. The teacher is the ultimate authority, but the students have choice; rules are agreed upon and often made by the students. Punishment is something that students agree on. The teacher is more of a mentor and coach, yes, a person who delivers information, but also who allows students to forge their own path. The only rigidity in this structure is the firm commitment to the idea that it will not be rigid. Students and teachers are almost on the same level.

As we covered these distinct types of classes, there was no question in my mind the kind of classroom I wanted. What appealed to me was the authoritative teacher, the knower of all things, the leader, the benevolent dictator, if I am being honest. I don't think I had any real interest in being benevolent as much as being in charge. I was interested in control, in structure, and I fell back to what I had always known as a student. Ironically enough, in retrospect, this was the whole reason I never wanted to be a teacher in the first place, and went completely against how drawn I felt to the open classroom I had observed in my sophomore year of college, but at the time, I did not connect the two. I also knew that a "democratic" classroom was folly; it could not work. Students as equals? That's laughable. Students making the rules? Impossible. Freedom, choice, teacher as mentor or coach or anything but authoritative teacher, that wasn't for me. In my twenty-year-old mind, I could not conceive of such a class or how a class like this could work. I wanted a different kind of relationship with my students than what I had experienced in my school years, but I didn't know how to make that possible.

The dirty little secret about the education of teachers in college is that very little of it has any value to a real classroom. The knowledge I found far more helpful was gained from the time I spent in actual classrooms. In the two years I was in the education program at Saint Leo, I observed or got to teach a preschool Montessori class, an elementary class, a middle school Social Science class, and two high school classes.

In the fall, before my final full semester of intern teaching, I took the Methods of Secondary Teaching course, one of the most important education courses you can take. This methods course was taught not by some college education professor but by a high school teacher, Cynthia Brendle. Her classroom was our classroom, the textbook was a group of seventeen-year-olds, and the test was how well we engaged them in learning. One lesson stands out from that course with Mrs. Brendle, the best lesson I ever got as an aspiring teacher. It was one of the very first things she talked about. After we made our introductions, she had each of us describe what we felt was our strength when it came to teaching a lesson. She then told us that we were to teach against this. If we were good lecturers, great, our kids would benefit from this, but we had to teach against that strength by doing other things: debates, group work, projects, simulations. We had to remember that no matter what area of teaching we were good at, if we only used this method in our classroom, we would not be doing what was best for the majority of our kids. For every student who loved it when we lectured and gave notes, there was the kid who needed to get up and do something, or who needed a textbook, or to work with others. We had to constantly keep in mind that our job wasn't to teach the information; our job was to find the best way to teach the kids. I had always thought of good teachers as the ones who were good or bad at lecturing. Now I was beginning to see that good or bad wasn't about who was the better teller of information. It was about deciding the best way to reach kids with that information.

I knew this, but I still really had no idea how to go about doing it. That's the thing about teaching; you enter it with the best of intentions, but you have no idea how to really do it.

I had a lot of great guidance, teachers, advisors, and mentors at Saint Leo when I was preparing to be a teacher. What I didn't know at the time was something that took me a long time to learn about teachers. Now, after twenty-five years, having taught more than two thousand students, I have reached a conclusion. There are two kinds of teachers: those who teach for the kids and those who teach for themselves. Those who teach for themselves have no interest in the kids; in fact, they see the kids as a hindrance to what they are doing. These teachers are usually the complainers; their problems are never their fault, and in their opinion, the kids are dumber, more disrespectful, and more evil every year. In fact, they often don't like the kids and enjoy hurting them. When I say this, I don't mean physically, though that happens too. In some ways, what they do is far worse. How many kids never forget that one teacher who had it out for them, or who enjoyed punishing kids. Today, I avoid these teachers. But when I started, I didn't have the ability to see them for who and what they are.

When I was in college and learning what teaching meant, I met a teacher like this, and he nearly ended my career before it started.

In my junior year, I was assigned to Mr. C to observe and to do my first real teaching. Up to this point, the only teaching I had done was in small groups or to introduce a lesson, but the full load of responsibility had never been on me. This would be my first time being in charge of the lesson for an entire class period. During my first few visits to his classroom, however, I observed him teaching. After a few days I came to realize that Mr. C's classes were joyless, sad, dull places, the kind of class where the kids were beaten down, marking time, getting through just to get done and get out. It was everything that I hated about teaching, teachers, and school when I was a kid.

Then, when I taught my first class lesson, I saw the full power of a teacher to harm when he had lost the joy of teaching or never had it to begin with.

When I started teaching the lesson, I was horribly uptight, every part of me on pins and needles, desperate to do it right. I had spent hours planning the introduction, the lecture, the independent work, and my conclusion. Mr. C sat in the back of the class, and the students listened respectfully, but from the start I felt it was not going well. Most of the class listened and behaved, but three students talked during the lesson, ignored my teaching, refused to do what I asked them to do, and disregarded me as a teacher. When I talked, they talked back; when I instructed, they interrupted; when I asked questions, they shouted a random answer that had nothing to do with what I was teaching. As I went on they kept whispering and laughing, and I knew I had to do something, so I separated them, but that just made them talk to each other across the classroom. I asked them to be quiet, to focus, and to listen, but nothing worked. I was at a loss. I was twenty years old,

I had no idea how to handle this, and three kids who seemed dead-set against me were destroying the classroom.

The longer I went the louder and more disruptive they got. I thought they would quiet down if I shifted from talking to having them do bookwork. The opposite happened; it emboldened them. They refused to work. I walked over and told them quietly to get to work, but they responded with loud refusals. One even went so far as to put one foot up on the desk and his hands behind his head. When I asked him to put it down, he laughed and put the other one up. Derisive laughter filled the room as the other two did the same thing.

Throughout the lesson, the rest of the class had been generally willing to do what I instructed them to do, but as the class proceeded and they saw that these three were doing whatever they wanted, others in the class also refused to work. The talking increased. Notes were passed. What could I do?

I had to get control, so I did the only thing I could think of. I threw the three instigators out of class, and told them to go to the office.

It was one of the worst moments of my life. I had failed. I had no control, no ability to teach, and I had struck out. I was red faced and shaking with anger and embarrassment.

The three slinked out, and the teacher left with them. Sanity and quiet returned.

Two minutes later, the door opened, and the three students came walking back in with the teacher; the kids, laughing, sat down and looked up at me with triumphant smiles. My hands were in a fist.

The class was lost. The kids realized I had no power.

I gave up as the students talked and ignored the work I had assigned them.

I sat at Mr. C's desk watching the minutes go by, and all I could hope was that the time would hurry before something else happened. Ten minutes later, the bell rang, and the kids shuffled out.

I can remember falling into a chair and looking up at the teacher. "What happened? What did I do wrong?"

He looked at me then down at the floor, and then he started laughing. I turned bright red and did everything I could to control my emotions, my anger and embarrassment. I can still remember how little and impotent I felt hearing that laugh.

And that's when he told me what he had done.

The day before I was to teach the lesson, he had met with the three boys and instructed them to purposely misbehave for me. He told them that no matter what I did, they were to disrupt the class, and within reason, no matter what they did, they would not get in trouble. He told me he wanted to see how I handled discipline. He wanted to show me what classes and kids were really like. He wanted to see how I would handle things.

And then he tore me apart for the way I had conducted class. He explained how badly I had handled everything, how I had let the students get out of control, how I should have stepped in, and what I should have done instead. He ripped me and mocked my way of talking to the students and to the three in particular. It was devastating.

While I drove back to Saint Leo mulling over what had just happened, it dawned on me how worthless his lesson was, and the way he had tried to teach it to me. If I had handled everything in that class perfectly, it wouldn't have mattered; those kids had free rein to do whatever they wanted without consequences. There was no lesson here, no learning, nothing for me to take away from this. He had set up a false situation that only served to abuse me and embolden three teenagers to indulge their worse impulses. He had set me up to fail with no chance to succeed. I could have been the greatest teacher ever, handled every situation perfectly, and the kids would have misbehaved anyway. I decided then and there I would never return to that class.

When I got back to college, I went straight to the education professor in charge of the supervision program. As I explained to her what happened, she sat horrified. She told me it would be taken care of. I was removed from the teacher's class, and he was forbidden from having any intern teachers from Saint Leo ever again.

As the first semester of my senior year ended, I prepared for my most challenging experience as a teacher in training. In the spring, I would be assigned to a classroom with one teacher and all that teacher's students. The idea was to take over more and more of the class load throughout the first four to six weeks. By the end of the semester, I would take over every aspect of the job: grading, lesson planning, the delivery of the material — everything would be in my hands. This is every education major's final gauntlet to see if this is the job they really want when they graduate. During my time as an education major, I'd heard lots of stories of education majors who'd made it through three and a half years of college only to get to final internship and hate it so much they changed their major and had to spend another year or more in college. Even worse, they got their education degree only to decide that teaching was not for them.

When I returned to school that semester I took the train from Miami to Tampa. The return trip gave me the opportunity to think about what was soon to come in my teaching internship.

The day I started my internship I was excited and terrified. Finally, I would be in a classroom with a group of kids who were mine to teach. It is one thing to study about teaching, another to observe or do a mini-lesson or two, but when it is all on you, all of it, 100 percent, the teaching, the lesson planning, the grading, it is another thing altogether. There is a reason this is the last thing an education major traditionally does before earning a degree. Everything you have worked toward for four years has prepared you for this moment.

For my internship, I was assigned to teach in a twelfth grade Economics and eleventh grade American History course. Saint Leo, as I mentioned earlier, was in the middle of Florida, which is to say that it was in the middle of nowhere, so the high school I was assigned to was rural. Anyone who has ever consumed bottled water is familiar with the city that bore the school's name: Zephyrhills. As I look back on that time, several things strike me, many of which would have a lasting impact on my teaching career going forward.

One of those was my supervising teacher, Mr. P. He is one of those teachers for whom teaching is a job. He was tall with the curliest black hair and the kind of white skin some call waxy. Mr. P was better known by another name to his students: Coach P. Something that so often infects high school Social Studies departments is the plethora of teachers who are coaches first and teachers second. The old joke in high school is, "What is the first name of every Social Studies teacher?" The answer, "Coach."

Mr. P had grown disgruntled and disinterested in teaching, and his classes showed it. The neglect in his classroom was palpable. To call his room sleepy, leisurely, laid back, was an understatement. His kids seemed catatonic, and being in his classroom for just one day, I could see why. The kids sat as Mr. P lectured, but he mainly gave bookwork, and for the eleventh grade class, it was all bookwork and worksheets, pages and pages of worksheets.

My first day as an intern was a whirlwind of meeting my fellow teachers, being introduced to students by Mr. P, sitting in class and listening to the same lecture or watching the kids do the same bookwork from one class period to the next. I was trying to get down the rhythm and feel of being in a classroom all day and of all that involved. The kids, for the most part, seemed nice if bored. By the end of the day, I was exhausted, and I hadn't really done anything.

The next day Mr. P. walked into the Social Studies teachers' common room and told me that I would be taking over all of the classes, all of the teaching, grading, everything, in two days.

This went against all the protocol that the school had laid out, but I was up for the challenge.

And two days later, that's what I did. For the next four months, the classroom was mine. He was never there. He didn't supervise, give advice, observe, guide, help, or do anything else. I barely saw him; days and days would go by, sometimes weeks, and I would not see him. To this day, I have no idea where he was, and I could not have found him if someone had come looking for him.

I was actually glad he disappeared. Sure, I could have used his help and guidance, but I was also glad to have it be my classroom, because the only thing worse than having no guidance when you are starting something new is having someone standing over your shoulder micro-managing everything you do.

I now had two very different classes to teach, and each of them taught me an incredibly important lesson.

The eleventh grade class was starved for attention from their teacher. And in this I realized the lesson: you can have the best curriculum, come up with the best activity, the best project, have the most interesting textbook, but there is no replacement for the human interaction between the teacher and the students. When you combine the best kind of technique with a passionate caring person, that's when magic happens in the classroom. Teaching the eleventh graders was by far the most fulfilling endeavor in my time as an intern. I ditched all the bookwork and worksheets, and focused on discussions and debates about ideas and concepts. Yes, I lectured a lot, but even this the students drank up. By the end of my time at Zephyrhills High School, I had gotten to know and was able to really explore learning with these kids.

My twelfth grade classes were a little less neglected, and being seniors in their final semester, they were over school. But again, it was in talking with these kids that the best and most important lesson came out. From the moment I stepped into the classroom, an instinct told me that being open with my students was the best way to be. So I talked about Saint Leo, about how I ended up there, about what college was like. I told my students about the fun, the silliness, the parties, the one time my sophomore year we decided to play poker in the middle of the night, setting up the poker table in the elevator as it went up and down the five floors of the dorm. I talked about my friends, the camaraderie, the road trips, the Saturday morning breakfasts that lasted four or five hours with friends drifting in telling the tales of their nights; about laughing and being young. I talked about the nights (of course censoring anything inappropriate) when we had fun just hanging out and listening to music.

At some point during these conversations, the seniors, who were only weeks away from graduating, asked me how to get into college, and they confessed to me that no one, not a parent or a teacher or a guidance counselor, had ever spoken to them about going to college. My heart broke for these kids. I gave them the best advice I could knowing it was not that great. All of this was a shock to me, as my whole childhood and into high school there had never been a question about whether my siblings and I were going to college; it was only a matter of where. I realized that these kids were going to struggle, that when graduation dawned in a few weeks, most of them would not know what to do with their lives. I wished I could somehow push the reverse button so they could have had the help they so desperately needed long before graduation loomed. There was a lesson here too: no matter how much we want to make a positive impact on a kid's life, we are limited by lots of factors we can't control.

But the greatest thing I learned from talking with these kids is the power of stories, of telling your truth, of seeing the value in being honest about what you are going through and what you have experienced. Kids are trying to figure out how to survive in a world they are not really part of and don't understand. Kids can learn so many good lessons from your own life, from your failures, from your journey. No two human lives are the same, but one person's life can be a great guide to another person.

I was able to look back over my years at Saint Leo and feel such accomplishment. I had gotten so much out of my four years of college. Most importantly, I had found an unexpected direction for my life, but I had also found great friends, people who loved me and who I loved. We had experienced a whole lot in our time together — had our hearts broken, gotten drunk (sometimes way too drunk), had huge laughs and great adventures. I had done so much with my time while at school. I had acted in a play, been the editor of the school newspaper, president of the Campus Court and the Debate Society. I had joined and been a leader in tons of organizations. Today, when I speak with kids about their college plans, one of the important considerations I get them to focus on is where they will feel the most comfortable. For some, that might mean a large college where they can be a face in the crowd, a small fish in a big pond; others may need a smaller campus where they can stand out and be a big fish in a small pond. For me the pond was just right. My time at Saint Leo ended with me being given one of the great honors of my life. I was asked to be the graduation speaker. It was a daunting task, but I had no idea of the storms that were coming, natural storms, others manmade, all of them beyond my control, but the worst storm was purely, completely, and 100 percent Quigley made. That storm would have the greatest impact on my life and set me on the journey to be the teacher I am today.

Andrew Churns, Destroys, and Makes an Impact

I graduated from college in 1992. For those of you who were adults at that time, you probably remember 1992 as the height of a recession, a time when America's fiscal and economic house appeared shaky. It would usher in a new president, Bill Clinton, and cause the country to fire the current president, George H. W. Bush. It was a terrible time to be a college graduate looking for a job, something I thought was automatic: you graduated from college and had your pickings of the jobs offered you. This was especially true in education, where the constant mantra was "we need teachers!" Well, here I was, newly graduated and ready to go.

After I graduated college, I returned to my home in South Florida. This was not what I had hoped for, but it was the best way to begin my professional career.

I was born in Ohio and raised there until I was seven years old when my parents decided to escape the frozen north and move to South Florida. I can still remember my father, on a freezing cold winter night, as we all shivered on the drive home from my grandmother's house, asking if we would like to live in a place where it was sunny all the time. I don't remember my answer, but I can't believe that my siblings and I would have answered in any way other than the affirmative.

A few months before I turned eight, we moved to southern Dade County. To the world, there is this perfect postcard view of South Florida, with its vision of pink flamingos, sandy beaches, boats, wave runners, bikinis, beautiful women, exotic locals, and lush tropical greenery — paradise. The place I grew up was far from that ideal. South Dade is rural farming territory. The beach is forty-five minutes away, and all of what defines Miami, that vision of a place exotic and wondrous, was not my life.

I'm not sure how long it took my parents to sour on South Florida; for my mother, I would guess days, and for my father it would take longer. For my mother it would be a life without her family and without the familiar seasonal weather patterns. I don't know for sure, but I would guess my mother never wanted to move from Ohio. For my father it would take repeated job failures, crippling financial problems, and the feeling of being the fishiest fish out of water.

I accepted this new place with some regret at losing the idyllic sweetness of all that meant "home" in Ohio.

My childhood was marked by many things, but the most important to the journey of becoming a teacher were the people, my family in particular, who defined my life as a child. I was raised in a very peculiar home in a very peculiar way by a very peculiar father. My father was an enemy of modernity. This can best be defined by his hatred for modern music, modern meaning anything after 1963, and he had a particular hatred for the Beatles. My father was at best uncomfortable with modern music and at worse fearful of its negative influences. He once told my siblings and me, "If Kiss ever come on TV, you are to turn it off." He never said why, but the lesson was learned: music was bad. So I grew up in a home where there was no contemporary music. I can still remember the first time I heard a rock song. I was in sixth grade. It was a Friday, and the school was getting ready for a dance that night. As we entered the cafeteria they were testing the speakers, and over the loudspeaker came Joan Jett singing, "I love rock 'n roll, so put another dime in the jukebox, baby." I instantly fell in love with and wanted more of this sound.

It wasn't just modern music that my father disdained; he didn't like modern movies, either. The only movies I saw as a child were oldies, and I wouldn't attend a movie in a theater until my freshman year in college. I can still remember that first movie. It was Tom Cruise in *Cocktail*, and the whole experience, the movie, the popcorn, the camaraderie of watching a movie with friends and strangers made it magical.

My father also had an issue when it came to television. He went through phases of taking away television, sometimes because the TV was broken, and sometimes because he felt it just wasn't good for us. Regardless, even when we did have television, we were severely restricted as to when we were allowed to watch; for example, never before dark.

These oddities put me in stark contrast to my peers, but it was more than just hating modern culture that made us different. In my family, we did everything together. To my father there were two forces in the world: family and everyone else, and everyone else was to be feared. My father preached that friends were bad, they would betray you, and family was the only thing that mattered. As far as I was ever able to see, my parents had no friends, and their whole lives were each other and their kids. For me making friends would be a life-long mystery; other kids seemed to make them so easily, going from hello to best friends in seemingly one breath. I didn't know what to do or what to say, and I was horribly awkward and shy.

My father was also a pacifist, hating and preaching against fighting and conflict, instead teaching us to turn the other cheek and to find another way through conflict. We never went to parks, playgrounds, or fairs, and we didn't go to the beach even though we lived in Florida, for god's sake! Vacations would've meant long treks from the depths of Florida to Ohio because of course, if we went on vacation, it would only be to visit family, so we never took any trips anywhere. The one time we went to Disney World was because my father was attending a conference paid for by the hospital he worked for, and the tickets were free. All of these things marked us, my brothers and sisters and me, as weird and different and separate from everyone else we knew.

This separateness marked my entire childhood. It hurt to move in a world of other kids whose lives all seemed normal. It made me feel isolated and separated. I tell you this to let you know how it marked me and greatly influenced me as a teacher. Because of my upbringing, I am sensitive to the lonely kid, the separate kid, the friendless, and I will try everything I possibly can to make a kid's journey as easy as I can.

Reading this, you might think that I felt my childhood was awful, but the opposite is true. I had a great family, I love the way I was raised, and I appreciate how it made me the person I am today.

My siblings were the saving grace of my childhood. I cannot imagine what my life would have been like had I been an only child. I was never lonely because I had two brothers and two sisters.

Three of my siblings, Elizabeth "Beth" Quigley, Bobiann "Bob" Quigley, and Bryan Quigley had the greatest influence throughout my childhood years and helped me navigate the awkwardness of my teen years. They were the ones I ran with, played with, fought with, and argued with, laughed with and had fun with. They embodied the essence of childhood for me. I must give the most thanks to my youngest sister Bobiann for getting me through childhood. Bobiann, who most people called Bobi and who I called Bob, was my constant companion. We were best friends. We stood against the world together, and

I can't imagine my childhood without her, but I do know it would have been filled with a lot less joy.

So in 1992, with my brand new teaching degree in hand, I returned to South Florida, specifically to the land of my childhood, to my family, to an area called the Redlands. It is just north of the city of Homestead and some forty miles south of Miami Beach. It is a land of plant nurseries, avocado groves, and large swaths of land. In fact, it is illegal to build a house on less than an acre of land in the Redlands, and you feel the Everglades here.

But there's more to be said about 1992 than what a bad year it was in the economy. For any adult or child living in South Florida at the time, 1992 was memorable for a much bigger event.

That event was Hurricane Andrew, whose path came across South Florida and churned over the city of Homestead.

In May 1992, I applied for a teaching job in every county in the state of Florida. I sent a letter of introduction, a sterling resume, and letters of recommendation, but every county sent the same reply: not only did they not have vacancies, they actually had more teachers than they had jobs. I felt desperate. I could find nothing.

I turned to the *Miami Herald* classified ads to look for teaching positions with private schools. Three of the schools I sent letters to responded. The first was Redland Christian Academy, a school just down the road from where I lived. The interview went well, but they had no job openings. However, the principal let me know they would keep my application on file, and they would surely call me if a teaching position opened.

The second school I heard from was Carrollton School in Coconut Grove.

Looking back on my life, I wonder how it would have been different had this job been mine. Coconut Grove had always seemed like Shangri-La to me. It was and still is one of the wealthiest parts of Miami, a place of old sedate houses with red-tiled roofs, but also a vibrant art and social scene, a place of theater, food, bars, and clubs. In this oasis of palm trees and million-dollar homes sat Carrollton School, a former palatial house. It had been converted to an all-girls school where the rich and powerful Cuban American population sent their daughters to be educated. The place was gorgeous, a school out of a dream, with as many pools as classroom buildings, manicured tennis courts and croquet, everything a young lady of distinction and breeding needed to matriculate to a life of understood luxury.

My interview with the school went well, and for a moment I dreamed of teaching there, but I found out I was their second choice, which made sense. When you are a private school in a tough economy, you can get great experienced teachers. I was a new college graduate with no experience. Still, I look back on that school and wonder how different my life would have been had I begun my teaching career there.

As August began, so did my unsuccessful search for a job. In the interim, I decided to do a very special activity with my father. For years my father had coached Little League baseball teams. At points over the years, both of my brothers played on teams my father coached. My mother and sister helped out, and when I was in high school, I was my father's assistant coach. Starting that year, there was a new fall league, and my father decided we should coach a team together. This was a great distraction and great fun. My father was an excellent coach who had never had a losing season and had won several championships. I wasn't much of a coach, and I really didn't know how to teach the game of baseball, but I did learn a lot about teaching from my father: the way he ran practices, the way he introduced boys to the game, the way he managed his team all were lessons for me as a teacher.

Years later I realized that good coaching *is* about good teaching. The skills are very connected, and I would think back on the lessons my father taught me on the baseball diamond.

The first time he and all the boys were together, after going over basic skills and how he wanted things done, he sat all the boys down and told them how excited he was to be their coach. He told them that he saw a championship on the field, that he had purposely put together a team of the best players because he loved the hustle of the game, and how, if they just followed his instructions, they would win and win a lot. On the boys' faces, you could see this look of pride, of knowing they were the best. No matter how bad the team played, he gave them this pep talk. It was unfailingly positive, and it set the right tone.

I learned that how you talk to people, especially in the beginning, is the direction your team or your class will take.

The other thing I took from Little League was the idea of practice. Practice is everything when you are dealing with kids. My father always said, "How can you expect your team to react correctly and do what you want them to do if you haven't taught them and practiced what you want them to do?" My father was a big proponent of putting his kids into real game situations. He practiced every aspect, every score, every strike and ball count he could think of. He scheduled practice games with other teams to get them ready for the season. He wanted his team to know exactly what was going to happen so that when it was game time, they could just go out there and play. My father's teams were not undefeated, and they didn't win the championship every year, but they were always well prepared and knew what to do in any given situation.

When I became a teacher, I applied these lessons of building from a position of being positive, of letting kids know they can and will achieve. But just saying a person can is not giving them the process, and the process matters. I realized that I can't expect my kids to know how to act unless I teach them, but if I explain the process in detail, the kids will understand what's expected, and if I have created the positive space for that to happen, they will achieve.

The final school that gave me an interview was on Miami Beach. If Coconut Grove was a desired and exotic country to me, Miami Beach was a different planet. When most people see the name Miami, what comes to mind is Miami Beach, with its bikini-clad beauties and palm trees and beaches and alcoholic drinks with tiny umbrellas in them. That was not the Miami I grew up in. Miami to me was avocado groves, rural, country, large plots of land, and confederate flags. Miami Beach and the Redlands-Homestead area are in the same county, but I'm not sure either is happy with that idea.

Not only was the school on South Beach; it was an Orthodox Jewish School called Mesivta. I knew very little about the Jewish faith even though I was dating a Jewish girl at the time.

But I was desperate! So I went to the interview.

Mesivta was located on one of the main drags on Miami Beach called Alton Road. It was a crumbling two-story 1950s-era art deco building crammed between several apartment buildings and abutting a golf course. I would soon learn that the school was as desperate for a teacher as I was for a job. The interview was with the Rabbi in charge of the school. He wore a dark suit with a white untucked dress shirt buttoned to the top, his head covered with a yarmulke, and from underneath his shirt, strings hung down. I was being interviewed for a secular class. Students spent the morning studying the Torah in Hebrew from 8:00 a.m. to 11:00 a.m. After that they had lunch and physical education, and then from 1:00 p.m. to 6:00 p.m. students took the same classes that every high school student takes: math, science, English, Social Studies, languages — the secular classes that I would be teaching.

The one thing that came out of the interview that would have the greatest impact on what I would teach and how I would teach it was when the Rabbi asked if I could teach a history class that said that the world was 5,753 years old. I answered truthfully that I wouldn't have a problem with that as long as it was understood that I would be able to teach that there are others who believe that the world is much older than that. This was very important because one of the classes they wanted me to teach was seventh grade Geography — hard to teach that landforms that are considered billions of years old while also teaching that the world was created less than 6,000 years ago.

At the end of the interview, I was offered the job. I was ecstatic. Finally, a job offer!

It was only during the long drive home in South Dade that my concerns began. First, the school was nearly an hour's drive away. Second, the school was only offering me $3,000 per class, and they only had two classes open, so in my first year I would earn a grand total of $6,000. I wasn't even sure that was enough to pay for gas and the upkeep on my ten-year-old Oldsmobile Cutlass Ciera. Lastly, I knew nothing about what it meant to be Jewish. What would the kids be like? In what ways would their religion matter to them? Would it matter?

But it was a job, and luckily I had some time to think about it and continue to look for others before I had to let the school know one way or the other.

As August droned on, I enjoyed coaching Little League and desperately searched for another teaching job.

A little more than a week before school would start, I was invited to a pool party hosted by the family of one of the kids from the baseball team. After playing with the kids in the pool for a while, I joined the adults. It was a typical Florida afternoon — hot and sunny with an endless blue sky. Though there were many topics of conversation, there was one the group kept circling back to. Evidently, a hurricane was churning in the Atlantic and was headed toward South Florida. It was the first time the words Hurricane Andrew were said to me. At that moment, we were a little more than forty hours from landfall, and you never would have guessed it based on the weather that day or our laidback mood.

It seemed like no big deal to me. In the fifteen years I had lived in South Florida, we had gone through a series of warnings as various hurricanes headed our way, only to have the storm dissipate or change direction. I even remember the excitement as a child of a hurricane coming, welcoming it and helping my parents prepare not really understanding what a hurricane was or what it could do.

As the kids shouted, laughed, and played in the pool, the burgers hissed on the grill, and the adults talked, Hurricane Andrew was moving closer to us, and we just sat and played and ignored its approach.

My parents had been through this before, so they acted like most Floridians did: it won't land, and if it does, what's the worse that can happen? Initially they decided we would do nothing to prepare. That night there was a special hurricane report on the local news, and we heard words like storm surge and saw what hurricane force winds could do. So my father and I decided to go to the local hardware store the next day to get some wood to board up the windows while my mother shopped for food.

Overnight the storm had not turned away from South Florida and had instead intensified, and it looked more and more likely that it was headed directly for the South Florida coast.

Our trip to the lumberyard was our first indication of just how worried people had become overnight. When we arrived to buy plywood, we could not find the end of the line to get in the store. As we drove away from the store to try to find it, we gave up when we approached the half-mile point. My mother fared no better at the grocery store. By the time she arrived, the shelves were picked clean.

We set about salvaging what wood we had in the garage to board up as many windows as we could. The reason you cover windows is not because you fear the windows being destroyed; instead, if wind gets in, it can lift the entire roof, exposing everyone and everything inside. We did the best we could to prepare throughout the day, putting up as much wood as we had, cleaning the yard of any object that the wind could turn into a projectile.

As the day wore on it became clear that the storm was not moving away, and it was not getting weaker. We had the radio on as we nailed in plywood, and the announcers talked about mandatory evacuations. That was one decision my father was firm about: we were not leaving, not the area or the house. He refused to go to a shelter. Besides, most predictions had the storm going north, making a direct impact on the city of Miami and Miami Beach.

As with most hurricanes, the weather in the hours before the storm hits is often beautiful, clear skies and hot muggy temperatures. As the day turned to night, the storm began its landfall, and the weather worsened. It is an amazing thing to wait for your doom — sitting and eating a meal and knowing it is coming, watching TV and knowing it is nearer, anxious conversations as the danger grows every closer.

Our house was L-shaped. The short part of the L was the family room, kitchen, dining room and living room, and then a long hallway led to three bedrooms ending with the master bedroom at the end. As the wind and rain lashed the house, sometime around midnight I stood in the protected right angle of the L of the patio with my father and watched the pool water rolling as though it were the sea. Beyond that, we had a forty-foot pseudo-pod tree. I looked from my father's face to this mammoth tree and watched as it swayed, dancing in wind that were barely a third of what it soon would be.

Later that night, as everyone else slept, I lay awake listening to the radio as the storm approached and then turned slightly south. Homestead was now in the direct eye of the storm.

By 3:00 a.m., no one could sleep. We gathered in my parents' bedroom because it was the strongest and safest room in the house. It had an interior walk-in closet, three walls of which were concrete. The storm was on us. It sounded like we were on a ship at sea as the rain and wind battered the house. We hunkered down and waited to see what the next few hours would bring.

The first part of the storm was horrific. We could hear the shrill whistle of the wind, and at some point, we lost power and the room was completely dark. After a few hours, the wind died down outside, so my father left the closet to check the house. He returned to let us know that there was some water damage, but other than that, everything was intact.

The weakest part of the storm had passed over us, and it only got worse after that.

The storm strengthened, the wind increased, and the moment the second part of the storm hit, we knew this was different. It was no longer a whistle of wind; it sounded like a demonic freight train screeching and wailing, almost human in its horror. Above our heads, it sounded like something huge was being dragged across the roof. The air pressure kept changing, and we could feel our ears pop. All of it grew louder, angrier, and we kept looking up, wondering if the roof could and would hold.

Huddled in the closet, my parents were sitting against the exterior concrete wall with my younger brother and older sister; my younger sister Bob and I were sitting against the one interior wall. As the storm intensified, the interior wall began to move, and at first I thought it was my imagination, but I looked at Bob, and I could see that she felt it too. Then water began to seep in as the wall moved first one or two inches, then more. I looked at my sister and she looked at me, and in that look, we decided that we weren't going to say anything to the others.

I could feel the fear; it was palpable, and each of us was quiet. My family is never quiet, and yet we sat there, each of us in our own little world of fears and worries, as the storm seemed to go on and on, as the sounds of horror filled the air, and the wall to my back seemed to move more and more.

Finally, the storm subsided and then stopped. Outside, there was silence. After a few moments of quiet, my father stood up and told all of us to stay behind. I can remember pleading with my dad not to go out, certain that it wasn't over yet. But he went anyway.

He came back after what felt like an eternity. My mother looked up at him. "How is it, Bob?"

My father just stood there dazed. He looked shocked, as though the life had been drained from him. All he said was, "We have a lot of work to do." No matter what we asked or how we asked, that was all he would say.

Emerging from my parents' bedroom, the carpet was slightly wet but other than that, untouched. The sliding glass doors were intact, and beyond we could see the patio screening was gone. We walked into the hallway and looked into our bedrooms, and everything seemed fine.

It was when we reached the living space that the effects of the storm became present. The sunken living room easily had four inches of water in it. All of the windows were gone, plant debris littered the floor, and the few chairs in the room had physically been moved. The dining room and kitchen had lost their windows and were covered in water.

Then we rounded the corner to our family room.

When I think back on my childhood, that room played the biggest part of my young life. It was the place where we watched TV, it was the room where I opened the letter to see that I had made it into William and Mary, it was the room of parties and celebrations, it was where we put our

Christmas tree every year, it was the center of my family's life.

And it was destroyed.

The first thing I noticed was the sky. The roof shingles were gone and water rained down. The carpet was soaked, covered in dirt and plants. All three windows and the sliding glass door were gone, and tree limbs and parts of the screening from the pool had been pushed through the windows by the wind. The pool was filled with plants, trees, lawn furniture, toys, none of which belonged to us. The world outside was gone. All trees of any size were flattened. The world I knew inside of my house and the world I knew outside had been changed, altered, twisted — obliterated.

We all just stood there gaping.

We had a lot of work to do.

And work we did. Over the next few days, everything was about survival. We had food and water, but electricity was gone. Luckily, one of our neighbors had a phone, so we were able to talk to my brother, who'd been away at college as a freshman during the storm, and my parents let our relatives in Ohio know we were okay.

As the days wore on, we waited in line for free food, travelled hours to get gas, bought a generator, cleaned up the mess, pulled out the carpet, and got a blue tarp to cover the hole in the roof. Eventually we put up a temporary roof. We waited for our insurance company to assess the damage so we could begin rebuilding, but that took months because a widespread part of South Florida was destroyed.

It was August in South Florida, we had no running water, no way to take a shower or bath, no air conditioning; we had a generator for a few lights and the refrigerator, but that was the extent of the power. Night after night, I lay naked in bed, miserable in the still, humid air, no breeze, soaking my sheets with sweat, trying to block out every sound coming through the wide-open windows and wondering when normalcy would return.

Those days seemed to last forever. In so many ways, my entire family was in a state of shock. In the hours after the storm, each of us exhibited behavior of being a little out of our minds. My father became obsessed with saving the trophies from the family trophy case. We had a house filled with water, we had lost a quarter of our roof, we had no power, and he was worried about my high school debate trophy. My oldest sister Beth wanted the water out, she needed it out, and so she began a single-bucket brigade of getting that water out. My younger sister Bob became obsessed with her own bedroom; the rest of the house was a shambles, but she cleaned her room.

For my part, after having slept not a wink in more than twenty-four hours, the desire to sleep overcame me, and I went back into my parents' closet and collapsed. When I woke up alone in the closet, surrounded by stillness and heat, in a state of near delirium, I believed for a moment that it hadn't happened. That thought was quickly followed by the idea that I might be the last person in the world. That idea was disabused when I heard my mother saying, "We gotta get it out of here, it's going to rot, we can't have it in here." My mother was straining to pull up the orange carpet that covered the family room as my father dried off trophies and searched for a safe place to put them.

In the days and weeks that followed, our life began a new normal. At night, darkness covered the world with only a few points of distant light, and the ever-present hum of gas generators was the background noise at all hours. Driving an hour to get food and water became the norm, and nothing looked or felt familiar. Sometimes while driving home, I got lost a few blocks from my house because nothing looked the same or felt right anymore. Trees, signs, buildings, and houses that had been familiar landmarks were gone.

We did not get electricity until late October. The joke that began to float around those of us who lived in the most rural parts of Dade County was that we would get electricity for Christmas. A few months later, we replaced all the windows, and the following summer, new paint, new carpeting, and new furniture.

In the middle of all this, I called Mesivta and let them know I was still alive, and yes, I would take the job.

So with no power and no hot water, I shaved and dressed, and was off to my first day of teaching. As I drove from my destroyed world, I headed north, and within twenty or so miles outside of Homestead, it was as though the hurricane hadn't happened. I drove from destruction to normalcy to the unknown. I was entering a world that would have been strange to me even if there hadn't been a hurricane.

I didn't know in the most real fundamental way what it meant to be Jewish, especially the type of Orthodox Judaism that was taught at the Jewish school where I would soon be teaching. I didn't understand what an Orthodox Jew was, what a bar mitzvah really meant, what Shabbos was about, what exactly kosher was, and how it meant more than just no pork. I didn't understand the role of the Torah or Talmud in one's everyday life, what defined the holidays of Passover, Yom Kippur, and Rosh Hashanah, Sukkots, and that a Rabbi was far more than just the leader of the religion. I couldn't fathom the traditions of marriage, or for that matter, that these traditions were different in different sects of the faith; how men and women were treated differently, or what a goyim was and what it meant for me to be one.

In other words, I had no idea what I was getting myself into, but it was a teaching job, and I thought I was ready.

BOY WAS I WRONG!

A Rabbi, a Pastor, and a Clueless Teacher

There was much to love about my time at Mesivta. So many of the kids were brilliant. I formed really positive relationships with one of the two classes I was initially assigned to teach, and I learned about a religion that I'd only had a passing knowledge of. But the pluses were far out-weighed by the minuses. Mesivta was not a place for someone who was completely inexperienced; there was no support and no guidance. The school was in desperate financial need — wires literally hung from gouges in the walls — but the school needed every kid to keep it afloat, and the students knew that, so they basically ran the school. Chaos ensued on a daily basis.

I taught a seventh grade Geography class and an eighth grade American History class. The eighth grade class was filled with thoughtful, sweet, smart, and interesting kids. From the first day, teaching them gave me incredible joy. The seventh grade class could not have been more opposite: high energy, loud, unwilling to follow directions, and in general a huge discipline issue.

Many nights I lay awake in sheer terror tossing and turning, trying to come up with every possible way to control that class. My problem was the same problem that marked the first three years of my teaching career in what eventually would be three different schools with three radically different student populations: ME!

I had no idea how to make a group of kids bend to what I wanted. If a kid or an entire class decided they weren't going to listen and behave, I had no idea how to change that. It was beyond my understanding to be able to do what seemed like a simple thing to so many other teachers: get the kids to *want* to follow my rules. At a school like Mesivta, that problem was exaggerated. Very early on, the kids read me well, and that seventh grade class knew I had no control.

One day while I was teaching, one of my seventh graders looked me in the face, picked up a basketball that he had brought to class for some reason, and hurled it straight up as hard as he could into the fluorescent light above him. The light exploded and glass rained down. I quickly moved my kids into the hallway and sent for the rabbi. While the custodial staff cleaned up the glass, the boy was taken away. Fifteen minutes later, he returned with the rabbi. The boy apologized and said he shouldn't have done it because he was a man now that he was thirteen. That was the extent of the punishment.

This was an ongoing issue with the boys who had gone through bah mitzvah: they were men in the eyes of the faith, and they were treated as such by the school and by the rabbi who was in charge of the school. This only led to the boys feeling like the rules didn't apply to them, and if they got caught doing something wrong, they only had to apologize and promise as men not to do it again.

The concept of thirteen-year-old boys being considered men was further proof that this school was a different world from the one I came from. To bridge the gap between my world and theirs, and to try to get them on my side, I started each class period asking them something about their faith. This allowed them to be the teachers. It turned out to be one of the best decisions I made. It allowed the boys to open up and share, and for me to do the same.

These teenage boys bemoaned the fact that they couldn't go on dates, and they weren't even allowed to be alone with a girl. They spoke with contempt and jealousy of the easy lives of non-Jewish teens because they could date girls, and they only spent six or seven hours in school each day. These boys were in school nearly twelve hours a day between their secular classes and Hebrew instruction. They had never been to a movie theater, did not listen to modern music, and had to be home by sundown on Friday for Shabbat, and then for the next twenty-four hours (or more), they were confined to their house or at the synagogue.

In many ways, these boys lived as opposite a life from modern America as possible and still be living in America. I learned about the prayer shawls, the long black curls of hair that young Jewish boys grow, what the coverings for their heads are for and why they wear them, what kosher laws were and what they could and could not eat, and how there is a prayer for almost every activity.

Letting them talk about their lives encouraged them to ask me questions about my life, what it was like when I was a teenager and in college. The boys were fascinated by Hurricane Andrew, and they loved hearing stories about the storm and its aftermath.

This activity also led to a mistake that taught me a lot about what being Jewish meant. These daily discussions started with me putting a question on the board. The kids had to write the question on their paper and answer it in detail. One day, I wrote on the board the following question: What does God mean to you? When the boys walked in there was an audible gasp. I could sense something was very, very wrong, but before I could ask what the problem was, one of the boys raised his hand and said, "Mr. Quigley, you can't write that."

I looked at the board. "What do you mean?"

"Mr. Quigley, you can't write the word God."

"But why?"

Another boy chimed in. "The word God is holy."

"So I can't write it?"

"No!" the class answered in unison.

I grabbed the eraser to get rid of it.

"NO! YOU CAN'T." I paused with the eraser above the word and turned back to them.

"But why not?" I was totally confused.

One of the best students in the class explained it to me as though I was the dumbest five-year-old in the world. "The word God is holy. You cannot erase it now that you've written it because it *cannot* be erased. It is holy." He said the words with such emphasis that it finally got through to me.

I looked back at the sentence. "You mean it has to stay there forever?"

The boys nodded their heads.

Months later, after I had left Mesivta, I came back to visit, and when I walked into this classroom, my first classroom as a teacher, the word *God* still graced that whiteboard.

As my time went on at Mesivta, I became really good at accidentally violating Jewish rules and traditions. In the front office was a receptionist/secretary. Every day I had to go into the office to check in. Every day I greeted the receptionist, and nearly every day I complimented her hair, which I thought was beautiful. Finally, after several weeks of this, she kindly took me to the side and said, "It's a wig." It had never dawned on me that one day her hair was short, the next long, sometimes blond, sometimes black. I had just seen it as beautiful without recognizing what was obvious. She then politely explained that in Eastern European Jewish tradition, women shave their heads in preparation for their wedding. From that point on, even after their hair has grown back, they never show their real hair; instead, they wear a wig. The idea is that a woman's beauty, her real hair, should only be seen by her husband and no one else.

In another example, I had become friends with the only other non-Jewish teacher on staff. She and I carpooled and swapped stories about the crazy funny things that happened at Mesivta. As a woman, her restrictions with the boys were far greater than mine. She was forbidden from ever touching the boys who had gone through bah mitzvah; she had to watch how she spoke to them and how she gave them work.

During the second week of school, there was an open house. The welcoming session was held in the small synagogue inside the school. She and I arrived early and sat in the back of the room. As parents filtered in, we continued talking not really noticing what was going on around us. Shortly before the meeting was to start, I looked around. On the side of the room where she and I sat, all of the other women had taken a seat. On the other side of the room sat all of the men. Men and women in the orthodox faith do not sit together in public gatherings, especially in the synagogue, and during religious services, they would be behind a screen so the men and women couldn't see each other.

I didn't know what to do; should I get up and leave the person I was friends with, or stay and take the chance of offending the parents? Not knowing what else to do, I stayed in place. To this day I don't know if it was the right thing or if what I did was offensive yet forgivable because I was non-Jewish.

The ultimate example of my fish-out-of-water experience at Mesivta happened after I had been at the school for a month. Because of when the secular classes began, I often had not eaten any lunch at home. A block or so from the school was a Walgreens. So, one day, I went there to find something to eat and selected a Lunchable. I carried it back to school to eat in my classroom. As I was about to walk into the building, I saw the rabbi, who greeted me and asked what I had to eat. I showed it to him, and he told me that it was forbidden for me to bring such a thing into the school. This Lunchable violated several kosher laws, the biggest being the prohibition against pork (it contained sliced ham), and the additional violation and prohibition of mixing meat and dairy. He explained to me that if I had brought that inside the school building, the entire student body would have to be released and sent home because the food was dirty, unclean, and a major violation of kosher laws. He told me to go behind the school to eat at one of the picnic tables.

This outside eating area was right next to the basketball court, and when I arrived, my eighth grade boys were in the middle of a game. Those few times when I got to school early, I often went to this back area to watch the boys play. In games, these boys were the most vicious and competitive kids I had ever seen. They fought hard, and it was not unusual to see a kid fall and get hurt. The only thing that could bring a game to a halt was when someone's yarmulke came flying off, and then all the boys scrambled to help the boy cover his head again. An uncovered head was an offense to God, and each boy understood the importance of making sure his head was covered at all times.

On this day, I sat down and began to eat my Lunchable. As often happened, the boys not playing came over to talk. The kids looked at the Lunchable package and wanted to know what I was eating. They had never seen one of these before. I explained to them what it was, and when they heard that it was slices of ham, they looked at me as though I was leafing through a porno magazine. Several of the boys asked if they could see what a slice of ham looked like. I held one up. These boys had never seen a pork product in their life. The orthodox buy their food from kosher markets, they only eat at kosher restaurants, their houses are kosher, all their friends eat kosher, and everyone they know is kosher.

They stared at the round slice of ham, fascinated.

The two most adventurous boys in the class asked if they could smell it.

So I held it up as these two fourteen-year-old boys put their noses a few feet from the dirty unclean meat. I heard them both take a tentative sniff. I looked at them and knew something was wrong. I have read and heard the term "turning green" when someone is about to be sick, but I had never seen it before. Suddenly, both boys turned around, bent over, and vomited.

When you've been told your whole life that something is unclean, forbidden, condemned by God, a violation of God's law, it's not surprising the first time you sniff it to respond by blowing chunks.

As I completed my second month and prepared to begin my third at Mesivta, I got a call from Redland Christian Academy, so I went in to see them. Somehow, despite being devastated by Hurricane Andrew, they had kept my resume. The school needed a fifth/sixth grade teacher. The school was five minutes from my house, they would pay four times more than what I was making at Mesivta, and the class would be in a more traditional school with a more traditional setting and schedule. Even more so, I hoped that with a new school and younger kids, I would fare better when it came to behavior problems and discipline.

I accepted the position and informed the rabbi.

My time at Mesivta was eventful, and I am forever appreciative of the teaching experience I gained there. It was a wonderful experience, and I am so grateful that I got an understanding of the Jewish faith, but I knew it was time to move on.

Two weeks later, I was at Redland Christian Academy.

But my problems, my shortcomings, my lack of understanding and control, all of that came with me, and if anything, it got worse.

When I took the job at Redland Christian Academy (RCA), I took it for all the right reasons: money, proximity, and familiarity. But I knew going in that I would have to overcome several huge new issues. I had been trained for two years and prepared myself to teach Social Studies: American and World History, Government, Geography, and Economics. The job at RCA wasn't a Social Studies position. Instead, I would be teaching all subjects, and it would be a combined class. This meant I had to teach a fifth and sixth grade math class, a fifth and sixth grade science, a fifth and sixth grade English class — you get the idea.

I decided that I was not going to do this. The majority of my kids were sixth graders, so I would teach from the sixth grade books. I figured that the fifth graders would be getting a leg up for next year. The truth is I did it because I had no idea what I was doing, and I picked what was easiest and best for me not for my students.

Once I had made that decision, I now had the problem of teaching subjects I was wholly unprepared for. Furthermore, I had no time to prepare, no one to mentor me, and no one to turn to.

Before I say anything else, if any of my former students from RCA are reading this, I owe you an apology. I had no idea what I was doing. Those kids got cheated out of a year of education. I cannot imagine how far I set them back or how much harm I cost them. I didn't intend this to be the outcome, but it was. I do know that they got a very good education when it came to history and, ironically enough, science, but I did a horrible job teaching math and English. When it came to math, I could not figure out a way to make it interesting to my kids, and I was bored teaching it. For English, the challenge of how to teach it was beyond my capabilities.

On top of this, I still had no idea how to control my classroom, preferring intimidation and fear instead of figuring out how to get kids to *want* to act correctly. I roamed my classroom like a caged lion just waiting to pounce on anyone who got out of line. Since I had no control, I used what few weapons I had. The biggest one was to make my students' lives as uncomfortable as possible. At first, this meant detentions, but I soon realized what little effect those had, so I flipped to using work to punish. If kids talked: more work. If kids didn't follow instructions: more work. If students talked back: more work. If students didn't immediately get to work: more work.

At first this worked like a charm and I thought that I had finally gotten my behavior issues under control, until I assigned some normal work, and the kids reacted by asking what they had done wrong. I had turned all work into punishment. Even though an assignment was a legit assignment given only because it was what I wanted them to do, they didn't see it that way. I spent the whole year chasing this problem, and as I could no longer use work as a punishment, now I didn't have any control over my classes. The kids felt that everything I asked them to do was punishment for something they hadn't done. My class was like an untamed jungle, and I had no idea how to control it. I identified a couple of students as the culprits, the ones who caused the other students to go off. I made it my goal to break them. I tried talking to them, isolating them, threatening them, and punishing the group, but for whatever reason, none of it worked.

There was another reason why my class was so out of control, and in this case, it was something beyond my control as a first-year teacher. This school and the kids who went to it were located in the heart of the destruction of Hurricane Andrew. Every one of my students had gone through their own individual hurricane nightmare. Each of them had an incredible story to tell. These kids had seen their houses destroyed, their world ripped apart, their neighborhoods flattened, their parents in desperation; some kids were living in trailers or in relatives' houses, and some kids still didn't have electricity.

In some ways, each of these kids had been damaged by the storm, but that damage was not just the physical loss of a roof or windows or electricity. The real loss was deeper and harder to see. I was very aware of this and did everything I could to make my class a place where kids could feel comfortable. I tried to incorporate time and space for kids to talk about what had happened to them. In their artwork, their English assignments, and in class discussions, we returned to this topic again and again.

But I wasn't an experienced teacher, and I was dealing with my own emotional problems that the storm had brought. And as much as I tried, I knew that even in this regard, I failed the kids.

Part of my job at RCA was to monitor the kids during recess, and one morning the depth of what Hurricane Andrew had done to the kids was revealed to me in the most innocent of ways. As I watched the younger kids play, the game looked familiar, but it also seemed odd, so I asked one of the teachers what they were playing. She sighed and said the kids called it "Andrew." She explained that the teachers had tried to get the little kids to stop playing it, but they couldn't. It was hide and seek with a twist: one kid, "Andrew," would close his eyes, and the other kids would hide, and then "Andrew" would come and find them. She told me originally that if Andrew found them, it meant they were dead, but teachers said that they were not allowed to say that anymore.

Kids have done things like this forever to make it easier to deal with trauma, and these kids had made the horrors of life into a game. Anyone watching this might feel compelled to stop them, not wanting these kids to relive the nightmare of the storm, but actually, this is a healthy way for kids to deal with things. But it was uncomfortable watching kids play over and over the nightmare of Hurricane Andrew.

We spent a lot of time in my class dealing with the hurricane. To this day, I feel blessed to have pictures, stories, and writings from the kids who shared their experiences with me. Some of the kids were reluctant to share what had happened to them. Others openly and willingly talked about their experiences. I respected each of these kids and let them know I was there to listen whenever and however they wanted to speak, and it was okay if they never chose to talk about what had happened.

Of all of my students, one stood out in his willingness to participate in every activity we did. I'll call him Thomas. Thomas was one of my star pupils: he was bright, funny, outgoing, and hard working. He had a lot of energy, but he was respectful and did anything I ever asked of him. And he was so open about his experiences with Hurricane Andrew. He always made everyone laugh as he recounted being in his family room when the storm hit, and through the sliding glass door as the trees came down around the swimming pool. He recounted how there was a huge bump against the sliding glass door, and it scared him so much he jumped back. He reenacted the look on his face, the way he leapt back, all of it, in a comical way that always got a laugh.

One day I was speaking with Thomas's mother after school. I told her how incredible her son was as a student and how impressed I was with his ability to cope with what had happened. She stared at me and then said very quietly, "You don't know, do you?"

She told me the real story of what happened to Thomas. A huge tree did fly against the sliding glass door, and he did jump back, but the reason he jumped back was that the tree crashed through the door and glass sliced his face, and now that there was a huge hole where the door had been, the wind whipped through, and within moments, the roof lifted off the house. The ripping sound was monstrous. She and her husband grabbed Thomas and ran to the bathroom with Thomas bleeding and the roof lifting. Her husband leaned against the door to keep the wind out, and Thomas passed out.

He woke up screaming a few hours later, and he kept screaming and wouldn't stop. By then, the winds had died and the storm was gone. They got him out of the house, and finally he calmed down. But he wouldn't go back in the house, and when they mentioned it or motioned to walk toward the house, he started screaming again.

So they got in the car and drove to his grandparents' house less than a mile away. It didn't matter that their house had also sustained damage; he would not go back to his house.

Over the next twenty-four hours, the family was able to borrow an RV that they parked in front of their house and lived in. Thomas refused to go into the house ever again, and when he was encouraged to and finally forced to, he screamed uncontrollably and passed out. He didn't revive until they got him outside. According to Thomas's mom, he had never walked back into that house, even as they repaired it, put a roof on it, fixed the house, and fixed his room. Thomas lived in the RV even when everyone else had moved back into the house.

And this was a kid I had thought was coping so well with the aftermath of the hurricane, but I realized that I had known nothing of what he had experienced because he was a child dealing with the trauma, not an adult like me, but I did my best and tried to help him.

In retrospect, I realize that I had no idea how to control my students or for that matter teach 90 percent of what they were learning, but I did make it my goal to get to know my students. That was the only thing I did well that entire year.

When I was in college, I had a theater professor who, when we read or saw a theatrical performance, asked us to respond by writing what he called a "think piece." The only requirement was that it had to be one page in length, and it had to be about the performance. I decided to use this teaching tool, but instead of talking about theater, I saw it as a way to get to know my kids.

From the very beginning, I developed a few rules for this assignment. First, I explained to them why I was doing this assignment. It was born out of what I had always felt as a school kid: that no one had ever cared for me, that what teachers really wanted from me was to come into the classroom, sit down, and shut up. Teachers didn't want to know me. I was doing this assignment with my students because I did want to know them. None of them could leave my class saying no one cared about them, because I did.

Second, since I was asking them to be real with me about themselves, I promised that no matter what they shared, I wouldn't hold it against them. I had no right as a teacher to ask my students to be real and then hold it against them when they were. Over the years kids have told me horrible things that have happened them, terrible things, things kids should never have to deal with, nightmares that adults would have difficulty dealing with. I have also had kids who refused to say anything, refused to tell me who they were. In both cases my response has always been the same: okay, I appreciate it, I honor you for saying it, and I will treat you the same and not act any differently toward you for refusing to speak, not even if you have shared with me a glimpse of the nightmare.

Third, students could write as little or as much as they wanted. Their grade would not be affected whether they wrote one word or ten pages because the reason I was doing this was so that kids could tell me who they were. It was their chance to be real with me about themselves and their lives, but it was also okay if they didn't want to tell me anything.

The last rule was by far the most important and the most difficult to keep. I promised my students that what they said would stay between us: I would not share it with their parents, other teachers, the school administrators — no one. Their words were for me and me alone, and I would not violate that trust. Within a few years, I modified this rule, though essentially the promise was the same. I made one change: if they said in their letter that they had been physically abused, sexually or otherwise, or that they were physically or sexually abusing someone else, by law I had to report that. Over the years, this has happened a few times, and I've handled it by talking to the student then going to an administrator or guidance counselor with the information. In every case, the student accompanied me to report what had happened.

That very first year at Redland Christian Academy, I gave this assignment, and in that very first year, I was challenged for doing it.

When the students turned in their letters, I got the usual mixture. Some kids just gave a basic biographical sketch: age, place of birth, things they like to do, interests, what they were like as kids, and so on. Some kids gave me little to no information at all, preferring to keep who they were to themselves. But for most of the years I have done this assignment, I've had kids write me pages and pages. That first year one of those kids explained a series of conflicts they'd had with their mother. They said some pretty tough things about her. Somehow, the mother found out that my student had written me this letter and that the letter contained some not so nice things about her. The mom came to me and asked to see the letter. I said no, and reiterated the promise I had made to the students that I would keep their letters private.

The mother was not happy and went to my principal to voice her discontent.

A couple of days later I was called into the principal's office. I was told that the mother wanted to see the letter, and he asked if I would acquiesce and allow her to see it.

I explained the promise I had made to the students and the intent behind the letters. The principal listened to my reasoning and made the decision to side with me. He told me he would let the parent know of his decision. I thanked him and stood to leave his office.

As I was walking out, he asked me what I would have done had he told me I had to give the letter to the parent. I thought for a moment and said, "If you made me show it, it would take me about thirty minutes to clean out my room. I would quit my job before I would turn the letter over."

To this day, this assignment has helped me bridge the gap, has brought me closer to my students, and has helped me become a true part of my kids' lives. These letters have led to correspondences that go on to this day, to having conversations and interactions that have made my life better and made my students' lives a bit easier.

The most important thing I learned from my time at RCA was that reaching out and wanting to be an active part of your students' lives is the most rewarding thing you can do as a teacher. I also learned to never, ever, ever, *ever* use schoolwork as punishment!

The last thing I took from my time at RCA was the process of figuring out how to get my class to function effectively and peacefully for everyone's benefit. Though I did not have an official person on staff assigned to guide me, I was lucky that I had a principal who spent some time mentoring me. Don was a pastor, not an educator by training. When he spoke, he sounded like every white southern pastor you have ever heard. He had this booming honey-dripping voice, a man who can quote scripture or cut you to the quick with a look. RCA was a fundamentalist Christian school, and the principal taught the Bible classes. He was also the lead minister in the church that supported this school, and the man in charge of rebuilding the school after the hurricane. Needless to say, he didn't have a huge amount of time for me, but the time he gave me felt precious because of what he shared with me, and later, in an action that would be burned into my mind for the rest of my career.

The single best thing he told me was that as a teacher, you need to view the kids like a bank. If you are smart, you make deposits into the bank every time you have a kind word, every time you reach out to them, every time you take an extra moment to be there for a kid, every time you listen to them; every pat on the back, every high five, every congrats is making a deposit into that kid's account. You are building up positive interest. And when you eventually need to make a withdrawal — you need a kid to do his classwork, to calm down, to stop talking — your kids will be willing to do what you need them to do. This is directly linked to the key to running your classroom: to figure out the best way to make your kids WANT TO listen to you and follow you.

His philosophy was revealed to me after a particularly bad day. He could see me struggling, could see how badly I wanted to be good at this and how much it hurt me that I couldn't get kids to do what I wanted them to do. When he gave me this analogy, I saw and felt the truth of his words, but I also knew that with most of my kids, maybe all, I had built up nothing, made no deposits; my only moves were those of fear and weakness, threats and punishment.

My failure would be proven in the most awful and spectacular way. As I said, RCA was a fundamentalist Christian school, and being a private school, the rules of what they could do in terms of discipline were a lot more flexible than a public school environment.

This was made real to me in a way I'll never forget. Two of my boys from the very beginning of the school year had caused problems. They were the oldest boys in class, and they constantly talked out, refused to follow instructions, didn't do their work, got poor grades (and didn't care), and worst of all, they were the instigators, the ones who got the entire class to lose control.

These two boys needed someone in their life, a person to put their arm around them, to let them know they understood their struggle. This is especially true for boys who aren't the brightest, but with the right direction in life, they can go far and live a good life.

These boys weren't bad; they just had a bad teacher who had no idea how to help them and guide them. I failed them. I am sitting here typing these words, and I am trying hard not to yell at myself. I want to go back and help me be the kind of teacher that both these boys needed and deserved. But they didn't get that; they got a version of me who had no clue what he was doing.

So after lots of meetings with them, their parents, and the principal, it was decided that the two boys needed to face a stiffer penalty. The school decided to give out their strongest punishment. Both boys would be paddled. And I, as their teacher, as the person who they had disobeyed, would have to stand there and witness it. It makes me sick to type these words.

I am responsible for a kid being hit.

I am responsible for a kid's tears.

I am responsible for a child being harmed.

And I stood there and watched it happen.

Yes, I was sick to my stomach, but I watched those two twelve-year-old boys being brought in, being told how they had misbehaved, how they had been brought to this place, and why this was going to happen. I watched both boys bend over. Watched the principal take out the paddle. Saw the tears start before there was even a first whack. Watched the boys' faces as they each received three smacks. Watched both leave in tears defeated, beaten, and destroyed. I am so sorry to both of those boys, sorry I failed them, sorry I hurt them, and sorry they ever met me.

I was beaten, destroyed, and defeated. I had come to a crossroads in my life and career. I had chosen to be a teacher to make kids' lives better, to help them, to ease them through the hard process that is school and life, and I had watched two kids who I was responsible for be beaten because of my failure.

What was I doing? Was this the best I was going to be?

The Infamous Letter Incident

In the summer of 1993, my family took a trip to North Carolina so my parents could buy furniture to replace everything that had been lost in Hurricane Andrew. Like a lot of homeowners who suffered damage from the hurricane, my parents received the maximum payout from their homeowner's insurance policy for damages. It is ironic that a storm that brought such destruction turned out to be one of the best things that had happened to my parents since they'd arrived in South Florida. Until now, they had had nothing but bad luck. Arriving right at the start of the economic crisis of the late 1970s, their finances seemed to always be in trouble. On top of this, my father seemed unable to keep a job; time and time again when things looked like they might finally work out, something would happen and disaster would strike. Finally, things began to look brighter. My father found a job with a company where he felt at home and did very well. Now they were going to reward themselves after the nightmare of the hurricane by fixing up their house.

When the school year ended, I was offered a job to continue teaching at RCA, and I accepted it. I did tell my principal that I would look for a public school job, but I knew that after the turmoil of the previous school year, the hurricane, and two teaching jobs, neither working out as well as I wanted, I needed some stability. So even though I said I was looking for a job as a public school teacher, I had done nothing in the way of actually trying to find one.

So I returned from North Carolina with a couple weeks of summer left before starting the new school year to RCA.

The night we returned home, I was in the family room with my father reading the newspaper help wanted ads. The only "looking" for a job that I had done was to glance at the help wanted ads in the Sunday paper, but the only jobs advertised were for other private schools, and although RCA was not a great school, it was a known commodity. I had an excellent relationship with my principal and I felt good about teaching there another year if I had to. As I was going through the usual advertisements, at the very top of the page was a job offer for a public school. I read the description, looked up at my father, read it again, and then got my dad's attention.

"Dad, a school in the Keys is going to offer me a job."

My father looked up from the page he was reading.

"Wait . . . you mean someone called?"

"No, there is a job in the paper, and I know I'm going to get it."

I looked back at the ad:

Key Largo School
Middle School Social Studies position
American History and Video Productions

I somehow knew I was going to get the job. I just knew it.

Now the question was, where was Key Largo School? Could it really be in THE Florida Keys? Was it in Key West?

I found out the next day when I called the school. Indeed, it was in the Keys, but I would find out later that Key Largo is the first of the Keys. It is closer to the mainland of Florida than it is to Key West, which is over a hundred miles farther south and the last in the chain of Keys. My only experience in the Keys happened the summer of my sophomore year in college. My best friend from high school wanted to go fishing in the Keys. I remember being underwhelmed by the whole tacky tourist look and feel of the Upper Keys. Beyond that, the other thing that kept going through my mind was, *Do people actually live here? Kids live here? People teach here? What could that possibly be like?*

When I called Key Largo School and explained my interest in the job, I was instructed to fax my resume, and they would call and set up a time for my interview. I asked to speak to the principal so I could get some information about the position and the school. The receptionist informed me that the principal was out, but I could speak to the assistant principal. I readily agreed. I wanted to make as good an impression as possible.

They transferred me to Michael Lannon. Within a few moments of saying hello and going through the usual pleasantries, Mr. Lannon asked me about my college and teaching experience. So I began by saying that I had graduated from Saint Leo College. Every time, in every interview and in every situation when I was asked about my college, there was the inevitable follow-up question: "Where in the United States is that, or is it outside the US?" I had gotten so used to this question that I had started saying automatically before being asked, "I went to Saint Leo College, a small private liberal arts college located about forty-five minutes from Tampa."

I was in the middle of that explanation when Mr. Lannon interrupted me to let me know that not only did he know where Saint Leo College was, but that he had been in its very first graduating class. I laughed at the immediate camaraderie we shared, and we talked about how we had both had to deal with no one knowing anything about our college. We talked about our experiences at Saint Leo, what we learned, the excellent education we got there, and how we both felt it had been the perfect place for us. He too had been a history education major who had gone into administration; we had even shared one history professor. Like every conversation I ever had with Michael Lannon, he was funny and insightful, and he put me at ease. I hung up the phone even more certain that this job was mine.

My interview was two days later.

To this day, I can close my eyes and remember that drive. The drive from the bottom of the Florida mainland into the Keys is boring, long, and tiresome, not to mention dangerous. I have never driven another road that was as fatal as that two-lane trek. (For a long time the county posted the number of fatalities on the road in the previous year. They hoped to scare drivers into passing only when it was safe to do so.) But at certain points the drive is breathtaking and exhilarating. It is called "the stretch" by locals. Much of the sixteen-mile drive is ugly, and just when you can't stand another inch of swampy ugliness, you hit Lake Surprise, and you know you are suddenly in a world unlike any other place. After miles and miles of flat swampland as far as the eye can see, the vista opens to this vast expanse of lovely blue-green water on both sides, a quiet cove of pure untouched bliss. It comes out of nowhere, thus the name, and when you see Lake Surprise, you know you have reached the Keys.

That first drive dazzled me. The idea that I could teach in a place so beautiful was overwhelming, and the longer the drive went, the more I fell in love with the place.

Lovely water and mangroves give way to the city of Key Largo, but there is very little civilization before you come to Key Largo School.

As usual, I arrived almost an hour early.

I reported to the front office, but instead of sitting there waiting with the other applicants, I decided to walk around and get a feel for the school.

With it being summer, the buildings were closed. Behind the main office was the cafeteria, and to the right was the largest building, the elementary school; behind this were six portables; to the left of the main office were three more portables, and two large one-story buildings, which comprised the middle school.

Even from the outside, you could see that this was no institutional school. The rooms had large glass windows, doors opened to the outside, and when kids changed classes, they did so by walking from building to building.

As I wandered around, I came upon a groundskeeper putting in some new plants. He was the only person I had seen since I left the front office, so I asked him about the school. He told me this was a good school with good kids. He asked me why I was here. I explained that I was interviewing for a job. I then began speaking passionately about my desire to teach middle school because my own middle school years had been so miserable. He seemed like a good listener, so I told him how I wanted to do whatever I could to make kids' lives better, and that I really wanted to be there for the kids. He didn't say much as he bent over putting in plants. He did mention that Key Largo was a unique place, but he seemed like he needed to get his work done, so I thanked him for the conversation and went to the front office for my interview. I was interviewed by three people I would come to know very well: Frankie McCormack (now Frankie St. James; she married a few years before I left KLS), who was the school principal, Annette Litchfield, and Mike Lannon, the assistant principal.

Right before the interview started, the groundskeeper walked in. He said to Annette, "Honey, I'll see you at home. I got the plants in I needed to get in." They kissed briefly, and he walked to the door, but he turned back to Ms. McCormack and said, "Hire this man. He's the right guy for the job."

Whatever fleeting ideas I'd had of not getting this job were completely gone.

There was, however, one gigantic issue I needed to deal with before the job was mine. The position was not just for eighth grade American History; it was also for Video Production. In all candor, I didn't know a single blessed thing about video production. But I needed this job. When asked about my experience with video production, I answered truthfully, that the last two years of high school I was one of the top students in the video productions class. What I left out was that the reason I was in that class was to be a member of the newspaper staff. My schedule with AP and honors classes meant that I could not take the newspaper class when it was offered, so instead I took video productions with the same teacher and then proceeded to produce the newspaper instead of doing anything with making videos. The other answer I gave was also truthful; what I didn't know I was willing to put in the work to find out.

Beyond that I don't remember anything about what was asked or said during the interview, but I do remember feeling incredibly positive. They told me as I was leaving that they had a few more interviews but they would call me by 5:00 p.m. Friday to let me know if I had gotten the job.

Somehow, I knew I was going to get it!

It was only during the long drive home that I began to panic. What was I doing? I didn't know anything about this school, the kids, nothing! I would have to move and find a new place to live. I was thinking of leaving a school I knew, a school I liked, a principal I really respected, and for what? For everything unknown? Plus, I had told RCA I was coming back! The principal at RCA had even offered me a decent raise. Going to the Keys would mean moving away from family and the known. I couldn't do this. The more I thought about it, the more fear I had: fear of failure, fear of the unknown, fear of being exposed as someone who had no idea what he was doing. And I was going to be teaching video production! I had never in my life held a video camera or turned one on. I was going to leave everything I knew to live in the Conch Republic, as the Keys are called, and I didn't have a clue what a conch was.

That night I spoke with my girlfriend to get her input as to what I should do. She listened as I told her about the interview, about the video production class, and then my thoughts concerning taking the job. I explained all of my reasons, all of the things that worried me, and why I shouldn't take the job. Yes, the job was in some ways better: more money, it was a public school job, it was teaching what I was trained to teach, it was middle school, which was the age I wanted to teach, but I kept coming back to my concerns. After going around this a couple of times, Rochelle cut me off and gave me a bottom line and one of the best pieces of advice I was ever given.

"I hear a lot of fears, William. If fear is the only reason you are not doing something, it's a bad reason not to do it."

I opened my mouth to reply, but I was struck dumb. She was right. Everything said this was the right move, but I was letting my fears rule me.

We left the conversation with the conclusion that if I was offered the job, I would ask for the weekend to think about it.

Two days later, it was getting near 5:00 and I had not heard a thing.

5:00 — no phone call.

5:15 — no phone call.

5:30 — nothing!

On some level, I was relieved. I didn't have to make a decision; it had been made for me.

So when the phone rang a few moments later, I knew this was what my father called a "thanks but no thanks" call.

And Frankie McCormack offered me the job.

I had been so certain that I was going to get it and then so certain I wasn't that I didn't know what to say at first, but finally I asked her if I could have the weekend to think about it. Her response was sweet and simple. I didn't have the weekend. I had this phone call. If I accepted the position, I was expected to be in Key West for new teacher orientation on Sunday and at Key Largo School on Tuesday for teacher meetings with the entire faculty, and a week later, school would begin.

"If fear is the only reason you are not doing something, it's a bad reason not to do it."

Two days later, I was driving the Overseas Highway headed for Key West.

It was the best decision I ever made in my life!

Teaching in the Conch Republic

No school is perfect, has perfect kids, perfect administrators and a perfect group of teachers, but Key Largo School was pretty damn close!

I could not have picked a better place than KLS to really begin my first full year as a teacher. Yes, my first teaching job was at Mesivta and then RCA, but when I look back, those almost seem like a dream, sometimes a nightmare. Yes, I taught in those schools, but I wasn't a teacher. I was more than a babysitter but much less than what a teacher should be.

I consider KLS my first real teaching experience and job.

In three weeks' time, I went from seeing the job in the newspaper to getting that job; driving to Key West and sitting through a series of meetings; attending preplanning faculty meetings — let's just say that I knew I wasn't in Kansas anymore when in the very first faculty meeting of the year, the entire administration welcomed the teachers by dressing like characters from the movie *Grease* and lip synching "Summer Lovin'" — moving to Key Largo, and standing in front of a group of eighth graders with the entire school year stretching out before me.

It was a whirlwind.

It was exciting.

It was scary.

It was fun.

The place I rented, my first place as an adult, was 100 feet from Florida Bay. Every day was filled with water and sunset and glory.

In the middle of all this change, I let some things slip. It was inevitable. I was trying to move into an apartment, figure out how I was going to structure my eighth grade American History class, and even more so, how was I going to teach video production. As I prepared for my first day of class, I still hadn't held a camera, as I found all the equipment had been broken the previous year, which temporarily put to rest the problem of teaching someone to use equipment I didn't know how to use. I still had the problem of figuring out what to do with these kids as we waited for repairs.

As I prepared for my classes, my mind kept returning to the biggest problem I'd had since I stepped in front of a group of kids to teach: how to get them to be quiet and do what I wanted them to do. My mind kept flashing back to basketballs hurled into fluorescent lights, kids being paddled because I couldn't control them, threats I made that had no impact, day after day in class waiting for the inevitable disaster to happen, which it always did.

I decided on a two-pronged approach. I would put every rule I could imagine on my list of class rules, and I would start class by going through every rule in detail. I was also going to be very specific about punishment. One of the things available to teachers at KLS was an in-school suspension program. Any kid at any time could be sent out of your classroom to this room where they had to spend four straight class periods as a form of punishment. There was also an after-school detention program if the behavior problem wasn't as serious.

I was going to be the biggest, baddest, strongest, toughest teacher who had ever stepped in front of a group of kids.

On that first day of school, I handed out my specific and detailed rules and my list of horrible terrible consequences.

How could I know that within twenty-four hours, what I did in class on that first day would nearly destroy my career before it began? The lowest point of my teaching career was about to happen less than four days after it began.

When I arrived the first day at Key Largo School, I was sick to my stomach with excitement and nervousness. Every teacher can identify with that buzzing feeling as you anticipate the first day when kids walk into your classroom with excited and expectant faces. You think about how you'll start class, the first words you'll speak, the first joke you'll tell that gets the kids to laugh, the way kids give you all the benefit as they try to figure out who you are, and you do the same about them.

At Mesivta and RCA, I had a first day, but this was completely different. I felt such positive glowing joy. For the first time in a very long time it felt good being in front of a group of kids. I felt free and positive, and they seemed to be responding to me.

I made it my goal from the first moment of class to take control. I had copies of my discipline plan and the consequences for breaking those rules. I had even gone so far as to include portions of the school's code of conduct. I wanted a long comprehensive list of rules so there would be no doubt as to consequences for unacceptable behavior.

KLS was on a block schedule, so I saw one group of kids on that first Monday and a separate group on Tuesday. On Monday I called my girlfriend Rochelle buzzing with excitement. It had gone so well, the kids had responded so well, and everything was great!

The next day was just as positive.

As I handed out the list of rules and consequences, I did not know that in the buzz, the whirlwind, the craziness, the late hours of getting settled into my apartment, that when I typed this, I had made it rife with spelling, grammatical, and typographical errors. And the errors were so silly that one quick edit would have taken care of the problem. I had obviously not done that editing.

The first hint that something was wrong happened midday when there was a phone call from my assistant principal asking if I was sending home a letter with my rules and consequences on it. I answered in the affirmative, and she told me that I needed to stop doing so immediately. I wondered why but assumed something was in the letter that shouldn't be there.

Near the end of the day, my principal called and asked me to come to the front office and to bring any extra copies of that letter with me. I walked into the office not suspecting a single thing.

Frankie McCormack had me take a seat in her office. I looked from her to Mrs. Litchfield to Mr. Lannon.

As was so like her, the first thing Frankie told me was that everything would be okay, and that this was just something I needed to know.

It was then that I was informed that someone had sent the letter to the *Miami Herald*, and there would be an article in the paper the next day. The article would not identify me by name, but it would report an embarrassing series of mistakes in the letter I had sent home. Frankie told me that no one would know that I had written the letter because the article did not mention me by name, and only the people in the room with us knew.

I listened in stunned silence. How was this possible? How had this happened? What had I done? This was the first week of school, not even the first full week, and I knew that no matter what was being said to me in that meeting, I had ruined myself in the eyes of the people in that room, and I would never escape this. How could I recover from this?

Seeming to sense some of what I was thinking, Ms. McCormack did her best to let me know that she would not hold this against me. I had made a mistake, it wasn't fatal, and she assigned me a mentor, someone who would check everything I sent home to make sure this would never happen again. I was to ask for the letters back from my students, and I did not need to explain why.

I was so shocked and dumbfounded that all I could do was nod and try to smile

I stood up and left, and it was only after I had stepped out of Ms. McCormack's office that it dawned on me what had happened and just how big and awful this was. I turned around and walked back into her office. The three of them were deep in conversation.

"Everyone's going to know, aren't they?"

Ms. McCormack turned to look at me then at the other two administrators and then back at me. She nodded.

I walked out.

Yes, the *Miami Herald* would never know my name, but everyone I taught with, people who I didn't even know yet, who didn't know me, would know I had done this, and they would laugh and shake their heads at my clueless mistake. My kids would know. I had hoped to establish iron-fisted control in my classroom, but instead I showed myself to be a fool. The parents would know that their kid had *that* teacher.

I left the office feeling utterly lost.

My classroom was in one of the portables, but the thought of going there turned my stomach, so I wandered to one of the other buildings. I don't know what I was looking for, but I was somehow trying to make what had happened feel better.

The kids had long gone for the day as had all of the teachers save one, who I ran into as she was going from her class to a computer lab to do some work. She didn't know me and I didn't know her, but she could see the horrified look on my face. She asked what was wrong. And for some reason, I told her. It all came out, the mistake, the *Herald*, the kids, how everyone would know. She nodded her head and looked at me with such kind concern. She listened as though I were the only person in the world.

She tried her best to make it okay, to reassure me. She even shared some of her experiences as a teacher, including several very personal stories. In that moment of my lowest despair, she was this one saving grace. This kind good teacher, who had no reason to reach out to me the way she did, to talk to me as a peer, to share aspects of her own life, met me in my place of need. She knew all the right words and how to make me feel good, and I left school thinking I could come back from this.

This is where things could have ended, but she would become my unofficial mentor in ways I wouldn't even appreciate or realize until years later, just as she had saved and would save me in every way a person can possibly be saved.

I had just met Jeanne Kurth — mentor, guide, leader, example, friend, and the best teacher I have ever known. I hope for your sake that you had or will have in your life a Jeanne Kurth, someone who tries in a thousand ways big and small to help you, who never gives up on you, who pledges their heart and their good name for you. That was Jeanne to me.

I went home feeling somewhat better. When I unlocked the door, my phone was ringing. It was my girlfriend Rochelle, who was a senior at Saint Leo. When I picked up the phone, before I even got to tell her what had happened, she asked me a simple question: "Did you send a letter home to students that had a bunch of mistakes in it?"

"How do you know that?" I exclaimed. I could hear her sigh, and that's when I learned that not only had the story made it to the *Miami Herald*, but it was now on CNN being broadcast to the world.

We talked, but I have no idea what she said. I'm certain she tried to make it better, but there are just some things that are bigger than words or what someone else can do to try to make it better. Some things you just have to find a way to bear.

I didn't want to, but I knew I had to see, so I turned the TV on. I watched for a good long time until right before the top of the hour when it came on. Two perfectly coiffed newscasters, all smiles and laughs during their ain't-it-funny-how-stupid-some-people-are infotainment "news" segment, talked about the teacher in the Keys who gave students a letter filled with mistakes. I watched myself making international news. I watched CNN make fun of me, laugh at me, and give the world a break from whatever real horrors were going on.

How could I face my class? How could I face my school? How would my kids and other teachers react? It was devastating. I turned the TV off and wondered if I was done.

Naturally, the next day in class, the kids wanted to know if it was me that the story was about.

My response was to tell them that it was not possible for me to know because the teacher was not identified in the article. I explained that some teacher had sent something home that had a bunch of mistakes in it. They wanted to know what mistakes. I explained it. They looked at me and didn't understand what the big deal was; this was just a bunch of mistakes in writing.

Sometimes you just gotta love kids for telling it like it is. In the grand scheme of things in life, this wasn't a big deal, but at the time, it felt like my entire world had crumbled.

Of course, the kids knew this was about me, but their response shocked me. They became very vocal and even angry, saying how stupid it was that someone would do that to me, would send that letter to the *Miami Herald* just because I had typed a few mistakes. This was ratting someone out, and it was really dumb to make a big deal about it.

I responded by explaining that no matter whose letter it was, I would be much more forgiving of my students whenever they made a mistake than this person had been to the letter writer.

At that moment, the issue was done, and not only was it done, but I had somehow made my students like me and feel closer to me as a fellow human being, and that was the ironic part. By becoming human to my kids, by showing I was vulnerable and forgiving, I got them more on my side than any rule or consequence ever could have done. Because I could bleed and fail and admit my mistake, the kids not only forgave it, but saw me in a positive light.

I have never forgotten this lesson. When you admit mistakes, explain when you don't know, show yourself to be vulnerable and human, kids appreciate that. They are so used to adults acting like they know everything and never make mistakes that when you do, it makes them feel connected to you.

I wish it had been that easy with my colleagues. No one ever outwardly treated me badly, but for years I put up with stares, laughter, walking into a room with all the talk coming to a halt. I knew I was the subject of whispers, and even years after it happened, people were still telling the story.

Worse for me was the embarrassment. How was it possible to ever overcome this? How would I ever be anyone but THAT GUY? It ate at me and made me question everything, especially since it was a direct hit at my intellect, the one area I felt was my strength as a teacher.

If this had been the only mistake that happened that first year, everything would have been fine. But as I noted at the start of this story, I was far from steady.

The list of my failures was growing.

I had no control over my class.

The kids were bored because the only thing I knew how to do was lecture.

I had embarrassed the school.

And I ended the first half of my first year at KLS by embarrassing the niece of my principal.

Four months into my tenure, in a secret meeting in the principal's office, all of my mistakes would be discussed, and hanging in the balance was my future as a teacher. For five months I was holding on by my fingertips, and even though I didn't know it, my career was slipping through my fingers.

I was fumbling and bumbling and stumbling my way out of teaching.

And I should have been fired!

Two things saved me that year. The first was that I had an ally on my side. Jeanne spoke for me strongly and openly; she admitted my issues, she acknowledged my shortcomings, but she explained to them, in a lesson I now carry every day of my teaching career, that people are savable, kids are savable, and teachers are savable.

In the days and weeks and months after my chance meeting with Jeanne, I spent hours listening to her talk, listening to the philosophy that governed her class, watching how she prepared, how she worked, the intensity of how she saw the structure and the curriculum of her classroom. When I met her, Jeanne had been teaching a dozen years, and yet she put in more work than anyone I knew. Jeanne's real workday began when the kids left, when she spent hours preparing for the next day.

Jeanne was not a Social Studies teacher; she taught classes for a dropout prevention program. But she helped me see that the subject doesn't matter; good teaching is good teaching is good teaching is good teaching. During the time I spent with her, I absorbed every part of what was around me. I spent very little time talking because I knew that I was watching excellence in action.

It is my firm belief that if a teacher wishes to improve, there are only three ways that can happen: get in the classroom and teach; go to workshops and be trained by the best on how to be the best; and see it being done in a classroom. Sadly, most school districts can't or won't go through the expense of sending teachers to conferences, and teachers aren't given the chance to go into experienced teachers' classrooms to see excellent teaching happen. So we are left to our own devices, and if we are lucky, we have a mentor to guide us.

I was one of the lucky ones with Jeanne as a mentor. I listened to her, watched her process, saw the work that went into putting together real and authentic lessons, and saw the consuming passion that is great teaching. Years later I would laugh with Jeanne as she told me how at times it was painful being around me, as she spent almost our entire time together talking. She didn't understand how I could possibly be getting anything out of it. She could not have been more wrong.

The other way I got lucky was that KLS really believed in innovation, in ongoing learning, and in being your best, and that included going to workshops. In the eight years I spent at KLS, I attended at least ten local, state, or national workshops and conferences. On top of that, my principal brought people to the school to present on a variety of topics: behavior, assessment, learning styles, leadership, and everything in between.

In the start of my teaching career, no other professional or presenter had as much of an impact on me and my classroom as Kathryn LaMorte. I was very lucky to attend several of her presentations at state conventions and in the spring of my first year when my principal brought her to KLS to do a presentation on authentic hands-on assessment. When it came to how I managed my classroom and how I taught, that workshop was a game changer. For the first time I saw that there were ways of teaching other than lecture or notes or bookwork. I owe her a great debt, and for several years, the best lessons I taught were variations of the activities she taught. She also fired my imagination to seek other ways of teaching. It was like being given permission to take chances, to open my mind to how a class could be taught.

But ultimately the thing that I believe most saved me was how badly I wanted it. I desired with every fiber of my being to be good — no, to be great. It was never enough for me to get by, to have a class that was merely okay. I wanted to be one of those teachers that truly impacted a kid's life. And I did not keep quiet about this. The second week of school, after the fiasco of the first, I wrote a letter to each of the administrators pledging to do better, promising not to repeat my mistake, and asking them for help so that I could become better. On a weekly basis, I walked into an administrator's office seeking help and guidance. I wanted them to help me in any way they could. And everything they said, I absorbed and put into practice.

I talked to other teachers about how they ran their classes, and I especially tried to figure out how to get discipline right, because discipline was still the problem that bedeviled me. I'd punish, raise my voice, get firmer, tougher, and more forceful, and as I did, I lost more and more control. I was a 6'2" male being pushed around by thirteen-year-old children. There had to be a formula to get it right.

I looked at one of my colleagues, the woman who would win Teacher of the Year my first year at KLS, her second time winning the award. She was all of 5'3" but when she walked into a room, it became hushed. The kids both feared and loved her. I marveled at her ability, and I wanted to figure it out. I had colleagues like Susan Coopersmith who made her kids laugh. She had warmth, and she cajoled, mothered, loved, and got her kids to love her class and learn her subject. Both of these women taught the same kids I taught, with two completely different styles, and yet they both got kids to work so hard for them. The two of them could not have been more opposite in their demeanor, and yet both succeeded, both had their students' respect. Meanwhile I was the epitome of a first-year teacher, a big mess that lumbered and bumbled and had no clue how to make it right.

I tried so hard to be good and I failed, but it did save me from losing my job.

As my first year ended, I breathed a sigh of relief. I had learned some things, I had some new tools to teach, but I was still in the dark and still horribly lost when it came to classroom discipline.

I would like to tell you I spent the summer of my first year in the Keys going to workshops, studying, improving my skills, but the truth is that I was living in the Florida Keys, so instead I played tennis, swam every day in the Florida Bay, went out, ate, drank, and had fun.

My second year began much as the first two, though my class did improve, thanks primarily to Kathryn LaMorte. My lesson plans improved slightly. I began doing more projects and hands-on activities. The kids embraced these assignments.

But I hadn't really changed. I prowled the class like some kind of animal, seeking out any disturbance and then pouncing, threatening, arguing, and punishing. I was on edge every moment I was in my classroom, and because of this, the class never felt like a good or positive place to be. For so many kids, this approach was a failure, and time after time I sent kids out of my class. Each time I did this was another example of my failure as a teacher. I constantly felt emotional turmoil, certain that at any moment, the kids might destroy everything I was doing. There was no comfort, and there was no safe place. I felt drained at the end of each day whether it had been a good day or a bad one. It was exhausting to have so much control and be so afraid to lose it.

Ultimately the issue was simple: I did not understand how to get kids to want to do what I wanted them to do. I was able to control most of my students, but the tighter I gripped, more problems squelched out, and when that happened, it showed that I really had no control.

With my colleagues, administrators, and anyone who would listen, I constantly asked questions and pleaded for help. How you do this? How do you make it work? Why do you have control and I don't? What do you do? Most people had clear ideas and suggestions, and I tried those, but most were just ways to get more control. Some worked but most didn't.

As I was turning to my fellow educators I was making a big mistake by not listening to another group that are experts on education, those who have spent years of their lives dedicated to seeing good teaching and bad up close, those who have strong opinions and incredible insight. These individuals have a unique perspective, but they are so often dismissed as naïve, or worse, as meddling where they have no business. These experts want teaching to be better because they have a vested interest in a great classroom. Of course, these educated experts are the kids themselves. Kids know the difference between a good teacher and a bad one, and they have real and deep insight into how to make a classroom better.

In the spring of my second year, at the end of a disastrous day of a disastrous week of a disastrous year, I saw one of my students from sixth period in the hallway. He was one of my best kids in that class, a sweet typical thirteen-year-old, awkward, gangly, pimply, hard-working, always with a smile, and one of those kids who, when things were falling apart, I could look to as the reason I kept trying.

That day, I closed my classroom door and told him to have a good day. He lingered in the hallway, and I noticed he had a tense look on his face. I could tell he wanted to say something.

"Mr. Quigley." He paused, not sure if he should go on. "Mr. Quigley," he started again, "why are you trying to be so tough? You know you can't do it." He met my eyes then walked away. I'm not sure why he said it. I don't know if he was trying to help me or if he had reached the limit of his own frustrations with me as his teacher, but that one sentence changed my world.

It was like someone had finally held up a mirror and made me see me for the first time.

He was right.

During my first three years of teaching, during the times when everything went great in my class, everyone was laughing and happy, and the room was buzzing with kids talking and being interested, it was when I wasn't in control, wasn't trying to squeeze the students. When everything worked best, it was during projects and discussions. My own personality is silly and sarcastic. I have a sense of humor that, in the words of my best friend, is "centered around trying to make a twelve-year-old laugh." That is me.

I wanted a loose class where the kids came in, loved it, did their work, and felt good. Being a tough, disciplined drill sergeant wasn't me. So often I started out tough, but my natural inclination was to be laid back. I liked jokes and laughter. I hated sameness, and to me, a quiet classroom was a boring classroom. But I kept telling myself that my problem wasn't that I was disciplined; it was that I wasn't disciplined and consistent enough. That was the lie I kept telling myself. The truth was I had spent almost three years fighting myself. I was acting the way I thought I was supposed to act. I was disciplining the way I had always seen teachers discipline. But it wasn't me. It was the opposite of me, and it is not surprising I was such a failure.

Okay, so being disciplined, strict, controlled, and structured had created a lack of discipline, control, and structure. So what was I going to do? If this didn't work, then what? It couldn't be as simple as being less disciplined, less strict, less in control.

I suddenly knew it was a Christopher Columbus moment: somehow, the way to go east meant going west, but I still didn't know how to do that.

But I now realized that I had to start over and create a completely new idea of me and the kind of teacher I wanted to be in the classroom.

And I knew this all because a wise thirteen-year-old had told me, "Mr. Quigley, you just can't do it." You were right, Paul Hann, and I owe you everything. Those words, that shock, that look in the mirror, made me realize I had to come up with a new way.

So began the first of many journeys toward excellence.

I knew where I wanted to go, but I had no idea how!

Respect Is the Key

The thing about epiphanies is they have consequences that often lead to uncertainty. In a moment of candor, a thirteen-year-old kid had blown apart my world.

It was a revelation.

I knew that what I had spent three years doing as a teacher hadn't worked. I knew it, the kids knew it, the administrators knew it, the parents knew it, and my fellow teachers knew it. I was a disaster. But what do you do when someone comes into your world, points out a problem, and then walks away and leaves you wrestling with what to do about it? You are left alone with a disaster.

I would be so happy to tell you that the epiphany that Paul Hann brought to my life was followed immediately by knowing the path I should take, or that the path was somehow revealed to me and I just knew what to do. None of that was true. I was lost. I had no idea what to do or what direction to go in.

Knowing you need to go in a new direction and knowing which way to go are two very different things.

Luckily, this epiphany happened just a few weeks before the end of the school year, so at least I had two months to figure it out before standing in front of a group of students again.

Summer in the Florida Keys is incredible. It never rains during the day, it has pure blue skies without even a hint of white clouds, it's always 90 degrees, there is always a breeze, and you are surrounded on all sides by water. In Key Largo, you are almost never more than a few blocks from either the ocean or the Florida Bay. My first apartment in Key Largo didn't have a lot going for it; I even had to buy window air conditioning units to keep from sweltering, but the water was less than half a football field's length from my back door.

I had been a tennis player since college, so I found a local club and played every day, often two or three times day, and afterward, I drove back home to snorkel and swim in the bay.

In snorkeling, I found a sense of peace. It's Zen, it's relaxing, it's rejuvenating. It is the closest thing to pure heaven I have found on earth. The water is bathtub warm, all sound is gone, you float above schools of fish, lobsters, rocks, swaying sea life; you are simply there to observe, to feel part of and away from the creatures in their natural habitats, all of you moving to our own rhythm. You forget yourself; you disconnect, and you find oneness with existence.

Each day that summer was the same: tennis, sweating, water, sea life, and thinking.

I can't emphasize enough the importance of what Paul did for me. This was the pivot point of my life. I had to figure it out. I had to find a way.

My teaching career can be evenly divided into two parts: the first three years when I didn't understand what I was doing and then all the years thereafter.

The summer of 1995 altered me as a teacher.

In writing this narrative of my life, I have struggled with this section the most, trying to explain what happened. As a writer I would love to point to the one thing that did it, but there was no one moment, one flicker of an idea that began the understanding. There was not one cataclysmic explosion of thought or a singular event that caused it all to come together. Instead, it was a process — slow, unsteady, and uncertain. It was painful and long, and even when I found my way, I didn't know if it was going to work. I had to strip myself bare, the idea of myself, and start over.

What I did know was that I needed to blow up what I had been doing.

So what would have to go?

Control in my class would not come from rules.

Control in my class would not come from consequences.

Control in my class would not come from threats.

Control in my class would not come from intimidation.

Control in my class would not come from squeezing a little harder, pushing a little more.

All of that was gone, and I was left with what I wanted in my classroom, and me.

So what did I want? I wanted a classroom where kids could walk in, feel comfortable, feel safe, feel happy, and know that learning was going to happen, but this learning would take place in a positive environment, a place where it felt good to be. I also didn't want to spend my time disciplining anyone. I wanted a room where kids would walk in and want to follow the rules. And, I wanted them to follow the rules, not because they would get in trouble if they didn't, but because they would never even conceive of wanting to break the rules.

Okay, so I knew what I wanted. How to get there?

I realized there was one constant in my class, one thing that never changed from year to year: ME.

The kids change, the subject changes, the grade level changes, the school changes, the city, the state, even the country changes along with curriculum and testing requirements, but the constant was me.

Ultimately this was going to have to be about me.

So that brought me to an existential crisis: Who was I? How was I unique? What strengths did I bring to this teaching gig?

WHO WAS I?

I needed answers to these questions, because if it was going to be about ME ME ME ME in that class, I had better figure me out.

So while I sweated and snorkeled and floated and gazed at sea life, I asked myself *who am I?*

Let's see, I was a man, age twenty-six, white, middle class, raised in rural Dade County, and educated in public schools until I attended college at a private Catholic-affiliated school. I had just broken up with my girlfriend of three years, and I lived alone in the Florida Keys.

Okay, none of that helped. Those were just stats.

I needed to go deeper.

The more I thought about it, the more I asked myself why I wanted to teach. I began to focus on my unique upbringing. It had made me want to work with kids, and with middle school kids in particular; it made me sympathize with the lonely kid; it made me want to reach out to that kid on the edge, the kid that didn't fit in, because that kid had been me.

So, what had defined me as a child? My father was the biggest influence on my life, and he taught me siblings and me that as a member of the human family, you acted in a certain way. You lent a hand when you could, you did for others, you asked people if they needed help, and you offered it as and when you could. You said yes sir and ma'am; you treated authority with deference, and above all, you treated the world and everyone and everything in it with respect. To my father, that meant his children respected those in charge, and we could never call an adult by their first name. He trained us to be polite to the point of painfulness. This idea applied to everything. We treated all life as though it were sacred. The killing of anything, even when necessary, was something to regret. Nature, animals, plants, the woods were sacred spaces where you tread lightly; you observed but did not disturb. There was a universe out there, and all of us were responsible to treat it with respect.

As a young adult, I carried these lessons with me. I referred to my principal as Mrs. Saint James no matter how often she said I could call her by her nickname Frankie. Since the start of my teaching career, I called my students by their last names, such as Mr. Smith and Miss Jones. It just felt natural and right to do this.

My father had been a personnel director his whole life. He in essence hired and fired people for a living. He spoke of a job as though it were a special and entrusted thing: you are lucky that someone hires you, and in return, they deserve your hard work and dedication. You respect the job, the company, the business, and your boss.

At the same time that I was going through all this in my mind, I happened to be watching a news report on TV about the increasing gang activity in the nation. Kids the same age as the ones I taught were joining these gangs. They did so because they sought a family, and even more so because they wanted the world to respect them. I saw young boys, their faces covered with bandanas, brandishing guns and explaining why they carried them. They looked to their fellow young gang members and spoke about them as family and about the respect they earned on the street when they were part of a gang. For the first time they felt like they belonged somewhere and got the respect they deserved.

As I thought about the three years I had been a teacher and the kids in this news report, I saw a lot of connections. When you are around teenagers, you realize how sensitive they are to injustice, of being treated like kids, of being treated as less than, of the unfairness of youth, of how little respect they are given as people. They told stories of being followed in stores, of being talked down to and disrespected by all manner of adults, from coaches to teachers to their parents and even strangers. They felt this unfairness deeply, and they resented it because it hurt to be so aware of their low place in the world. It hurts to realize that you are put down and disregarded simply because you happen to be young.

If you've ever spent time around teenagers, you know of what I speak.

During the past three years, I had been through at least a hundred parent-teacher conferences. I had heard and felt the frustration of parents who honestly did not know what to do with their children. You can feel the parents yearning for a way to bridge the gap between their kids and themselves. What the parents desperately wanted was for their kids to respect them, to obey them, and to act right in the world. Their kids were equally desperate for their parents' understanding, love, guidance, and yes, their respect — the kind of respect that is born out of trying to understand what it is like to be them, at that moment, in their life.

As I contemplated my role as a teacher, I kept coming back to the idea of respect. All human beings desire it, and we need it in every situation and from every person we interact with.

In the real world, the need for respect flows both ways: parents want it from their kids, but their kids want it too. A boss wants it from his worker, but the worker wants it from the boss. On the street, a cop wants respect, but so does the person being stopped and questioned. The teacher in front of the class and the kid sitting in that class both want respect. A coach demands it, and the players desire it. So does the politician and the voter, the leader and the follower, the customer and the store clerk.

We walk around the world every day in every situation simply wanting our position as a person of value and substance respected by everyone else, and the people we meet simply want respect in return.

Kids are a special case when it comes to respect. They are incredibly sensitive to it and seem to innately know when they don't have someone's respect. It is a word they have heard their whole life, but in almost every case the word, the concept, how it was applied, when it was applied was a one-way street. It is incumbent on the child to do the respecting. It is assumed that respect always flows from child to adult.

Children are told that respect is automatic when dealing with an adult. An adult gets respect, period . But children only get respect if they've worked hard enough, given enough, acted right, and demonstrated the proper respect, bowing and kneeling in acquiescence to the adult — and then, maybe, they might EARN the adult's respect.

The word respect has been used as a battering ram to drive home the message about how kids should talk, act, dress, speak, and interact with the world, but especially with adults.

Okay, so we all want respect. Kids are often denied respect or have to earn it. Kids have a refined sense of injustice. Kids want to feel safe and respected. Kids want teachers to respect them and treat them with respect.

After pondering all this, I still looked in the mirror every day that summer of 1995 and wondered what this meant to me as a teacher. How could I possibly use any of this?

Here's what I did know: I couldn't command kids to do what I wanted. (Thanks, Paul Hann, and every class I failed at bullying). And since I was the only constant in this equation, and the students were the variables, the atmosphere in my class had to come down to what I did differently, and the answer had been right in front of me all along: I had been raised on the idea of respect, something my kids desperately wanted.

So . . .

Could

I

Somehow
Make
My
Class
About
Respect?
What would that even look like? What would it mean?
How could I do this? How *would* I do this?

How would I make my class about respect?

As I pondered these questions, thoughts and ideas
began to flow:

I am the constant.

Kids want respect.

I want them to do things because they want to do them.

Could it be this simple?

To do this I would have to flip the script on everything I
thought I knew about how to deal with kids.

Instead of telling kids how I wanted them to act, I
would only ever talk about how I was going to act. I would
never say I how I expected them to treat me. If I did this
right, I wouldn't have to.

Before I tell you how this works in my class and what I
started doing in that very next school year to put this into
action, I want to tell you what this change has meant for
my students and me.

I don't write referrals or detentions, ever. I don't do
discipline, ever.

The last time I wrote a referral for discipline was over
sixteen years ago. My students rarely misbehave because
the idea of doing so offends them. When I am in my class,
no matter what class I am teaching, I feel nothing but the
quiet respect of my students. I could tell a lot of stories
about how this change has caused such joyful bliss in my
class. I could tell you about kids who have never behaved
for a teacher and who were constant problems in class after
class, who I had no problem with; of the kids who tell me

the respect they feel for me; of how special and unique my approach to teaching is.

But I think one story best illustrates the change in my students.

Several years after I implemented these changes, I was subbing for another teacher. The kids in the room were all my students because KLS followed a true middle school concept where teachers taught in teams with the same kids. Near the end of class, I turned my back to write something on the board, and as I did, an object flew across the room and hit the board near me. I turned, shocked that a student would do this to me. It had been years since I had felt that kind of disrespect. I asked who did it. No one responded. I stared at them, shocked. Who could have done this, and why would they do it? Everything I believed, everything I had taught was being tested in that moment.

The class ended with no one saying anything. When the bell rang, four of my boys walked up to me. The lead boy, Chris, let me know that none of them knew who did it, and then he said, "Don't worry, Mr. Quigley. We'll take care of it." I told the four of them to not hurt the kid but to let me know who it was when they found out.

The next day, I was in my classroom before school started when the door opened. A kid who had just transferred in from another school a few days prior stood there, his head down, and mumbled an apology about what he had done the day before. I sat him down so we could talk. He told me how frustrated he was that his family had moved five times in the last two years because his father was in the Coast Guard. He told me how he had finally felt at home in California when his dad announced in the middle of the school year that they were moving to Florida.

He told me he didn't know why he threw something at me; he said he was just angry. We talked for a while longer about him, his family, and his feelings about the school. When he stood to leave, he told me he understood that he would get in trouble, and he couldn't have been more sorry for what he did.

I asked him a simple question: "Did you learn your lesson?" He nodded his head and was close to tears.

That's when I told him I was a teacher. I was not here to punish. If he learned what he needed to learn from this experience, there was no reason for me to punish him.

Later that day Chris came in, and I got him to the side and asked him if he had hurt this kid. He promised me he had not, but he did say, "He needed to learn that no matter what, you don't disrespect Mr. Quigley."

In that moment, everything I had worked to create was validated. Chris hadn't stood up for me because he feared me. He had my back because he couldn't imagine anyone wanting to disrespect someone who treated him and every other kid with respect.

So how does my class use this concept of respect?

The best, most simple way to put it is that everything in my class is about respect — everything, every word I say, every action I take, everything, everything, everything — every, every, everything in my class is about respect.

During the first few days of class I go into exacting detail as I talk about respect with my students and explain what it means to me and why I do the things I do.

No matter what, one truth is above all others: my kids deserve respect, period! This respect is given automatically with no preconditions, no earning. You walk into my room, you have my respect.

When I realized the direction my class needed to take, I knew that anything I did that wasn't respectful had to be jettisoned, starting with my discipline plan. Besides, if what I was about to do worked, I wouldn't need to discipline the kids.

I didn't leave anything to chance, and I still don't to this day. I speak specifically and in detail about each of the things listed below. My ultimate goal is to make sure my students understand that in my class, they have my 100 percent complete respect, and if there is any way I can demonstrate it, I do.

So, here is how it works in my class:

In the first few minutes, hours, and days of each new school year, I explain how I will go about respecting them.

First, I call them by their last names. I do this because this is one of the ultimate signs of respect. They of course don't have a choice in what they call me; they must refer to me by my last name, and I could do what other teachers do and call them by their first as though they were friends and buddies, but that creates a division between teacher and student. Calling someone by a last name is a sign of respect; if they have to do it, then so do I.

Students sit where they want. There are no assigned seats on those first few days, and as far as I am concerned, I will never assign a seat. I only do that if my students demonstrate to me they can't handle it. I actually don't care where they sit or whether they lay on the floor, live underneath a table, or pace in the back of the room, as long as they do their work without being disruptive to anyone.

Students are never allowed to be yelled at by me or another student. I never ever raise my voice at one of my students. I have never understood why it is okay for an adult to yell at the students, but if the students dared to raise their voice at the teacher, they would be in trouble.

If students need to go to the bathroom, they can go. Like everything in my class, unless a kid demonstrates that they can't handle something, they are not forbidden from doing it.

When I talk to my students, I refer to them as ladies and gentlemen. I call them sir and ma'am. The language we use to refer to people marks the way we see them. Calling someone a child or boy or girl creates a distance, makes them the other, reduces their position of value and equality.

Every day at the start of class, I stand at my door and shake each kid's hand as I welcome them into my room. I want every kid to know that they are in a place I want them to be, that they are welcome to be there. I want our interaction to be positive. This is their class, not just mine.

I dress professionally in a way that says what I do is a professional job, on the same level as a doctor or a lawyer or a business executive. I wear a shirt and tie, dress pants and dress shoes. I tell them I consider teaching as important as any job, and they should expect someone who cares enough to dress like that's true.

I do not sit at or use my teacher desk. I actually allow my students to sit at my teacher desk, but I do not ever sit there. Having a desk that is different and always better than theirs creates a division in the class; it elevates me and gives me a position of importance and power that seeks to separate me from my students.

The last thing I do to create an atmosphere of respect is admittedly the most controversial. It has caused outrage, not from my students, who actually love it, but from my fellow teachers. Once I came up with my plan and saw how it completely changed my class and my relationship with my students, I began presenting it at local, county, and state conferences. I knew that some teachers would have issues with my methods, but I did not expect the strong reaction I got from some teachers.

Teachers have walked out during my presentation.

Others have confronted me during it, calling me out.

Still others have sought me out afterward. I've been accused of ruining education, of trying to make students equal to teachers. My response to that criticism is actually, yes I am. I very much believe in the equality between my students and me. When it comes to respect and how we treat each other, we are equals.

So, what was this method that caused such controversy? Put simply, all of the rules that my students must follow, I must follow. (I do make one exception, which the kids do not seem to have a problem with: because I have to teach, I need to move around the room, something they generally are not allowed to do.) As they well know, if they break the rules of the class, they will get punished. Since they get punished for breaking the rules, it only makes sense that I should get punished if I break the rules. I then show my students the rule that I most often break. I also tell them I will break it in the next few days. You have never seen more surprised and happy kids than the idea that they get to punish a teacher — and boy, over the years, they have come up with some great ones, like making me run through the hallways saying I'm a rule breaker, making me dress up, forcing me to make a fool of myself at prom or pep rallies, making me swim in the school fountain — I am always amazed at what my students come up with.

After the first couple of days of discussing the concept of respect, I demonstrate it in several specific ways.

First, in everything I do, from what I say to where they sit, from what I wear to where I park my butt, to the rules of the class and what I expect of them, everything is based around ME treating THEM with RESPECT. And, I remind them that at no point have I said that they have to treat me with respect.

In fact, I never tell them how to treat me. If they want to respect me, they can. I can't control their actions. I can only control mine, and all of my actions are based on the idea that they deserve respect, and they will have it from me.

After going into detail about how I will teach them from a standpoint of respect, I conclude with the following: I believe that my students should be treated with the same respect that I show to their parents; they deserve to be treated with the same respect I have for my fellow teachers and the principal, my boss, the man who could fire me and make me stop doing the thing I love most in the world. They deserve the same respect as my friends, the people I love and choose to fill my life with, and lastly, with the same respect that I have for my father and mother.

Epiphanies have consequences, and this one changed my life. I had found teaching accidentally. I had failed completely, and through those first years had begun to question whether teaching was for me. And then, with one astute observation from a thirteen-year-old kid named Paul, a long hot summer, and the simple concept of respect, I had found my calling, the purpose of my life.

This Is My Truth

A *m I a good man?*
I paused, the letters clutched in my hand, as the question came unbidden into my head. Suddenly, I needed to hear the answer to that question before I did what I was about to do.

It was November 1, 1999, my seventh year at Key Largo School, and three weeks before my thirtieth birthday. I had finally and completely gone through and come out the other side of the problems that had plagued me the first three years of my teaching career. Classroom management, which had started out as an area of supreme weakness, had actually become my strength. My unique approach to kids and teaching led me to do conference presentations on my discipline plan and the innovative and creative hands-on projects and activities I implemented in my classroom.

I had gained a reputation among my fellow teachers as someone who taught in a very non-traditional way. The irony was not lost on me that I had gone from being a teacher who lectured all period and disciplined through fear to the direct opposite. Whenever I presented my approach, teachers who were as lost as I had been sought me out, and some even dared try some of the techniques I shared. It was an odd place to be after struggling so mightily.

So here I was, finally confident in myself as a teacher, and then I asked a life-altering question to one of the wonderful people who worked in the front office of Key Largo School. I stood there fearful of what the answer might be. I was standing on the precipice of a great decision, a choice that, if I made it, was irrevocable. It would fundamentally alter my life and the people who mattered most to me.

As I write these words, I realize this section will alter how some people see me or know me.

"Am I good man?"

"Mr. Quigley, you are one of the best I know." She smiled and gave me a wink.

So it was decided.

I held in my hand five letters, four addressed to my brothers and sisters, and one to my parents.

I will not go into the content of the letter but the import of what it said can be summed up in three words: I am gay.

Some of you reading this might wonder why I have included this aspect of who I am in this book about my teaching journey. I have spent hours and hours in my own mind debating whether I should. I have no desire to alter how people who know me perceive me, and I don't want any future kid who now knows this to shy away from me.

But . . . !

For me teaching has always been a journey. From the moment my dad suggested I major in something that would get me a job, to the first class I observed, to when I changed my major, did my internship, got my first teaching job and found my way, it has always been a journey to find my best self in the classroom. I believe life is a journey to become the man and woman we are supposed to be in our jobs and in our lives. The purpose of this book is for you to see my journey and the truth of my teaching life. But the life inside the four walls that define a classroom is not separated from or unaffected by what happens outside the classroom in a teacher's life. This is especially true for me.

Being a gay man informs what I do in my classroom. It informs how I see my kids, the way I deal with them, how I treat them, and how my heart breaks for the outsider, for the kid alone, the kid separated and friendless. It's why I have always tried to help the lost and hurting ones.

When I think of my students, I think of a book given to me years ago by Mrs. St. James, my principal at KLS, a book titled *Love Me When I Am the Most Unlovable*. This is what it means to teach; to teach is to love. To love is to find the capacity to love yourself, to embrace yourself, and then to let that love embrace others.

Around the same time I finally figured out how to run my classroom to maximize what is good about my teaching style, I also started to come out, started dating, started being real with those who loved me and who I loved. Along with learning how to teach my class, I also had to learn how to love my kids, to find beauty in their blemishes, to help the truly helpless, to aid those who needed it. But to do that, I first had to find the capacity within myself to love my blemishes, to admit how helpless I was, and to open my heart and be proud of myself and my life. As my heart opened in the real world, it opened in my class. I have often been accused of being a bleeding heart when it comes to my kids. I am guilty of that because I could no longer deny who I was and what my life was. I couldn't really love my students and be the kind of teacher I needed to be until I found love for myself.

There is no way of knowing whether I would see my role in the classroom the same if I were not gay. I have no idea if I would be as sensitive to my students, especially the ones who feel lost in this world. All I know is that in my class, I lead with my heart, and I am always aware of the kid who needs an encouraging word, a pat on the shoulder, or a smile.

There is another reason that sharing this truth with you is the right thing to do. If we are our stories and our journey, as I believe we are, then the more open we are, the greater our impact will be. Before I began to come out, and especially before I came out to my family, I had to hide who I really was. When I did that, when I do that, I am not nearly as good a teacher as I could be. I believe that to be the best teacher possible, you must be 100 percent yourself in your classroom. When I was hiding, when I was lying, when I was refusing to accept the great truth of my life, I was the worst possible teacher imaginable. The more open I was to *myself* and eventually to *others*, the better I was as a person and a teacher.

How can you possibly love anyone when you can't find it in your heart to love yourself? How can you be open to hear other people's pain when you won't embrace your own? I include this because to not do so would be to deny part of my journey and its great impact on me and my class.

To put it simply, to be the man I needed to be and the kind of teacher I hoped to become, I had to be out to myself. And for this story of myself to be true, to make sense, and to be honest, I need this to be known, though I have never in any way made this known to my students. Being honest with myself about who I am has made every positive interaction I've ever had with any kid possible. The opposite has also been true: the more I've hid, the more I've denied, the further from my truth I've lived, the lesser the person and teacher I've been.

This section sounds far braver than what I felt when I wrote those letters to my family. But once it was done, it was done, and I look back and wonder why I was ever afraid. It is as though there was one man before I did this and another after. The moment I did it, I exhaled, looked back, and wondered why I was ever afraid. That's the thing about fear; most often the scariest part of something is not the thing itself, but the fear we build up in connection to it.

The truth is that I feel fear sharing this with you. And I can only hope that I will look back, after this book has been published, and laugh and think, *that is what you were afraid of, Quigley? That small thing — that couldn't be it! There is so much that could have caused you to feel such fear, but that? — That makes no sense. That is silly! This truth is who you are, and if said with love, it will show that you were silly to believe that sharing it would ever be a problem.*

This is my journey. This is my truth.

As I prepared to celebrate the end of a century and the start of a new one, I could do so knowing that I had pride in who I was. In November 1999, I put those five letters in the mail, told my truth, and knew that this would cause turmoil in my family. At the very least, it would make Thanksgiving and Christmas more than just the usual family gathering with all the trimmings. What I did not know was just how much my world was about to change as the year 2000 loomed.

Karen, a Stuffed Monkey, and the Story

Now that I have lived long enough, I've learned that sometimes years, even decades, can go by and nothing truly eventful or earth shattering happens. There is, of course, the daily, weekly, monthly, yearly job of just being alive, of laughing, of eating, of sleeping, of the stuff of living that happens.

Then there are years that stand out, as though the universe wants to prove that it is still around, that no one's time on this planet is forever, and that the day-to-day of life can be interrupted and altered forever.

In the world of my family, 1999 was that kind of year.

In 1999, my youngest brother graduated from high school and went away to college. This was important for him but even more so for my parents because it was the first time in their marriage that it would be just the two of them. My mom had gotten pregnant two months after they were married. That was in 1967, which meant for 32 years they had a child at home. For 32 years it was them plus one then two then three then four and finally five kids. At one point my mother had four kids under the age of six.

This was also the year my younger sister Bobiann announced that she was pregnant with my parents' first grandchild. My parents could not have been more thrilled.

Starting in the late summer we all watched my sister get bigger as we awaited the arrival of what would become my niece, Sarah McMinn.

My oldest sister Beth bought her first house that year. You could see her pride and joy in owning something, in being able to say that she had done the work and saved the money to make this major event happen.

In 1999, I was still teaching in the Keys, and it had become a joy. I often describe the later years of my time at Key Largo School as the feeling of being wrapped in joy. I moved and lived and worked in joy. My kids were a joy. My colleagues were a joy. My classes were a joy.

For me 1999 was also, as you just read, the year I came out to my family.

The 1999-2000 school year was a time when KLS decided to have elective courses divided by grade levels. I was assigned to teach a sixth grade course I had developed called History Alive. It was a class that allowed my students to explore history in a different way; whatever they wanted to learn, I was game to teach, and if there was some aspect of history I was interested in focusing on, we would learn about that too.

The thing about Key Largo School is that it was a place that catered to giving kids unique experiences, which allowed me to focus on topics that were interesting. The History Alive course was a great example of that.

Working with sixth graders was a new experience. I soon learned there are two kinds of sixth graders: the ones who act like six-year-olds because they are still young kids; puberty has not started, and they are small and childish in their demeanor. In essence, they are still children. Then there are sixth graders who act like sixteen-year-olds; they have boyfriends and girlfriends, they act older, dress older, talk older, and often, puberty has hit full force, and they have dealt with it by trying to be as grown up as they possibly can.

In 1999, I had a student named Karen who was one of those sixth graders who acts like a six-year-old.

I will never forget the first day of school. Here was this short little blond pixie of a girl. She sat separate from the other kids in class, plopped herself down in a chair, and opened up her backpack to pull out a bunch of toys that she placed around the edges of her desk like a wall to keep the force of middle school out. As I started class, she began playing with these toys. Through the first few days of class, she followed this same ritual. Pull out toys, set them up like a wall, and play with them. She was very much a loner, and my heart broke that these toys seemed to be her only friends.

Day after day of her sitting and playing alone made me want to do something to make her feel better and to give her some special attention.

From day to day the toys changed, except for one. Every day, Karen pulled out a long thin green plush pea pod that I found out during the second week of school was named Mr. Green Bean. As Karen was lining up her toys, I did something that to this day I am not quite sure why I did it. I walked over to Karen's desk and grabbed Mr. Green Bean and began talking to him. I asked him what his name was, and that's when she told me it was Mr. Green Bean. I asked him about his day, how he was doing, if he liked sixth grade, if he liked Mr. Quigley's class, and so on. This delighted Karen and made her laugh.

The kids watched and responded by talking more to Karen and asking her if they could play with and hold her toys. When this happened, I could see her swell with pride. Starting that day, whenever she brought Mr. Green Bean to school, I grabbed him and talked to him. This went on for several days until one day Karen brought a toy I had never seen before, a light brown stuffed monkey with a dark brown face. It had Velcro on the pads of its feet and hands, and its limbs were long and thin. It was an unusual toy for her because other than Mr. Green Bean, she had no stuffed animals.

So when she took it out, I asked, "Who is this, Karen?"

She looked up at me and smiled brightly. "This is Mr. Quigley."

I laughed and said, "Where did he get his name?"

You know the look that little kids give you when they think you have just said the stupidest thing possible; that's the look she gave me. She looked up at me, eyes half closed, face scrunched, and forehead creased. "I named him after you."

And then I did something totally spontaneous. I grabbed Mr. Green Bean and Mr. Quigley and took them to the front of the class. I didn't even realize what I was doing until I sat down, and this was how I began class.

"Mr. Green Bean and Mr. Quigley were best friends. In fact, they were the best friends in the whole world. The two of them did everything together — they ran, they played outside, they watched TV, they played video games, they had sleepovers — they were the best friends." The whole time I described the two of them, I acted out each action with both stuffed toys. "They were the bestest best friends that ever were," I said, my voice growing louder and very fast, and then I paused and slowed way down, and said in a soft voice, "until one day, accidentally, Mr. Quigley killed Mr. Green Bean. And he was happy." I threw Mr. Green Bean down, and Mr. Quigley danced around. Again, don't ask me why I did any of this, because to this day, I don't know. I honestly don't know if this is something I should have done or what gave me the idea that this was the proper way to start a sixth grade class. But that is what I did, and boy, did the kids laugh! The kids thought it was hilarious, they loved it, and Karen laughed the most and just beamed.

Starting that day, whenever Karen brought Mr. Green Bean and Mr. Quigley to school, I'd tell a story about them.

The story always started the same way. "Mr. Green Bean and Mr. Quigley were best friends; in fact, they were the best friends in the whole world...."

It always ended the same way: with Mr. Quigley causing the death of Mr. Green Bean.

Very quickly I began to work the stories in with the time periods we were studying. If it was Rome, they were Roman gladiators, or if Ancient Egypt, they were mummy best friends. If it was the Middle Ages, they were knights fighting but still best friends; if World War II, they were soldiers fighting together. Through the fall and start of winter those two stuffed animals became a huge part of that class. Mr. Green Bean and Mr. Quigley became such a big deal that students frequently asked me what story I would tell next.

As we rolled toward Christmas of 1999, my life, my teaching career, and my family were all in this wonderful place.

And then I sent the letters. As I waited to hear the response from my family and to see if I was coming home for Thanksgiving, it gave me time to think about what my family had always meant to me. We were close-knit, tight, and we had our problems, conflicts, and fights, but we had always been a strong unit. I knew by sending the letters I was challenging that status.

Within a week or so it was made clear to me that regardless of how they felt about me being gay, they wanted me to know that my place was at home, that whatever else was true, they wanted me home.

I can still remember the day before Thanksgiving 1999 driving my car onto the street in Tampa where my parents lived. This would be the first time seeing them since the letters. I felt nervous, worried, my heart was beating fast, and I wondered what I would say, what they would say, how this was going to happen.

I parked in the driveway and waited, looking at the quiet of my parents' house. I am not sure how long I sat, but I eventually found myself knocking on their door. My mom opened it. She looked at me, I looked at her, and she spoke first. "Did you get something to eat on the way?"

It was that simple. I walked in, my mom made me something to eat, my dad wandered in from his greenhouse, we talked about pleasant nothings, we didn't mention the letter, but it was done, I was home, I was their son, they were my parents.

A month later we celebrated Christmas.

If you celebrate Christmas, my family's celebration is a lot like yours. We get together, eat a lot of food, laugh a lot, fight a lot, make up, eat some more, give each other presents we don't want, and eat some more. That Christmas of 1999 was the same, with the exception of my sister being pregnant, my brother being a college man now, and me being gay. Besides all that, it was just another year, just another Christmas. Regardless of other things that change, it is so good that some things don't.

The only other thing unusual about that Christmas was that my mom had not been feeling well. She had gone to the doctor, and they had determined that she needed to have her gall bladder removed, but she had decided to postpone the surgery until after Christmas since it was not a big deal.

So we got together, had a great Christmas, exchanged presents, had lots of food and fun, and enjoyed just being a family.

I went back home to the Keys and waited for the New Year.

New Year's 1999 was the end of one millennium and the start of another. It was something that I had been told by Prince since high school that I was required to have a party unlike any other. All across the country, there was a lot of pressure and anxiety to make this New Year's unlike any other. People planned and schemed and tried to figure out what the perfect New Year's Eve should be. How do you properly go from 19-something to 20-something? The truth is I don't even remember what I did at all. And my guess is that many if not most adults are in the same position I am; all that pressure and it was just another New Year.

A couple of days later my winter vacation ended and I was back to work.

My first day back was also the day my mother had her gall bladder surgery.

When I got home that day, I called my parents to find out how the surgery went, but the phone just rang and rang and rang and rang. So I kept trying. I called them and called them and called them and they never picked up, which is not unusual because my parents never picked up the phone, but it seemed unusual on this day when they knew we kids would be calling to see how Mom was doing. After an hour, I gave up and called my sister Bob, who is also one of those people who never picks up, but she did, and I asked, "Bob, how did the surgery go?"

There was a pause, so I persisted. "Bob, I've been trying to call Mom and Dad, but they aren't picking up. How did the surgery go today?"

Again there was a pause on her end until she finally said, "You need to talk to Mom and Dad."

"I know, I've been trying to call them for an hour but they are not picking up. How did the surgery go?"

Her response was, "You need to talk to Mom and Dad."

I began to get a little exasperated. "I know, I have been trying, but they won't pick up. You know Mom and Dad, they never pick up. Bob, how did the surgery go?"

She again hesitated, much longer this time, but her response was the same. "You need to talk to Mom and Dad."

I felt a little coldness creep in. "Bob, you are starting to freak me out. Tell me, how did the surgery go?"

There was no response but a long pause, a sigh, and then she spoke. "They opened her up, they looked around, and they found something."

On the word *something*, my insides turned cold. "Wait, what did they find?"

This time the pause was long and profound. "They found what they think is cancer."

I felt my whole body get quiet and still as a wave of coldness washed over me. "Wait, what? Where?"

This time, my sister, the nurse, really paused and responded with one devastating word. "Everywhere."

"What does that mean?"

"You need to come back home, Honcho. If it is cancer, they are giving her a week, maybe less. You need to come home."

1999, phone in my hand, mother, cancer, everything.

I ended the conversation with my sister and again tried to call my parents, but still no response, so I called my school to let them know what was happening. I spoke directly with my principal, and she didn't even hesitate. She just told me to go, that they would take care of everything, that I was just to go. I had lesson plans for the next two weeks, so just go.

So I did, and four hours later, I was in my parents' driveway.

My father greeted me in the driveway, we hugged, didn't say a lot, not even sure what to say or how to put any words to the enormity of what was happening.

Inside the house, my mother took one look at me and immediately said I had to be hungry and went off to the kitchen to make me food.

I followed behind.

So there I was, on the day I was told that it was likely my mother was dying of cancer, standing in her kitchen as she cooked me a meal I didn't want. We talked in hushed tones about everything except what was happening. How was it possible to be standing there talking as though the world hadn't been blown up with one trip to the doctor? Nothing rang true, about her, about it, about any of this!

Several days later, we got the confirmation: it was cancer, and she was given no more than a few days to live.

That, however, wasn't my mother's plan. For the next two weeks I stayed with my parents. In that time my mom was simply my mom. She looked like my mom, talked like my mom — she was my mom. She was a bit more tired, but you never would have known she was sick. My brothers and sisters visited often, we had meals, played cards, watched TV, laughed; nothing was different, and nothing said that she was sick and that she was dying.

I did what I could. I cooked and cleaned and tried to help out. My dad took on the main job of taking care of my mother, so I took on the job of taking care of everything else.

In those two weeks I was able to have some special conversations with my mother about her life, about my life, and though I wanted to say more, talk more, reassure her more, we did get time, and we did get the space to say some things we'd both been wanting to say.

But at the end of two weeks, I had to go back to the Keys. The quarter had ended and I needed to do grades, and even more, to create lesson plans that would keep my students on track in my absence.

While I was gone, my fellow teachers had told the kids what had happened. The kids knew my mom was sick, that she was dying. I am grateful to those teachers and the gentle way they told my students what was going on, and the way they prepared my kids for when I was coming back.

That first day back to school I was incredibly nervous. I didn't know how the kids were going to respond to the news, didn't know if they would shake it off with the typical indifference that teenagers are known for, how they were going to act toward me or even how I was going to act toward them. For two weeks I had been in the bubble of my parents and cancer. Nothing in my time as a teacher had prepared me for this.

The first morning back, I got to school nearly two hours before classes started. As I approached my classroom door, what greeted me surprised me and set the tone of what the two weeks back with my students would be like. Waiting outside of my door were three of the roughest, toughest eighth grade boys I taught that year; two of them would be in jail by the time they got out of high school. As I approached they walked up to me. When I asked them what they were doing at school so early, they each put their hands on me, one hugged me as though the world depended on it, and they said that they had asked their parents to drop them off early because they wanted to make sure I was okay. I stood there with tears in my eyes and they had tears in theirs, then we went inside. In the next hour my room filled with students, all equally concerned. My desk was covered with messages from my students, and one of the walls in my classroom had a banner welcoming me back.

On that first day and in the week I was back at work, the kids did such incredible decent things, things that were small but made all the difference in the world to me. Some just hugged me without saying a word, others told me they were praying for me, others left messages or flowers or drawings in my room, still others asked about my mom, wanting to know all about her; and they told me sad stories about their own lives. One young lady told me every day I saw her, "I love you, Mr. Quigley," and another, "I pray for your mom every day, Mr. Quigley." Eighth grade boys, who are not always known for being the most gentle or thoughtful, made it their mission to make sure I was okay. In a very typical teenage boy way, they did it both awkwardly and sweetly.

I have to take a moment from the story to express a thought here: it makes me angry when I think about how adults talk about teenagers. They say things like teenagers don't care, that they are rude, have no respect, no sympathy, no kindness. My experience with teenagers has been completely different. They are the most amazing and kind people I have ever known, open, loving, and willing to show kindness for no reason other than because they are good. Sure, teenagers can be jerks, but that is often when they are in groups and they fear showing any sign of weakness among their peers. This attitude is not about their strength; so often teenage bravado is about their deepest fears.

After being at work for two weeks, I headed back to Tampa.

In that time, my mother had grown weaker, but still, more than a month after she had been told she had a week left, my mom was still with us. During the next three weeks I spent with her, she welcomed her sisters to visit, along with my father's family. We enjoyed family gatherings, and my brothers and sisters came over nightly. I again helped the best I could, doing most of the cooking and cleaning to allow my dad to spend every moment with my mom.

When I was alone with my mom, I talked with her about the past, about all the things that mattered to her and her life: her kids, her house, her husband, our happiness, our success. We only spoke about the gay issue once, and during that conversation, she said she did not understand or approve of it, but she did trust me to be a good man and to lead a good life. It wasn't much, but at least she knew me. I have often been asked in the years since if I regret telling her so close to the end of her life, or if I felt any guilt at adding to her burden, or whether telling her might have made her sickness worse. The answer to all of these questions is no. What matters is for good or ill, I was able to tell my mother my truth.

After three weeks I had to return to the Keys to do a presentation that I was being paid to give to teachers. Ironically, the topic was how to do discipline, and it made me smile and shake my head to think that the thing that almost cost me my job and nearly made me quit teaching was the thing that I was now being asked to present around the state of Florida.

While I was gone, my mother's health deteriorated rapidly. She went from being my mom, acting like my mom, talking like my mom, cooking every meal and being the center of my family's life, to this person that no longer was my mom. She stopped eating. She stopped talking. She slept, hour after hour, and when she was awake, she had this blank stare.

I wondered if my mom was even there.

But my mom was tough. She is by far the toughest person I have ever known in my life. She had already lived more than six weeks longer than they expected her to. Through this, we all held out one hope, that she would make it to the birth of her first grandchild in March.

I spent two more weeks with my mom, and during that time, I could see the end coming painfully and slowly as she deteriorated, but I had to return to work. I had no more lesson plans for the substitute teacher, and grades were coming due.

I drove back on Sunday, February 28, and the next morning, my father called me as I was about to go out the door. He told me I needed to come back, that my mom was fading, and he didn't know how much longer she would live.

So I went to work knowing I wanted to get to my mom as soon as possible. To make that happen and to be able to spend time with my family after my mom passed, I needed to prepare several weeks of lesson plans.

When my first period students walked in that morning, I told them the honest truth. "You need to sit there and shut up and leave me alone. My mother is very sick, and I need to do this work so that I can go see her and say goodbye to her before she passes away."

My first period came in and left.

I told my second period, "You need to sit there and shut up and leave me alone. My mother is very sick, and I need to do this work so that I can go see her and say goodbye to her before she passes away."

I have no idea what those kids did. I was working and they were doing what they were doing.

I knew if I could get the lesson plans done by the end of third period, I had fourth period planning, and I could leave.

At the end of third period, I was nearly done. The bell rang, the kids were leaving, and I was about to finish when I felt this shadow over me, and there, in the middle of the lesson plans, something was put down on my desk. It was a stupid stuffed monkey. I looked up into the bright serious eyes of Karen, and I just lost it.

"WHAT?" I screamed at her. "WHAT DO YOU WANT?"

She looked at me, smiled, and in her soft voice she said, "Take him with you and know that we love you."

And she walked out.

I shook my head, put the stuffed monkey to the side and finished my work, left my classroom and ran to my car. It was only as I was putting the key in to unlock my car that I realized I was holding this stupid stuffed monkey. I looked down at it then opened the door and threw him onto the passenger seat and drove to my house to gather some clothes to go to Tampa.

When I got to my apartment, there was a message on my answering machine from my dad. "Get here when you can. Your mom died this morning."

I hadn't made it in time. I didn't get to say goodbye.

I walked downstairs to my car and put my suitcase in, and that's when I saw Mr. Quigley face down on the floor.

Everything connected to that silly stuffed animal had been a mystery. Why did I talk to Mr. Green Bean? Why did I use him and Mr. Quigley to tell all these stories with one of them dying? When Karen gave him to me, why did I pick him up? And now, as I looked down at this child's toy, I wondered why I put the suitcase in my trunk and walked around to the passenger side of my car.

I DON'T KNOW WHY I DID IT!

But I picked him up and strapped him into the passenger's seat, and for the next nearly five hours I talked to Mr. Quigley about my mom. I told him everything I had said to her and the things that were so hard to say. Told him about every little thing, all the big things, the joy things, the only you things, the things that you are going to miss, the things that only a mom can mean. I said them to him even though they were all to her. I told him every memory of my mom I could think of, all my emotions, everything came out, I laughed, I cried, I told long rambling pointless stories that tried to say what a mom means to someone.

How do you describe love? How do you give love to a parent as an action, a reality, without making it seem so simple that it becomes commonplace? A child's feelings and love for his parents, the people who gave him life, they are the beginning of everything. But thank you for a meal, a house, a bed, a place, a beginning. I don't know the words to say without you. I am not and may never be able to give them enough to convey the sheer bigness of it. But I tried on that drive, I tried and I said them all to a stuffed silly monkey given to me by a sixth grader who in one simple sweet action tried to offer me something to make it okay. And I used this gesture as a way to talk to my mom. At the end, he sadly knew more about my true feelings, all of them, the good, the bad, the sad of how I truly felt than I ever was able to say to her.

Hours later, in late afternoon, I made it to Tampa. I walked into my parents' house.

Near the end, my mother could no longer make it up and down the stairs to the second floor bedrooms, so we had brought her bed down to her. It was still light out, but it was dark in the house. I found my father in the same place he had been for hours, sitting on the bed my mom had died in. He had not wanted to leave it.

There is a lot I could tell you about my father, about our relationship, about the man he shaped me into; about the things we shared, about his hopes and dreams, the sorrows and the failures. My mother always said about me, "You're not a chip off the old block; you are the whole block reincarnated." One of my father's quirks is that he did not like swearing. Even if you were an adult, if he caught you swearing, he would throw you out of his house.

He was sitting on the edge of the bed looking down in despair when I walked in, and when I sat down next to him and put my arm around his shoulder, he choked out, "It's so fucking unfair. It's so fucking unfair."

For the entire next week, Mr. Quigley, the stuffed monkey, sat on my bed or was with me all the time. He came with me in my suit jacket to the viewing, the last time I would see my mom. He rode in the car with me to the funeral service, and when we said goodbye to her at the cemetery and laid her to rest in the ground. He was there when people mumbled apologies and told stories of my mom. He was there for the hugs, the I'm so sorrys, the pointless but expected how are you doings; he was there when everyone left and it was just the six of us. But sometimes seven minus one isn't six; it's a number so low and so negative that no math can calculate it. He was there night after night, giving comfort, giving me someone to talk to or just letting me know that there was a place and a world where I could go and feel love. He was there for all of it. And he, more than my family or my friends, got me through those awful days.

Every time when I thought things would get too much, I would reach my hand into my suit jacket and touch the fur, and it would make me smile a little and hear Karen's words, " . . . and know you are loved."

After two weeks I returned to school.

My first day back was a very tough day. My kids were kind when my mom was sick, but now they were even more so — loving, and giving, and so very thoughtful. Child after child spoke to me, embraced me; some tried to talk, their eyes filled with tears; others talked and started to cry. Each kid was somber, sad, and I could feel the weight of what they knew I had been through. When my third period class walked in, so did Karen.

I had placed Mr. Quigley on my desk. When Karen sat down, I walked over to her carrying Mr. Quigley, my thumbs caressing the softness of his fur.

She looked up with a question in her eyes.

"Here," I said, "and thank you," and for the first time that day, I got choked up.

She smiled and gave me a mini version of the scrunched up you're-being-silly look. "No, he's yours now, Mr. Quigley."

I looked down at this stupid stuffed monkey, and I felt like I had been given the richest present ever.

I don't like monkeys.

I don't like stuffed animals.

And I could not imagine a more wonderful thing to own.

Mr. Quigley lives in different places in my room, sometimes on my podium, sometimes on my desk, sometimes on my shoulders, and sometimes, when they for some reason need him or want him, on the shoulder or desk or in the arms of one of my kids. He will at times, often for reasons I never know, become something they need, and so I let them have him. I never know where he is going to end up or in what position I will find him: in a lotus position practicing his yoga or swinging from the celling or in a hammock my students made with some cloth. I will be teaching and see him cradled in some kid's arms. No matter where he is, it always makes me smile, and I get choked up a little bit.

In the first few days of each new school year, I introduce Mr. Quigley to my new crop of students. I tell them that he is the most valuable thing in the world I own.

I tell them his name, and I also tell them there is a story of his name, which I will tell, but they have to ask and ask a lot for a long time. Weeks will go by, a month or two, and they ask to hear the story. Eventually I tell them, and they get angry when they find out that how he got his name is not the real story, but rather, it's how he came to be mine. But I make them ask again for weeks and even a month or more.

I eventually tell them the whole story, about Mr. Green Bean, my mom, of cancer and a little girl, about all the kids who did something nice for me that year, and all the kids since.

Today, when I look at Mr. Quigley, what surprises me is that the story is not only about my mom. What I think of the most is all the kids I have ever taught, all the good decent kindness, of laughing with them, talking with them — I see a parade of kids' faces, I see cards and letters and pictures and presents. I see awkward timid teenagers and kids filled with bravado terrified if they let their guard down just a little because everyone will know how broken they are. I see needy kids and hurt kids, happy kids and kids who have been so horribly hardened by a world that does that to too many kids. I see desks and rooms and buildings filled with kids, names I've forgotten but smiles and stories and perfect unforgettable moments that I can close my eyes and see and feel. They are the story of Mr. Quigley, and so I have shared it with them.

For whatever reason, sharing the story of Mr. Quigley and my mom has meant something to them, and in the years since she died, I have been given lots and lots of stuffed monkeys, well over a hundred.

I will never forget the first time a student gave me one; it was a year later, for Christmas, that I unwrapped her.

I held her in my hands trying not to get choked up.

"So who is this?' I asked.

The student paused then said, "That's Mr. Quigley's girlfriend." I smiled and told him that the monkey was getting more dates than I was.

The next year, my class had gone to the local zoo as a class science field trip, and the day after the trip, they walked in all smiles and presented me with another monkey. I again asked who this was. They looked at each other and got into a huddle, and after much talk told me that this was Mr. Quigley's son. My response was, "WOW, they are not even married," indicating Mr. Quigley and his girlfriend. Another quick huddle and it was decided.

Three days later, during lunch, with a wedding cake and the principal to officiate, Mr. Quigley married Mrs. Quigley.

In 1999, I finally found the guts to be myself to the people who mattered most. I lost my mom, and the devastation of that still affects me as I type these words, but my mom gave me something and taught me something about my students. Her death brought me closer to my students. Mr. Quigley has allowed me to connect emotionally with so many students. When I tell the story of Mr. Quigley, an emotional bond forms, and students feel safe to share their own stories of loss. They become part of the story, and because of them, the story has grown. Karen and all the kids that have come after her have taught me a lesson that has made my classroom something more, something it hadn't been before, and all it took was the kindness of one child when I was at the lowest point of my life, to show me how a classroom of kids could become my family.

The Specialness of Key Largo School

Key Largo School made an indelible imprint on my life. I became a teacher at Key Largo School. I became a man at a Key Largo School. I lost my mom at Key Largo School. I came out at Key Largo School. But most of all, I discovered what a group of good, loving, committed people can do to make a child's life a little bit better. I would love to say that I touched and changed every kid's life who I met during my time at KLS, but the truth is no teacher, no matter how great, how loving, how committed can reach every kid. What I learned at KLS is not that every kid can be reached. I learned it is our job to do our best, to give our hearts, to reach out our hands, to be willing to do anything and everything we possibly can to help every kid.

I also learned that not every kid, no matter how far you reach your hand, is able to reach back. Sometimes kids just need time; they need to fall down a little bit more before they can reach back. And for some kids, the things that have happened, the lives they have led, even as middle school kids, are not redeemable.

Every year that I have been a teacher, I have had a number of kids who my heart has broken for, and all I have wanted to do is to take them by the shoulder, look down into their faces filled with fear or anger or sadness or loneliness, and tell them, "It's okay. I will give you a home where you're safe and loved." But of course no teacher can do that, and every time a hurting child has turned and walked out of my class, a part of me has felt just as destroyed and hurt and lost as they were.

Later, I will speak about what I believe is the role of a teacher when it comes to being a part of a kid's life, but I think that no matter what, it is a teacher's job to be sensitive to what kids are going through. So many teachers I have known and taught with over the years have purposely avoided getting to know their students, and have shown little concern for what their kids were going through outside of school. Some do this because they do not feel it is their job to know or care. Others remain detached because they don't feel comfortable getting involved in a child's life outside of school; still others because they believe it is their job to demand that their students learn at the highest level, and to take time to care about whatever their kids are going through is perceived as taking time away from teaching.

I believe that being academically demanding and emotionally sensitive are not mutually exclusive.

I believe that my compassion and willingness to reach out to my kids comes from being bullied as a child, feeling awkward, devoid of friendship, and lonely. I do believe that this made me attuned to the kid who is separate and apart from the others. For this reason I try very hard to never put a kid on the spot or to make him or her feel the sting of scorn and rejection. I would also like to think my parents, who believed in dignity and respect, played a part in wanting to ease the passage in life of a child.

I also think that being a gay teen helped me understand that children are a vast sea of feelings hidden beneath the smile, the good grades, the rebellion, the anger, the disrespect — the bravado of being a teen is the mask that so many kids wear.

All of these have made me sensitive to what a child is going through, but I believe I would be a different teacher if it weren't for the extraordinary group of women I taught with at KLS. Each one of them made a huge impact on the teacher I am. For eight years I got the best education in kindness, caring, and teaching.

The first of the ladies who helped me so much at KLS was Carter Hannah. She was not a classroom teacher but the school librarian. Very early on in my teaching career, she reached out to help and guide me. What Carter taught me was that a teacher should do more than just teach; you have to show up, you have to do things before and after school, field trips and all manner of school programs. I watched her organize and then involve me in organizing all sorts of school activities. She taught me that teaching happens in your classroom and everywhere else.

I will never forget when I was scolded in the library by the county director for Social Studies, a person who for whatever reason had no use for me as a teacher. She had just observed a lesson I had taught, and she was in the process of ripping me apart. This was several years into my time at KLS, and I had come a long way. In the middle of this diatribe, Carter interrupted the women to tell her that my principal was looking for her. This ended the conversation. I was devastated and limped back to my room. Twenty minutes later, in walked Carter and Mrs. St. James. It was then I realized what Carter had done: she had called my principal, made an excuse to get this women away from me, and here the two of them were to make sure I was okay and to let me know what a good job they both thought I was doing with the kids. In that moment, I felt all the kindness that Carter had spent years giving to kids. I spent hours in the library listening to Carter and talking to her. She is a wonderful person who gave me so much

Another teacher who made a tremendous impact on my life was Susan Dempsey-Coopersmith. From the start of my time at KLS, it was Sue more than any other teacher I wanted to emulate. I wanted my kids to talk about me the way her kids talked about her. She was the teacher other kids went to when they were down, when they were fighting with their parents or their friends; when something was happening in their lives, it was Sue they went to. I wanted to be the teacher that kids could rely on to be there, and I watched Sue to find out how. I watched her treat each kid differently, and noticed how she had a special and kind word for each one. It was a lesson in how to love a kid when no one else would.

Another incredible woman was Linda Gass. She was everyone's mom. She taught like a mom, listened like a mom, spoke like a mom, hugged like a mom. She had this innate goodness about her that shone like some kind of light. She had the incredible ability — with a smile, with a pat on the back, with a kind word — to kick kids in the ass and leave them wanting to do better and be more. Many teachers want to say that they don't have time or interest in being there for a kid, and what's more, it isn't their job because it gets in the way of teaching whatever subject they teach. Every time I hear this, I think of Linda and want her to be there to look at these teachers, give them a motherly smile, and then kick them in the ass to do the right thing by their students.

And then there was Roseanne Ganim. Roseanne is and was a mystery to me. I kept trying during my first three years to find the magic formula to great teaching. Roseanne proved there is no one formula to become great, and she is the reason I believe greatness is a journey to find the best you that you can be — and then be that. I have never known someone to command more respect, to get kids to work harder or to allow kids more freedom. I have seen Roseanne walk into a room of talking teenagers and they just stop dead, each kid looking to her and listening, waiting for her instruction. It was instantaneous. I have watched her run a Student Government program where each kid had a voice and was encouraged to be amazing. I saw kids who could not do math, but after a few weeks in her class, they got it — all of this from a 5'2" former strict-as-strict-comes nun. That woman had magic.

This job we call teaching is something that can be learned, but when it is done right it is a high art. I know I saw four skilled creators of four very different classrooms raise that art to a new level.

I was lucky enough to be on a team with these four women, to be nurtured and guided by them, to hear their counsel and to watch them deal with the educational system, parents, and kids. Put simply, I got hella lucky!

I have never done an adequate job of explaining what Key Largo School was really like. It is the best school I ever had the opportunity to teach at. The school was this funny, creative innovative place where we were pushed at every turn to be better, to explore the new and the different. It was led by an administrator who was constantly going to workshops to learn new approaches and directions in teaching. She brought the best professionals to school to shake things up. In the eight years I was at Key Largo School, she brought in people to rethink the entire middle school experience, to create school-wide activities, and to understand authentic assessment and projects. Every teacher was trained in the various aspects of different learning styles so that we could meet our kids' unique needs. We learned what leadership meant.

Every aspect of what we did was up for evaluation. If there was a better way for kids to learn, we threw out what we were doing and did something new. The one sentence I remember from my time at KLS that best defined what the school was about came from a workshop: "Sacred cows sometimes make the best hamburger." There was nothing sacred at KLS other than getting the best out of our kids and helping them excel.

We teachers were expected to embrace the new. We were expected to go to conferences, take classes, and learn new ideas and approaches. It was expected that we would bring these ideas into our classrooms. It was never enough to just go to the conference, get the information, and go back to doing the same old thing every day. We were expected to implement those methods and ideas so that they mattered to our kids and our class.

Every year at our opening meetings, the new idea that we were going to focus on and be trained in that year was revealed. At the time, I resented so much constant change. I resented that just when I got used to whatever new idea we were supposed to do the previous year, we were presented with something new the next. Now I am so glad I had that experience and was expected to be better, always better, never satisfied with mediocrity.

The middle school was governed by the teachers, and the administration allowed great leeway in how the middle school team did things. The school was organized and run by us, the schedule was structured by us, and the discipline was implemented by us. The best example of this was the in-school suspension program, which allowed the teachers, any time a child acted incorrectly, with no layer of administration to deal with, to send a kid out. You the teacher felt empowered in this system.

The world that existed outside of the walls of Key Largo School made teaching there a joy and a challenge. The Keys are a tourist playground. It is a long thin strip of land divided by US 1; driving south, to the right is the Florida Bay, to the left is the Atlantic Ocean, and lining the road and the water are tourist trap souvenir stores, restaurants, bars, dive shops and few other businesses. The entire place is wrapped in a tacky tourist covering. In the Keys, you are either the rich, or you serve the rich. There are pockets of extreme wealth and horrible shanty poverty. Most people in the Keys who work have jobs in some tourist business. There are few professional jobs. Families struggle, and many of the kids I taught had never left the Keys. There was this isolated island mentality.

They Keys are a land of beauty, but they're a place where lots of people live because they're running to or from something. It is not unusual to go to a bar and see a parent and kid sitting next to each other. When I taught at Key Largo School, it was not surprising to have a parent conference with someone who looked like they drank hard and slept harder. Often the kids came from really tough backgrounds, had little support at home, and had giant gaps in their learning, but KLS was the perfect school for these kids. Failure was never an option because we loved them.

There are a lot of stories I could tell about the kids I had at KLS and the way we as a school dealt with those unique and amazing kids. I have chosen one situation to show you the goodness, the heart, the decency of the place and the amazing group of people that made up that school and the eight years I was lucky enough to teach there.

The day we returned from summer break, there was always a faculty meeting, and KLS is a pre-K through eighth grade school. This meeting was followed by a middle school team meeting, and that afternoon or the next day we had a grade-level team meeting. The way KLS was structured we had a team of five teachers: math, science, Social Studies, reading, and English for each grade level, six through eight. It was a true middle school concept with each teacher on the team dealing with the same kids.

At that first grade-level meeting, we received information about one of the kids we would have that year in eighth grade. This kid, I will call him Joey, had been a troubled child for years. He was not a strong student, he was very hyper, he often blurted out in class, but he was also very loving and sweet. Like a lot of troubled kids, he could go from a hellion one moment to a child who needed to be held the next. He identified strongly with adults, being very wary and fearful of his fellow students. He had not passed sixth grade and barely passed seventh. More and more he struggled, and reading was especially difficult for him. High school would be a true challenge. It was up to us to get all of our kids ready for that and to hold back kids who couldn't make it. This was always a wrenching decision. Eighth grade is a tough time in a kid's life, but to be held back is horrible, especially twice in three years. But none of this was why we were talking about him on that first day at school.

Linda told us the rest of Joey's story, the part that went beyond the troubled kid at school.

The Florida Keys are very beautiful, a natural paradise, but they are also a place where people go to run. The Keys are literally the end of the world, especially for the eastern part of the United States. People who run to Florida and are running away from the life, their mistakes, the people they were, and the things they want to be rid of keep running and end up in the Keys. Joey was the child of a mother who was running. She ran to the Keys when Joey was two and decided that a child wasn't what she wanted, so she gave him up. He was literally dropped on the steps of one of the runaway shelters for kids in the Keys. It took over a year to find her, and when they did, she was strung out on drugs and in no shape to be a mother, so Joey became a ward of the state. But Joey was a sweet and loving kid, and so he got lucky; he was adopted before he started kindergarten at KLS. For the next seven years, he was a student at KLS.

A few weeks before school started for his eighth grade year, his adoptive parents decided to leave the Keys. So they packed up everything they owned, put it in a van, and began the long drive out of the Keys. Before they left, they stopped at the same runaway shelter Joey had been dumped at as a two-year-old, and they told him they no longer wanted him.

I sat in silence not believing any people could be this cruel. To be dumped by the people he loved the most at the same runaway shelter his mother had dumped him, the person who should have loved him the most, his mom, was unfathomable. This was beyond cruel, beyond wrong, a whole new level of awful selfish evilness.

When Linda finished this story, she looked around the room. I couldn't look at anyone because if I did, I knew I would cry. I have no idea who suggested what happened next, but the moment someone did, we all agreed.

"We can't hold this kid back. We can't fail him. We can't give him an F. No matter what this kid does, he isn't going to fail my class."

We decided then and there that we would do what was in our power to do. We couldn't be this kid's mom, we couldn't make the hurt and pain go away, we couldn't bring this kid's life back, but we could make the next year easier. We could give him a home, a place where he could be safe and feel safe. It was all we could do to lessen this kid's burden.

Some would say that what we did to help Joey is what's wrong with education, because we refused to let him fail a grade, but when I look back at my time at KLS, I am more proud of that than anything else.

My eight years at KLS helped me grow up, grow into, and find pride in myself as a man and as a teacher. That's what those kids gave to me. Teaching is by definition the giving of knowledge, but lessons are learned from both sides. I hoped that I left some knowledge in my kids, but what they left in me was far more valuable.

From the start of my teaching career, I was a failure. I started my time at KLS making international news and almost getting fired. After eight years I had gone from disaster to success. In that time, I was named Monroe County's Social Studies Teacher of the Year and Key Largo School's Exceptional Student Education Mainstream Teacher of the Year, and nominated several times for the overall Teacher of the Year award. I felt gratified for these honors knowing where I came from and the work, the emotion, and the pain I put in.

But as I look back on my time at KLS, what I feel the most grateful about is that it was the perfect place for me, the perfect place for a new teacher. They had a great infrastructure there, good people willing to give of their time and experience to help guide me. I had the kind of principal who saw me struggling but also saw how desperate I was to be good. I got to fail in the most spectacular way, and yet I was saved. And the bliss that followed the last few years at KLS will stay with me forever, teaching in bliss, being around kids who were blissful, in my class, in the hallway, in meetings, every moment had become bliss.

And then I decided it was time to leave.

Eight years after taking the job, I knew it was time to move on. There were a lot of reasons I made this decision, someone of them small and petty, and I would be embarrassed to admit them here. The two biggest were that I had fallen in love with someone who lived in Miami. From my school to his house was a 90-minute drive. I wanted to be closer to him and the life I hoped to create with him.

The other main reason was that I had begun to do presentations around the state of Florida. These conferences and workshops were on my discipline plan and various projects and activities I had helped create. Though these were generally well received, I kept getting the same constructive feedback: sure, you can do these things in The Keys, but can you do them in a place that has a diverse group of students? This fed off the stereotype that the Keys were a magical place where the rules and problems of kids and teaching didn't exist. It became obvious that if I was to continue to present and work with educators, I would need to work in a larger more urban school system. I didn't know where that was going to be, but I knew I wanted to stay in South Florida.

Monsters Both Real and Imagined

A year before I decided to leave KLS, I was presenting at a middle school conference when I met a teacher named Connie Hines who taught in Broward County. She and I became friends, and I shared with her my thoughts about leaving the Keys. Eventually, through conversations, phone calls, visits, emails, and general pleading, Connie convinced me to give Broward County a shot.

Broward hosted a job fair at the Broward Convention Center attended by thousands of teachers, all vying for jobs at hundreds of schools throughout Florida. During a seven-hour period, I interviewed with over fifteen schools and left the fair with offers from over ten. Going in, I had no idea what if any value I could bring to a school. After, I did not know which job to take. I didn't know any of these schools, where they were located, what kind of kids they had or what kind of schools they were. Each middle school that offered me a job seemed to offer something that I was looking for.

The job that I eventually accepted was at Perry Middle School. I did so for two reasons. First, the woman who interviewed me had been to one of my presentations, and she seemed very positive about having me at her school. Secondly, the school was starting a new program, a school within a school, which meant teachers would be given great latitude in their teaching. I would be part of a select group of teachers to create and initiate the program. I loved the idea of that.

I took the job without an idea about the school other than that.

When I moved to Broward County that summer, I met several people who knew about Perry Middle School, and from each person I got the same reaction.

"Perry, ohhhhhh . . . um . . . wow!"

That ohhhhhh wasn't ohhhhhh, you made the best choice you could make; it was ohhhhhh, what were you thinking?

Former teachers at Perry: "Ohhhhhh . . . ."

Former students who went to Perry: "Ohhhhhh . . . ."

Teachers from other schools in Broward County: "Perry? Ohhhhhh . . . ."

People who lived in Broward County: "Perry? Ohhhhhh . . . ."

This response was accompanied by a combination of one or more of the following words: very tough school, very tough kids, poor administration, poor teaching, poor area. And then I would get the look that said it all: poor you.

In the summer, as I prepared to join the staff at Perry, I built up an image in my mind of who these kids were. They became these huge hulking thugs from some inner city teaching movie starring me in the role of Michelle Pfeiffer.

The fears I thought I had conquered at the start of my teaching career resurfaced. I wouldn't be able to control this group of kids. The class would dominate me. The monsters had returned, and I was helpless to stop them.

As a new teacher to Broward County, I was required to attend a county meeting with all the other new teachers. This meeting was run jointly by the county and the union. At this meeting, the union told us every horrible thing that could possibly happen to a teacher: out of control parents, out of control kids, out of control schools. They gave us phone numbers to call for advice when things went horribly wrong and we needed the union to come in and save us.

The next bit of advice finally got me to walk out and finish the "seminar" in the hallway.

They made it clear that a teacher should never be personal with their students. We were to tell them nothing, never be alone with a child, never talk to them about our life outside of the classroom, never ever touch a kid ever, not even a slap on the back or a pat on the arm or an arm around their shoulder. Kids will sue, parents will sue, you will get fired, and you will never teach again.

I walked out, seething.

The subtle message:

Don't care.

Don't connect with your kids.

Don't ever make physical contact.

This was the opposite of everything I believed, everything I knew about being a good teacher. I decided then and there that even if I got fired for hugging a crying kid who just told me that something awful happened to them, then so be it! But again, the message from the union, the group that existed to protect me, was that the kids I was about to teach were looking to exploit my goodness. They were monsters that must be carefully dealt with, monsters ready and willing to destroy you and your career.

As my time to start at Perry approached, my fears grew.

My first experience at Perry was at a meeting for teachers who were new to the school. There were a lot of new teachers, an interesting mix of young new educators and older new teachers for whom teaching was a second career.

We were talking quietly among ourselves, getting to know each other, when the door to the library flew open and the assistant principal marched in. He had his hands behind his back, and he stared at us with this piercing menacing look as he paced back and forth in front of us. All conversation came to a complete halt, and the room went silent. He made eye contact with each and every teacher as he paced. After making sure that he had our complete and focused attention, he walked over to a plastic garbage container sitting at the front of the room, pulled his leg back, and kicked the container as hard as he could, flipping it over and spewing garbage everywhere.

He turned to face us.

"Next Monday, I want you to walk into your class and do exactly what I just did, and then I want you to look at them and say, 'Okay, which one of you is next?'"

He went on to emphasize the need for absolute iron-fisted control of the class. He warned us what would happen if we allowed any freedom. He went through the various levels of discipline and how to write detentions, referrals, make phone calls home, and so on.

Welcome to Perry, I thought. This was my introduction to the school I had picked!

Oh my God, the kids are monsters!

The next day, the faculty arrived. After the usual first day stuff, we adjourned to our rooms to prepare. That afternoon we had a second faculty meeting, this one not held in the library but in the cafeteria.

At this meeting, the principal outlined emergency procedures. As he explained what to do in case of a fire, tornado, and every kind of emergency you can imagine, the lights went off. Through the darkness, the principal assured us that this was just an exercise.

And then, for the next twenty minutes, the police did a demonstration of how they would do an incursion into the cafeteria if a shooter had taken it over. In full SWAT team battle armor, guns, masks, moving like the military on the field of battle, they entered the building and secured it. The whole time the principal explained how the police would deal with an emergency, how they would secure a room, secure the school, and take down a shooter. When the lights came back on, we were facing twenty members of the SWAT team. After giving them an enthusiastic round of applause, all I could think was that in the two days I had been a teacher at Perry Middle School, I had been told to kick students like garbage containers, and I had learned how the SWAT team would move in if and when we had a shooter on campus.

What kind of hulking, man-eating monsters attended this school?

The next day I met the team of teachers I would spend the year working with.

The reason I took this job was because the school was creating a special instructional program in which five teachers would work as a team. There were two classes of sixth graders, two classes of seventh graders, and one eighth-grade class. The principal had handpicked four of the teachers from the existing faculty. I was chosen from outside.

I don't know if I have ever been around such an odd idiosyncratic group of teachers.

The math teacher, who was actually a fantastic teacher, was known to take off her shoes to throw at students when they didn't know the answer to a question. She was by far the loudest person I have ever worked with. She was also incredibly funny and would do anything to help the kids. One moment she was berating one kid, and the next her arm was around another kid as she walked him step by step through a problem.

The English teacher was the most negative person I had ever been around. We ate lunch together every day, and she was always going on about how one of her students was the brightest kid ever or the dumbest kid ever. She had a tendency to pick out a kid and spend days grinding him (or her) down. There were days and weeks when she boasted that she simply refused to teach the students, throwing her hands up and saying they weren't teachable. Any slight by a kid she took personally. She loved her sixth graders and a few of the seventh graders, but she loathed the eighth graders. She regularly stated that since the eighth graders were leaving for high school in a year, the only classes to worry about were the sixth and seventh graders. In all of her classes she tried one thing after another after another; for each she claimed that this was the solution to whatever problem existed in her class, and then she would quit the idea at the least bit of resistance from the students.

The science teacher was everyone's mom. Like a lot of teachers who think of themselves that way, she never really asked the students to do anything. As far as I could see, the students didn't do any work in her class. Instead, science became a class where the kids could simply be. Every lunch she had a different story from the kids, and though she was an invaluable person when it came to helping me know whether something was going on with a kid, she didn't really do much teaching.

The final class that all of my kids shared was Spanish. I don't have much to say about this teacher other than that among the kids she was universally despised. When we were around her, she seldom spoke and had little to contribute to the group. By the end of the year, she seldom came to lunch, and isolated herself in her classroom more and more.

Of course I did not know anything about these teachers when I first met them. As we talked about the school and the kids, they did not help to reduce my fears, but rather, they stoked them. They talked openly about the fights, the disrespect, the teachers the kids had driven out, the horrible behavior, the poverty of the kids, the broken homes, the broken kids, the broken classrooms, teachers attacked, and all the other colorful things they could think of to describe Perry Middle School.

It was that night I had THE dream.

Many teachers have the dream. Each person's is slightly different. The basic format of mine is always the same; it is a dream I have every summer at some point before heading back to school. In the nightmare, the classroom, the school, the place changes, the kids may be older or younger, but the dream follows a terribly familiar pattern. It is the first day of school, and I am in front of the class teaching, but no one is listening. The kids are ignoring me or outright being defiant by yelling out or talking back. Nothing I do or say makes them stop and listen. Nothing! I have no control, no power, and in the dream I grow frantic as I try to think of something to get control back. All those awful terrible feelings I had in the years when I was that failing flailing teacher return. I feel the horror that a thirteen-year-old can make you feel when they are in control.

At some point, I wake up in a panic.

The dream came to me that night. I was in my classroom teaching, but I wasn't teaching kids; they were monsters, frightening monsters with snarling fangs, saliva-dripping monsters.

The next morning, I was in my classroom getting ready for the first day of class when the door opened and in walked the monsters.

Except they weren't monsters at all.

The first students I met at Perry were Tommy and his best friend Kara. They were your typical middle school kids. They were happy and smiling and talkative. They were funny and kind. They asked me about things in my room and talked about how excited they were for the start of the year. They weren't monsters. They were kids — just kids.

And that's when I decided I wasn't going to let anyone else's thoughts about the kids in my class become my thoughts. I was sure there would be kids in my class who would be challenging and make me have to work, but they weren't monsters, and I wasn't going to think of them that way.

I would only be at Perry Middle School for one year. But in that year I learned a lot about kids and teaching, and about the heights of success, but I had one of the lowest points of my teaching career during my brief stint at Perry Middle. When I look at my teaching career and wish I could go back and redo anything, it would be that year, but I made mistakes that I have learned from.

The mistakes I made in my first nine years as a teacher were mistakes of ignorance, and of not understanding how to handle certain situations. Those are forgivable, but the mistakes I made at Perry were not because I knew that what I was doing was wrong, and I did it anyway. I knew what good teaching meant. I had gone down enough of the teaching journey to know not to make certain mistakes. And then I made them anyway.

From day one, the kids fought me on the system I had created of basing everything on respect. They openly told me that I did not act like a male teacher should. They did not believe me when I said that I would not treat them with disrespect, and they really did not understand how I could keep my promise that I would not yell. All they had known from all of the males in their life was someone who raised his voice, who threatened, who controlled by intimidation. All of these were the antithesis of how I taught. My students, especially my male students, reacted negatively to this. Though they never said it, they questioned my masculinity and my manhood.

My reaction to this challenge was to compromise the best of me. I would not yell, I would not disrespect them, but I played down my personality. I reduced who I was in class. I lost myself. I changed because of them, and it was only after I left the school and looked back that I realized the degree to which I had lost myself. I held back my true self as a teacher. I did not connect with the kids. Gone was much of my compassion. With the older kids, I took on a tougher more sarcastic more combative tone.

The truth is, I was scared of my students calling me out for not being man enough. I was afraid they would call me out for being gay even if they never used that term. I feared them accusing me of that, for using that against me, and I had no idea what I would do if a kid accused me of that, challenged me on that, used it as a weapon. But I feared it, and as these kids reacted against my personality, I found my personality changing.

I am not proud of this, not proud of being afraid of this part of me, afraid that kids would see me for me, someone sensitive and caring, a man who not only isn't going to yell but who wants to know them. I lost myself to protect myself, but in doing so, they got half of a teacher. Sure I could teach them the information, but I didn't make a difference in their lives. Of all the kids I have ever taught, they needed me the most. They needed this side of me the most, but I wasn't strong enough to be me.

Only at the end of the year would my seventh-grade students confess that they had done things all year to see if I would yell at them. This was their challenge — not outright defiance, but instead, zeroing in on the best most sensitive part of me, and I gave in to them in the worst way possible. I buried the best part of me.

The seventh-graders challenged me by questioning my manhood. The eighth-graders challenged me by seeing if I could control the class. From the outset they were my toughest class. They were the class of kids who talked when I was talking, who disrespected me when I was teaching. They pushed me and challenged me in every way I had spent nine years trying to overcome. But I was a different person now. I kept trying, kept using my methods, kept pushing respect, kept hoping the kids would do what I wanted them to do because *they* wanted to do it.

And I was utterly failing.

Since I couldn't get kids to stop talking when I was teaching, I simply stopped talking.

On a Monday in early October, from the moment my students walked into class, they were greeted by a new me. Normally, I would be standing at the door shaking their hands and welcoming them into my room.

That day I didn't do that. Instead, when they entered the room, I was standing at the front.

On the front board was a letter I had written to the students. The content of that letter said that I had tried for two months to get them to not talk when I was talking, and for two months I had failed, so now I was no longer talking to them. All instructions on what I wanted the students to do would be communicated in writing. All work would be done silently. They would work exclusively out of the book. I would only say three things to any of them: warning, detention, or get out. The letter went on to explain that this was how class would be for the next several days, and if need be, weeks. The students' first assignment was to copy the letter, take it home, and get it signed by their parents.

The first kid who tried to ask me a question, I ignored and pointed to the board. When another student started talking, I warned then gave a detention. I refused to smile or talk. From the start of the class to the end of the class the students did boring book work.

The same thing happened the next day.

And the next.

On Thursday, there were no instructions on the board. Instead, I began class by telling them what I wanted, which was simple: when I was talking, they were to be quiet and listening. I didn't expect them to be perfect at this, but when I called them on it, they would stop breaking whatever rule they were breaking. I further explained I wanted a vibrant class where all kinds of learning happened, a place where we could do lectures, discussions, group work, projects, a place where kids were free to raise their hand, ask questions, and give their opinions. But this could only happen if they were quiet when I spoke. I then asked by a show of hands how many students liked what we had been doing for the past three days. Not one kid raised their hand. I said it was simple, either they would listen and be quiet when I was speaking, or this would be the way I ran the class the rest of the year. The last thing I said was that I really wanted an open class because a silent class was boring to me, and I had hated the last three days as much as they had.

They got the message. Over the next eight months they were by no means perfect, but the class was so much better, and by the end of the year they had become my favorite class.

Meanwhile, my seventh-graders kept pushing me and making comments about how they thought I was not acting correctly, that I wasn't acting like a man, and with each of these comments, I drew further and further into myself.

From the start of the year, my sixth-graders were incredibly sweet. Where the seventh-graders fought the way I taught class, the sixth-graders embraced it. They were hard working, and they responded so positively to everything I did in class. During three periods a day I was on my guard, but with my sixth-graders I could relax.

Early on, I bonded with one of my students, Omari, someone I would only find out later had one of the hardest lives of any kid I met. His dad tried to burn him alive by dousing his blanket with lighter fluid. They were living in a car, and it was after they had a fight when the boy had supposedly eaten too much that his father dumped the lighter fluid over him, but luckily, he was so drunk he couldn't light the blanket.

One day after school, I saw Omari loitering by my door, crying. He gave me a withering stare when I asked if he was okay. I could see his fists clench, and I could feel the anger and tension raging inside of him. So I just opened my classroom door and let him in, and figured he would talk when he needed to. I heard him curl up in one of the beanbag chairs at the back of my room. After an hour I heard him get up and leave. Those beanbags became his beanbags, and each day he came in after school as soon as the bell rang. He never explained why he had been crying or why he came into my room. He just did. And I let him.

Of all my students that year, the one who stands out the most in my mind is Tony, one of my sixth-grade students. Tony was such a lovable boy. He was sweet and always willing to be involved in class. He was one of the smartest kids I taught. He worked hard. He dedicated himself to everything his teachers asked him to do. He was also very hyper, and this got him in trouble in some teachers' classes. For several years in my class I had toys, some of them stress relievers, others just toys that I had accumulated over time. Just like the beanbags had become Omari's, the toys became Tony's. Each day I would find him with three or four toys on his desk as he worked.

One Friday, as we were walking to class, Tony came up to me and whispered that it was his birthday. When we got to class, I went to the back of the room with Tony where I kept the class toys. I told him that he could pick any of the toys to take home, and it would be his.

He looked up at me in disbelief.

I said, "Which one do you want?"

He lowered his voice to a whisper. "You. I want to take you."

I stood there stunned.

I didn't know what to say, so I gave him a hug and then another hug as the class ended, and I wished him a happy birthday.

After school, I was telling the science teacher on my team what had happened with Tony. She looked at me surprised. "Don't you know about Tony's dad?"

I didn't. She told me that Tony's father was in jail and had been for all the years of his life, and his father had refused to see him.

The story broke my heart for Tony, but more than that, it broke my heart that I hadn't known this until now, and this was on me. I had done so much to protect myself that I hadn't known! This expressed perfectly my failure with those kids that year.

There was a lot that was memorable about my years at Perry. I went to my first Passover Seder, I met some truly gifted kids, kids bright as any kids I ever taught, and I took a group of kids to hike in the woods and for their first trip in a canoe. Mind you, these kids were from cement and concrete, from the suburban sprawl and poverty of Fort Lauderdale. None of them had ever been in the woods, let alone the Everglades with its huge gators and beautiful, majestic egrets. These street tough kids were terrified of scrub oaks and flowers and palm trees. Our guide walked with them pointing things out, and from their reaction, he might as well have been taking them on a tour of another planet. The kids who walked with me watched me grab long grasses and put them in my mouth to chew.

"Mr. Quigley, you gonna die!" said one of the boys, and we all laughed.

They saw me bend to show them the secret world of plants. They walked through the woods terrified to let any of it touch them. After a short time, they relaxed, took in their surroundings, and loved being in nature.

The same thing happened when we took them on their first canoe trip. They stepped lightly, fearfully into the rocking boats. They found their balance, learned to hold and use a paddle, and were quiet as they tried to figure out this new world. By the end of the trip, they were laughing giggling kids. What had been alien to them was a place where they felt joyful just being kids. It was a great experience for me to be part of that with them.

Accidentally Finding Home

When I left the Keys and got the job in Broward County, I had to go to downtown Fort Lauderdale to the School Board building referred to as the Crystal Palace for its glass structure but also for its status as the power center for education in Broward County. I had to get fingerprinted, turn in a ton of paperwork, speak with the benefits department, and sign up for health and dental care plans. This meant going from one seemingly endless line to another seemingly endless line. Everyone in these lines was a new teacher. The first line I got in, I struck up a conversation with the woman in front of me. I found out she was going to be a debate coach at a local high school. She had taken on the challenge of teaching this class because her son was a state-ranked debater. She had zero experience as a teacher, and she didn't know anything about debate. Her son did the form of debate known as Lincoln-Douglas or LD, the same kind of debate I did in high school. She enlisted me to help her and especially help her son. I said I would do what I could.

Over the next seven months, I gave her advice on how to teach debate, how to introduce kids to debate, and how to teach the different forms of forensics. I tried my best to explain what original oratory was, extemporaneous, humorous, and dramatic interpretation, and to guide her to understand how to lead the student Congress. I advised her son on how I would handle a particular LD topic by going through the arguments and explaining how best to formulate a plan of attack.

She called me in March to tell me she had decided that teaching debate wasn't for her, but she asked if it was okay if she put my name in with the principal as a possible candidate for the job. I told her I really wasn't sure I wanted to teach debate, but I would talk to them if they called me about the job. I wanted to make it clear that I was not looking for a job because I had a job, a job that was challenging and hard, but that I wanted to do. I was loyal to my school and my principal, but if the school called, I would speak with them.

A few days later, I got a call from the assistant principal. He asked me about my interest in the debate job and I told him that I wasn't interested, but if he and the principal agreed, we could talk about a Social Studies position.

I was not interested in teaching debate for one major reason: having done debate in high school, I knew how consuming that world is. You and your team can go to a debate tournament every weekend if you want to be that involved. This activity consumed me as a teenager, and that's the only way to do it right: to allow it to consume your life. I loved teaching, but I had no interest in giving up all my time after school and on weekends.

A week later, I was sitting in the front office of Pembroke Pines Charter High School.

It was a school I had never heard of, an interview I hadn't arranged or pursued, and it was a high school, which had never been my interest.

The interview was with the assistant principal Peter Bayer. It was one of those interviews where everything just clicks, where the more you talk the more you can see that the person interviewing you is just getting it, getting you, getting your view of what teaching and kids are about. And the more I talked with Pete, the more comfortable I became. My initial impression of Pete was that he was a funny, energetic, and positive person. As I got to know him, I learned that even in the face of crushing news he could find the joke and the bright spot. He was disarming and charming.

There was a moment when the interview transformed into something that surprised him and I think clinched the job for me. At one point he asked, "So, what classes are you interested in teaching?" In all honesty, I had never considered being asked, so I responded instinctively and truthfully. "Mr. Bayer, you give me kids, and I will teach them." I could see the answer had surprised him, so I explained what I meant. "Whether you want me to teach honors or regular, American or World History or whatever, I will teach the kids you give me. My job isn't to pick the kids or pick the subject. The kids on my roster are the kids I will teach, whoever they are, whatever the subject."

This is what I believe. Whenever a teacher says they are "done" teaching a particular group of kids or that they should not have to teach a particular group, that's the moment I question the kind of teacher that person is.

After the interview, Pete told me he couldn't offer the job until I met the principal, but after this meeting, he felt certain that a job would be offered.

I left wondering what I should do.

A couple of days later I met the Principal, Mrs. Amalis Parmerantz, a kind, calm, quiet and soft-spoken woman. We spoke for only a few moments, just long enough for me to give her my background and my philosophy of teaching. She offered me the job and took me on a tour of the school.

PPCHS was a revelation. It felt like I was on a college campus. The building felt new yet lived in. Walking from the front office you approach the center of the campus, which has as its mid-point a fountain, which I would learn is the gathering point before school, after school, and between classes. To the east is the science building, and beyond that is the school's library, which is also the county regional library. This gives the students access to everything you would want in a school library plus the additional resources of the county library system.

Across from the science building in the northeast corner is a branch of Broward Community College where the high school kids take classes. Due north is the arts building, beyond that is the gym and cafeteria, and further north behind it is the county municipal swimming pool, which gives the students the use of a pool on campus for swimming classes and swim meets. Northwest of the central fountain is the English building and the temporary home of Social Studies. Due east was a building under construction. It would house the local community theater, which our students would have access to, and the future home for Social Studies, math, and foreign languages as well as a satellite campus for Florida International University. The southwest corner is the computer and other technical classes. It wasn't just a high school; it was a campus with amenities that happened to have a high school on it.

I was home. I just knew it.

I had to take the job.

But I didn't know how to tell my administrators at Perry Middle School. It felt like I was letting them down and abandoning them. The idea behind the program I was hired into was that I would teach the sixth graders I had this year for a total of three years. They would be my students that entire time. I had grown extremely close to them and felt like I was walking out on them. One class in particular had become very close-knit; they were the ones who had given me Mr. Quigley's "son," and we had celebrated a wedding between Mr. and Mrs. Quigley. I had also seen some amazing transformations in my eighth graders and was really enjoying them. My seventh grade class had started out by testing me and had slowly evolved into a group that worked extremely hard and dedicated themselves to the work. It was around this time they admitted to me that they had spent the first part of the year trying to break my resolve and get me to yell at them. They still expressed surprise that a male teacher wouldn't just yell at them when he was pushed too far, and there was always an underlying distrust of me. And even though things had improved, I felt like I needed to protect myself from them.

In all of my classes, I was guarded. I taught from a place of fear and suppressed a lot of my personality. I was more reserved than I naturally am, and less willing to be myself. I knew what I most feared: that my kids would find out I was gay and use that against me. I was still not comfortable with such a private aspect of my life becoming public. I would like to think that if confronted by a kid with a sneer on his face who hurled "faggot" or "queer" or "gay" at me, I would handle it with strength and pride. But the truth is it occupied my thoughts and it made me walk less sure, talk more softly, care less, embrace them less, and reduce myself.

So I took the job, told my principal, let my fellow teachers know but asked that this information not be shared with the kids.

A few weeks later, like any other day of the week, I walked to my class, unlocked the door, and turned on the light — and I was confronted with the final proof of my year of failure with these kids.

My classroom was trashed. I stood there in total shock, looking around at the destruction that littered every part of my classroom. I could not believe what I was seeing nor comprehend what had been done. It was my failure ripped open and vomited in my room. There is no other way to look at it. I had let them down, and they had shown me how they felt about that. I had said or not said something, done or not done something, and I could no longer deny my failure.

For several weeks, my sixth graders had been studying the Middle Ages. One of their projects was to create castles out of poster board. All of the projects were crushed. Beanbags that I had allowed my students to sit on had been ripped open, and the beans littered the floor. Students' notebooks and textbooks had been thrown all around the room. Chairs and desks were turned over. Someone had taken everything off my teacher desks and thrown it on the floor.

On the white board in the front of the room, someone had written, "I did it!" with an arrow pointing down to Mr. Quigley, the plush toy monkey, who was perched on the ledge.

This was personal. Only a kid who knew me and who knew who Mr. Quigley was would do something like this.

I stood in the center of my failure and looked around my classroom dazed and disbelieving. I was in total shock. I stood dry of tears but broken of heart.

I walked to the front office so devastated that I couldn't even look the secretary in the eye when I told her what had happened in my classroom.

My students were directed to the library, and while I conducted class for the next few hours, my room was cleaned and set right. Later that day I returned.

Throughout the day, whether we were in the library or in the classroom, kids expressed their sadness and sorrow that someone had done this to me. I just felt cold and dead inside.

In all my years, in all my failure as a teacher, even when kids acted up, none had struck at the heart of me in this way.

I muddled through, not knowing how to handle it, not knowing what to say.

I would never know what kid or group of kids did this. Of all the parts of my journey, this one confounds me the most. All the other parts seemed to speak of how I needed to be better. There was some lesson, something to be learned, something I was supposed to realize about this and figure out, but the winsome truth is that it was me and the way that I had conducted myself in this school the entire year.

I had spent months hiding, protecting, waiting for the attack, preparing for it, knowing my defenses were inadequate. And now I realized that instead of preparing for the attack, I was inviting it.

I had hidden and denied me — as a teacher, as a man, as a leader, as a mentor. I had protected myself and kept my kids at arm's length, and in doing so, I had invited this.

Then and there, I decided never again would I allow this to happen.

I was going to be me, fallible me with all my human faults and frailties, just like everyone else, and if I failed, if another classroom was destroyed, if I flamed out, if some kid with vile hatred in his heart screamed at the top of his lungs FAGGOT — fine! But those words would be said TO ME, not to some crouching, frightened, cowed and timid version of me.

When I left Perry Middle School, I did so with sadness and regret, not because of what had been done to my room, but because I had denied my kids the best of me. I have had to live with that guilt for the rest of my time as a teacher, but I used it to fuel me as I entered the next school and the next chapter of my journey.

My best friend always used to say about my personality, "Your entire sense of humor is based on trying to make a twelve-year-old chuckle." True, so true. So when I took the job at Pembroke Pines Charter High School (PPCHS), I did so knowing that I was going to try to rediscover the things that had made me successful at Key Largo School. The largest part of that was letting me be me, letting my personality out and being free again. But I had never taught high school before. This was unknown territory. Would the kids respond to me? Would they get my personality? Would they think I was corny or childish or silly? What about the monkeys? Should I talk about them?

I knew one thing: I was not going to deny my true self. When I went to Perry, I had purposefully not put up pictures, awards, or things associated with Key Largo School. I thought this was for the best, as a way of saying this school is not that school, like starting over and starting new. I wanted to put away the things that had reminded me of who I had been, as though I could do that, as though I wanted to do that. The Keys, that place, the kids, the people, the events, made me who I am.

This time, I wasn't gonna deny that part of who I am. Instead, I was going to take the best of me and bring it with me.

But I did worry about my middle school personality and how it would translate to high school kids.

I expressed this when I met my department head. I told her my concerns about my sense of humor, my way of doing things, my manic behaviors, my silliness, and how I was worried it wouldn't work in high school.

She just laughed, shook her head, and told me I would be fine.

She couldn't have been more right. My silliness, my corniness, my sense of humor, my goofy manic energy, my personality, all of it translated. In fact, it worked better with high school students than it did with middle school kids. I look back now and can't believe I had any fear about this. But it just goes to show that sometimes you've gotta learn the same lesson over and over and over again. It wasn't about what kind of personality I have or that any teacher has. Rather, if you are authentic, loving, open, true to yourself, and positive, you will be fine, even when you push kids harder than they ever thought they could be pushed.

As it was with me, the single biggest mistake teachers make in their careers is trying to be something and someone different than who they are. We are us; being anything else denies our basic self.

It is now fifteen years later at PPCHS, and I have had my failures, classes that didn't work, kids I couldn't reach, moments when things went wrong, lessons that bombed, situations that went awry, but in those years I have never failed at one thing — being me.

When I arrived at PPCHS I didn't know what a charter school was, and I didn't know the history of the creation of the school nor the real and amazing experiment that I was walking into.

The charter school movement had begun by people looking for an alternative to public schools. Charter schools are not private, but they are not entirely the same as a public school, though they are more like a traditional public school than anything else.

In the state of Florida, almost anyone who wants to can form a charter school. Religious groups, parents, arts organizations, and corporations all start charter schools. What makes PPCHS unique is the reason it was founded and who founded it.

To give just a little history, in the early 1990s, Pembroke Pines was a quiet sleepy town on the far western edge of Broward County, a place of large houses, large pieces of property, but not many people. That all changed in 1992 when Hurricane Andrew ravaged southern Dade County. After the storm, Dade County struggled to house the thousands and thousands who had lost everything, so people headed north. Once insurance checks rolled in, people decided to stay. Thus, a storm that had destroyed one community created another. Suddenly this sleepy town was bursting at the seams. Housing was going up, new people moved in, restaurants, stores, movie theaters, malls — all moved in quickly to meet the needs of the people. The one thing the community lacked, however, was schools.

The main school in Pembroke Pines was Flannigan High School, and it wasn't sufficient to deal with this huge influx of students. The school was bursting to the point that it created a whole separate campus just for ninth graders. Class size was outrageous. The parents of Pembroke Pines were not happy, and neither was the city, which repeatedly demanded the construction of new schools to meet the growing population. This all happened during a time when the entire county was expanding, and the school board would not move quickly enough to take care of the needs of the western side of Broward County.

Finally, the city decided to act on its own.

For the first time in the history of the state of Florida, a city created a charter school system. It would be wholly owned and run by the city. All the money, all the benefit would go to the school; there would be almost no bureaucracy. To this day, the only layer of administration beyond the school is the city council, which is our de facto school board. Each school is its own separate entity.

Once the school was chartered, there were bumps, bruises, mistakes, and at least one emergency that threatened the very nature of the school. But along the way, the philosophy of the system has stayed the same: create the best school for kids and teachers, and give teachers and administrators the freedom to run themselves, and see what happens.

What did happen was the creation of a school that is unique, a place that often looks and feels like a private school but will take any kid who applies from Broward County. The school's popularity and desirability necessitated the creation of a lottery system, and to this day thousands of kids are on waiting lists to get in. It is also a place highly resented by teachers and administrators at other schools in the county, as well as county officials.

Many times I have attended county workshops where I've introduced myself and the school, and it has never failed to elicit obvious negative reactions. I have sat on countywide boards where members made it clear that we were the enemy and an example of how public education was under attack. Part of this is a misunderstanding of the nature of charter schools. Those outside the system believe that we are exempt from the requirements of public school. In actuality we give the same exams, we have to follow every state law, we give every ESE accommodation like every other public school in Florida. Those outside of charter think that we can pick and choose kids like a private school. This is not true, and once a kid is in, we can no easier remove a kid from our system than the school district can. Yes, our kids wear uniforms, but so can any kid in Broward County. All it takes is a vote of the parents. None of those things that others in Broward County would point to are the things that make PPCHS unique.

What does make PPCHS unique is that every penny goes into the school. The teachers and administration have lots of freedom, and the school is governed by a simple idea: what is good for kids and teaching is good for us.

I had no idea about any of this when I took the job at PPCHS. Actually, when I was offered the job, I almost turned it down. There were two main reasons for this. First, I had always taught middle school, and had always believed that my evocation was to work with this unloved and misunderstood group. Secondly, high school started too damn early. I am by nature a night owl. It was tough enough getting up at around 6:30 or 7:00 a.m. for middle school, but PPCHS started classes at 7:15, which meant I had to get up at around 5:00 a.m.

Luckily for me, I decided not to let these challenges prevent me from taking the job.

The first few days, weeks, and months at PPCHS were amazing. I kept feeling that I was home. My entire teaching career I had been trying to find that one school where I could spend the rest of my career as a teacher. I wanted to become an institution. I wanted my name to mean something, to leave behind something, to make a huge impact on the school, the kids, and the people I worked with. I knew I had found that at PPCHS.

I have completed fifteen years at PPCHS. As I look back on that time, the single thing that most stands out is joy — the joy of the kids I have taught, the joy of the people I have worked with, the joy of the time I've spent, the joy that I am the only person to have ever occupied the classroom I am in. I have felt the joy of getting to know my students, hearing their stories, making them laugh, knowing their souls, and then after they've left my class, having them come back to share what's happening in their lives. There is no greater pleasure than being in my classroom, hearing a knock at the door, and looking up and seeing a face that's older, wiser, more travelled, with a sly happy smile and a story to tell.

It is ironic that we teachers spend hours grading papers, preparing lesson plans, creating assignments, lecturing, giving notes and tests and presenting information. This is of course the stuff of teaching; it is what we are taught to do, and it is what makes up the vast majority of what we do. And yet, when I look back, so little, if any of that, really matters. What I recall is the kids and the time we spent together. Just like I needed to learn to be there for them, I also needed to find balance between having a personal connection with my students and setting rigorous academic standards and high educational goals for them to attain.

When I started teaching at PPCHS, I had a very clear understanding that to teach is to create a personal bond with kids. By showing each kid RESPECT, and through stories, conversation, listening, reaching out, and seeing each kid as a unique and special person, you can make a difference in every kid's life. My job, first and foremost, is to help my kids navigate life and to have a clear understanding of themselves and their place within the world.

First and foremost you teach with your heart, knowing that a child's emotional wellbeing is more important than anything else. By doing this, your kids care about you and your class, and when they do, they work harder for you than any teacher they have ever had.

I eventually realized, however, that I had spent so much time and effort perfecting the connecting that I had sacrificed too much of the intellectual. I had created demanding, involving, engaging, complex, and challenging projects and assignments, but rigor was missing. I was, simply put, imbalanced. I had to find that fine line between heart and head, soul and scholar. I would like to tell you that transition was quick or that I even realized that I had to make that transition, but it didn't happen that way.

It took several years of assessing, reevaluating, sacrifice, changing subjects, being held to a higher standard, and eventually teaching Advanced Placement classes before I finally understood what I had to do for my kids to get the most out of my class.

Teachers must find that balance, and it's the most important thing that PPCHS has done for me. I did serve my first few years at this school giving my students a sense of belonging by helping and guiding them, but I was not a good enough teacher of academics. I hope my current students would be surprised at that sentence, considering the class I primarily teach today is a college level government course. I spend the majority of my time as a teacher preparing them for an exam that will determine whether the class will be worth college credit. The person I was when I started at PPCHS would be shocked to see the number of Sundays I spend grading essays and the amount of class time that is spent with me being the primary voice. These have been necessary things. I will say the thing that still gives me the greatest joy is that the students who I pushed, challenged, worked, and lectured often come back to visit me, and what they remember are the stories, the connection, the laughs, the silliness, the bond.

So what was the change I made? The most important was to heighten the rigor of my course. I now demand that my students know more, remember more, and do more with their learning. I require kids to read difficult text and analyze it, and then to do something new and unexpected with it. I will describe in the second part of this book the ways to go about doing this.

When I started at PPCHS, I saw every assignment as having primarily two purposes: to engage students in learning and to help the students understand some aspect of themselves. I realized by teaching high school that the best assignments should have three purposes: to engage, to help them understand themselves, but also to engage at a deep level with the information being taught.

Along the way I would learn a lot about this depth, and one of those lessons was that rigor did not simply mean more. More might be part of rigor, but it is not the key to pushing kids. Instead it's about what you do with the information. It's about what you ask kids to consider. It is about using complex abilities to think about the information you're presented with.

The first place this issue came up was when we were trying to differentiate between honors and regular courses. The easy way to define the difference was by doing more chapters, more questions, more homework, more classwork, more tests or projects. This felt right to me as a teacher. I asked for more, and more equaled harder, and harder equaled rigor. This, of course, is not how rigor works. Giving students less to work with and challenging them to dive deep into the subject matter is often the most rigorous thing you can do.

Before I arrived at PPCHS, I thought that I had a firm understanding of teaching, but I was half the teacher I needed to be.

So I immersed myself in the world of Bloom, the world of Webb, programs like CRISS (Creating Independence through Student-owned Strategies) and Socratic Seminars, and really looking at the quality of the activities, assignments, essays, and questions I expected my students to complete. Not for the first time I had to rip apart my understanding of my job and start anew.

Everything I did when it came to the work I assigned my students had to be held up to the light of rigor, and no matter how good it was, if it didn't pass muster, it had to be done away with.

It was a long process, but like every step of this journey, it was on me; it was about the hard work, the rejecting of what didn't work, and throwing out the old. I am still working on this process. It is still part of my journey as a teacher, and I won't get close to the excellence I desire until I find my way through.

What John Taught Me

I have been a teacher at PPCHS for fifteen years, which means I've taught approximately 2,000 kids. Many of them stand out because of the people they were and the story of how they became who they are, which they shared with me. I have watched kids go on to become teachers, lawyers, and doctors; business people, police officers, firefighters, and members of the military; and others are still trying to find their path. I have been visited by many of them, each with a desire to tell their story. Each has had a journey. All of them deserve to have their stories told. Each one is worthy. Their stories should be told, even the ones who feel they don't deserve it.

When I close my eyes, I remember faces, kids, souls that have sat in my class year after year after year after year. There are so many faces, faces that make me smile, faces that hold a special place in my heart, voices that fill me with pride or regret. So many faces have faded, but all I need is to see a photo of them or hear their name or have them walk back into my room, and who they were (when they were my student) is fully present.

Yet, as I look back, one name, one student, one person keeps coming back to me over and over again. He won't let me be, and so the story of John has to be told.

John was a good student, a solid A/B student, a good guy with a shock of curly black hair and a pale face with a devastating smile, part goofy, part mischievous, the kind of smile that made you smile back — it was all him, big and bright. John was in my tenth grade World History class for both semesters that year. I got to know him, I reached out to him, but I had 125 kids to teach. So when he left my class at the end of the year, in very little time he became just another kid who had been my student. As with most kids of the kids I taught, I had a memory of him, but with the passage of months then years, John was just another kid who was part of the past.

When John was in my class, I did everything I do with all of my kids: I reached out to him and tried to get him to open up. When the year ended, I encouraged him to come back to visit, and I told all of my students that even though they were leaving at the end of the year, my class would always be their class. As I tell all of my kids, they would never stop being my kids; they would only stop being my students.

I would have welcomed John back, been glad to see him, talk to him, laugh and smile with him, but he never came back to visit, so in time, his face and the person he was slowly became lost in a sea of memories.

Two years later, near the end of the school year, one of my students walked into my class and asked if I had ever had a student named John. The mention of his full name brought back an immediate memory of the curly black hair and that smile.

I told the student I had, and he said softly, "John killed himself yesterday."

What?

John, that smiling good kid, him, he, him, he, what? The kid who always sat in the same place, on the floor on a beanbag against that wall just over there, that John?

During the next few days, the story of John and what had happened in the two years since he had left my class was revealed. It was a typical story for many kids who are young and lose direction. John had dropped out of PPCHS and gotten into typical kid problems. He became friends with kids who were not the best influence on his life, and he did some stupid kid stuff that strained his relationship with his parents. He had made some bad choices, but he had never hurt anyone or done anything that put people in danger. He had just been a lost directionless kid. What he needed was some time, some breaks, some guidance, some chances to fail and finally to succeed. He had people who loved him, but he was a kid, a big goofy smiling kid who had a bad night in a long string of bad nights. It wasn't the first time he had made silly mistakes so typical of a teenager.

I have so many kids every year who I look at and hope that something happens in their life that will make everything click for them, that the direction, the actions, the things they are doing won't ever get them to the wrong place but will set them on a strong, successful path, whatever success means to them. I always hope this happens before they make a mistake that is unredeemable.

John got home after being out all night, and as he got out of his car, his mother came out of the house to confront him. She was understandably angry. She told him that his behavior was not acceptable, and they had a long, loud argument. There had been arguments before, angry words said before. She said things; he said things. Eventually John just walked away from the argument and into the house.

Before his mother had time to follow him into the house, she heard a gunshot.

No explanation why, no more angry words, just an unredeemable, irrevocable action.

The memorial service was just a few days before what should have been John's graduation from high school.

I really didn't want to go. This was the first time I would attend a memorial service for a student of mine. I was in a state of shock trying to reconcile the kid I knew and the action he had taken. I was filled with emptiness.

When I arrived at the funeral home, I parked my car and sat outside for several minutes to gather my strength.

When I walked into the funeral home, my personal feelings evaporated as I was greeted by hundreds of kids, kids I knew, kids that had been in John's class. These kids, all tears and shock, bewilderment and sadness — it was the class reunion no one ever wanted to attend. Kids hugged me and I hugged them back. We all needed each other. They held on to me, mumbled words, I mumbled words back. It was a sea of sadness, a river of tears, an ocean of why.

The flow of this loss poured in one direction, to the large open room and the casket.

As long as I live, I will never forget what I saw. I stood watching this never-ending flow of young devastated faces parading past the casket as a video of John played, John as a kid, John playing games, John at the beach, John at school, John playing hockey, the game he so loved. There were lots of pictures of him in various hockey uniforms. Next to the video was a framed hockey jersey. And in every picture was that smile. It hurt to look at those smiling images.

But it wasn't the video that had my attention; it was the scene next to it. I had never met John's mother when he was my student, but as soon as I saw her, I knew that's who she was. I watched for the next two hours as the same scene played out: kids crying, sobbing, distraught as this woman held them; this heartbroken mother talked to each child in that somber space punctuated by the sounds of anguish. Cries rose up like the wind. Some kids literally collapsed. Big strong teens lost it. It was a horrendous nightmarish thing to experience.

But I had to witness it.

Here was a mother who had lost her son. He had killed himself just a few moments after fighting with her. She had to live with the knowledge that the last words they had spoken to each other were words of anger. But she was trying to soothe the pain of others. How many times in the minutes, hours, and days must she have wished with all her heart to take back those angry words?

And now at the service for her son, she could easily have been the one who needed holding up, but here she was trying to hold it together as child after child reached out to her for the comfort I am sure she needed.

It was beautiful and awful to watch, such heart-rending sacrifice when you must be dying inside.

It is now years later, and John still haunts me and forces me to ask questions.

What do we teach for? Why do you teach? Why do I teach?

I want my kids to know everything in every lesson, all the facts, all the information I impart to them. I want them to burn with the joy of learning.

But what do we teach for? I taught John facts, but was that enough?

As I mentioned in the previous section, I had to find a balance. I had to teach with rigor, require more, demand more. It played on a loop in my brain: *you gotta make kids think and write and learn.*

But is that why we teach?

Fine, I'll find balance, yes, okay, yes, yes, yes, yes, yes — I'll teach the standards, and I'll demand they learn academic rigor in my class, but if you make me choose between THE KID OR THE CURRICULUM, I'll pick the kid every time.

Years later, I wrote on John's memorial wall online that his memory is my challenge. The challenge is simple: to prevent another kid from taking their life and wasting their potential. I won't succeed with every kid. I know there will be kids who, no matter how hard I try, will spend time in my class then leave, and I will not have been able to take away their pain and torment; students that I could have helped but didn't or couldn't, but by GOD, I am going to try. And I have to accept that when it comes to John, I failed him.

So at night, as I prepare to fall asleep, when I pray, when I think of my life, I whisper the names of those who have passed on. I say my mother's name, my father's, my grandmother's, my aunt's, and I think of them and their life. As I end my prayer, the name I end with, the whisper before sleep takes me, is John. If anyone every wonders why I teach, it is for John.

The Year of the D

A t the end of the school year in 2005, I was attending a going-away party for a Social Studies teacher that I had helped hire at PPCHS. It was one of those happy-sad occasions. I was saying goodbye to a colleague I respected, but even more, I loved her as a human being. This loss of a friend made me sad, but she was returning to her home state, a place she loved, and for that I was happy.

When she arrived at the get-together, she did so sans hair. She had challenged her students to get above a certain grade point average in her class, and if they did so, she would shave her head. That was the kind of person and teacher she was. As I wandered through the crowd greeting friends and colleagues, I found myself in the company of my principal, Peter Bayer.

"The FCAT scores came out," he said. "Guess what grade we got."

Before I go on, I need to explain what the FCAT was. The Florida Comprehensive Assessment Test was devised by the Florida legislature in the 1990s for two reasons. First, it was used to assess where students ranked against other students in the state and the nation. The testing began in third grade and concluded in tenth grade when students had to pass the exam to eventually graduate.

It was high stakes testing at its finest, especially considering what else the test was used for — to evaluate schools. Each elementary, middle and high school was graded on an A-F scale. If a school was ranked a low-rated school often enough and for long enough, the state could come in, remove the administration, fire the staff, and close down the school. This actually took place.

There were rewards for the schools that got the highest grade. Schools earning an A received money that could be spent in any way the school decided. Most schools voted to give the teachers a pay bonus. Though in my next-to-last year at Key Largo School, we voted to spend the money to fix up the teachers' break room and to allow teachers to be able to go to conferences. We did this because the middle school had gotten an A, but the elementary school had not, so to prevent sore feelings, it was decided to use the money to benefit the entire school, especially since the kids in the middle school had been originally taught by the elementary teachers.

The tests initially had one part, a writing exam, and over the years, a math and a language section were added, then finally a science section.

This system was nearly universally hated. Kids hated the FCAT because it put so much pressure on them to do well. Teachers hated it because they felt they had to teach to the test and spend much of their time prepping for the test. Parents saw their kids losing the joy of being in school because of the focus on the test. No one seemed to like it, so the state eventually replaced the FCAT with an even more difficult test that took even more time and had even higher stakes.

So, back to my conversation with Principal Bayer, he said, "The FCAT scores came out. Guess what grade we got."

I had always been a fan of guessing games, so guess I did.

"An A."

PPCHS had always been a B-rated school, so it would make sense we had somehow gotten up to an A.

"Nope."

"B."

He shook his head. "Nope."

"We couldn't have gotten an F!" PPCHS was a lot of things, but an F school was not one of them.

"D," he said in a wry tone. "We got a D." From the look on his face, I wasn't sure if this was devastating to him or if it was amusing.

I was shocked. I knew enough to know this was bad.

"What does this mean for us?"

He shrugged his shoulders. "I don't know. We'll see."

Over the summer, the consequences of getting the D became obvious and ominous. The changes to the culture and the way the school had always operated were huge.

To understand how radical these changes were, you would have to know what PPCHS was like before the Year of the D.

PPCHS was a school that proudly proclaimed we didn't teach to the test. We often talked about and believed that if we did our jobs, if we focused on good teaching, if we pushed kids, if we required kids to read challenging material and taught them to do high level math, the test scores would take care of themselves. In the three years before we got the D, I had attended exactly one meeting about the FCAT, and that was in my first year, a few weeks before the test. The meeting was called by the English department head.

During the meeting, members of the English department tried to emphasize to us the importance of the test and teaching the reading skills necessary to do well on it. The Social Studies department had always treated the FCAT like it was the English department's responsibility; it was after all a reading comprehension test. I taught Social Studies, not reading, I thought, as though reading was something that kids didn't do in Social Studies. It didn't matter that literature made up only a small percentage of the reading test, and there were far more Social Studies samples on the test; we simply could not accept that the FCAT mattered at all to what we were teaching.

It was easy to be this way when our scores were a perfectly good B. But for three years our school's test scores had been slipping, and no one seemed to notice. I certainly didn't know why. If I had known, I would have reacted like a typical Social Studies teacher and put this off on the English department, but even the English teachers did not pay the FCAT much attention, so the D reflected a systemic problem within our school. It was more than just not focusing on or caring about a test. We were cocky enough to believe that we could go on teaching and not caring about what was happening outside of the school, and everything would be fine.

The year we got a D we had actually gotten a C but had been penalized a grade level. The additional reduction of a letter was because of the kids who ranked at the very bottom. Students are divided into cohorts based on how they have done on past tests, and not only had the school done badly overall, but we had failed those who struggled the most.

It would be easy to say that the kids should have done better, but we failed them. We had not done our job to prepare these kids. There is a lot I hate about the FCAT and other evaluation systems that exist in education today, but a low grade reflects a failure on the part of teachers to adequately prepare kids for challenges. My school failed to do its job.

However, what we did to remedy this failure and what it says about education today is why I am talking about the Year of the D.

So how did we change?

This is just a partial list of things we did to improve our FCAT scores.

The entire school's ninth and tenth grade teaching staff was reorganized, especially in Social Studies and English. Teachers who the school considered the strongest and best at preparing kids for the FCAT were moved regardless of what they had taught the previous year. In Social Studies this meant several teachers who had never taught World History were moved into that subject.

A school within a school was created, a small learning community made up of ninth and tenth grade students who were in the bottom quarter of scores. These kids would all have the same core teachers who would organize everything around preparing the kids for the FCAT.

Geography was brought to the school as a required elective to have an additional course to help teach FCAT reading skills.

Each week all teachers in the school had to meet a reading skills objective while teaching our curriculum.

To facilitate this focus, we had weekly meetings where all ninth and tenth grade teachers prepared lessons that focused on a particular skill. This was a required meeting during our planning period. It didn't matter what was being taught in the core curriculum; reading was the focus. This was confirmed by our newly hired reading coach who used those exact words during our first meeting with her.

Having a reading coach was yet another change. She not only met with us weekly; she met with us individually, and it was clear that our job as Social Studies teachers had changed.

We were required to give weekly assessments to see how students were doing on the reading skills focus. These mini-tests were reported to the school administrators, who compared each teacher to the others teaching the same subject. Our reading coach met with us individually if a particular area of weakness was identified in our classes.

Twice the entire school day was devoted to administering mini-FCATs to assess and determine areas where students were weak.

To improve reading, a thirty-minute uninterrupted class period was added to the schedule so students could do focused reading. They could choose what they wanted to read, but this sustained silent reading time happened throughout the school by kids and adults.

The pressure was intense. I had never taught under that kind of pressure, where everything we did was watched and measured. The intensity of that year boiled over in late October. Our students had taken the first of the two school-wide mini-FCATs, and they had not done well.

This caused a storm of a reaction so fierce that the administrators held a meeting with all ninth and tenth grade teachers.

The meeting took place in the middle of a storm of our own making but also in the midst of an actual storm. The year 2005 was a year of hurricane after hurricane. To most of the country, the storm most associated with 2005 was the horrific and deadly Hurricane Katrina. To us in South Florida, Hurricane Wilma did the greatest amount of damage. That year was a record-breaking year for storms in the Atlantic, with 28 named storms (a record), 15 hurricanes (a record), and 7 major storms (again a record). Hurricane names are decided before the season begins. There are 26 names, one for each letter of the alphabet. There were so many storms they ran out of names, so they had to turn to the Greek alphabet to name the last two storms Alpha and Beta.

As Wilma churned through the Caribbean and headed toward the west coast of Florida, the FCAT meeting began. It was dark and rainy outside, and inside the feeling was equally oppressive. It was made perfectly clear that we were failing to do our jobs. Clearly, we were not doing enough to teach the kids, and if things continued as they were, there would be serious consequences.

The direct words delivered to us teachers surprised me: "You are your kids' scores."

I couldn't believe what I was hearing, so I raised my hand.

The words were repeated back, and it was very clear that how the kids did was a reflection on us, and the school would make decisions based on the students' test scores. To the administrators, the kids' scores were directly related to the quality of our teaching.

Less than six months before this, we were a school that never worried about the FCAT, and now we teachers were being told the scores were us, and our future depended on those scores.

The meeting ended with each of us feeling the full power and effect of this storm.

This meeting took place on the Thursday before Hurricane Wilma hit the west coast of Florida. Usually when a hurricane makes landfall, no matter what direction a storm comes from, the greatest amount of damage is done on the coast it hits first. As the storm moves across the state, it weakens because it is no longer over warm water. This is usually when a hurricane fizzles out, and by the time it moves up or across the state, it is so diminished that it is nothing more than a wet weather front.

Like a lot of things that year, Wilma didn't act like it was supposed to. It hit the west coast of Florida then moved across the state. Initially it was a Category 1 storm, the weakest kind of hurricane, but as it moved across Florida, its strength grew so much that by the time it exited the east coast, it had grown to a Category 3, and it did serious damage to Broward County.

The storm knocked out power for millions for a week; many lost roofs, and some suffered even worse destruction. One of the other oddities of this storm was how widespread it was. There was damage from the western fringe of the county, where PPCHS is located, to the middle of the county, where my condo is, to where the county meets the Atlantic Ocean. For more than a week the county struggled. With power out, it was difficult to get gas, food, ice for coolers to keep the small bit of food we had cold, and water.

During this week, as the county tried to return to some sense of normalcy, school was cancelled.

In that week, a fever seemed to break. When we returned to school, there was no mention of the meeting we had had before the storm. It was as though the storm had reminded us what really mattered; it allowed us some distance and a chance to reflect.

We still had weekly meetings and a weekly focus, and we understood that our job was to get the students ready for the test and to make sure we rose above the D, but a semblance of balance returned. The pressure was there, but the intensity had dissipated to a much more acceptable level.

As the end of the year approached, we felt that we had done everything we could to get the students ready. The students, not surprisingly, rose to our expectations, and we were rated an A school. It was the first time in the history of the FCAT that a high school had gone from a D to an A in one year.

I don't say that to brag. I say that because to me it's instructive of a very important lesson.

At the start of the year, one of the teachers said that he thought it was good that kids be evaluated and that schools and teachers be judged. Though I agree with this in the abstract, I had huge problems with this in implementation. This particular teacher was also the school's basketball coach. He was used to competition and being judged against others. At the end of a basketball game, there is a winner and a loser, a score to show who excelled and who didn't. My retort to his statement was simple: okay, what if we decided not to score basketball based on who made the most baskets and instead based it on who could throw the best passes or which team dribbled the best. If that were the case, I asked him, would he ever bother to teach his team to shoot baskets? He of course said no.

This is the problem with high-stakes testing. The moment the teachers learn what is going to be on the test, that's what they focus on. And what so often happens is we become the basketball coach who never teaches his kids to shoot baskets because that skill isn't on the test.

The problem is not that we test; it's how we test, what we test, and what we use the test for. When we use the test as a weapon, it changes a school. If our focus becomes a test, what other skills are we not teaching? What learning becomes disposable because it won't be on the test? What is sacrificed when a test becomes the focus instead of real learning?

To give an example, at one point our science students were having problems doing well on the FCAT science test. But it wasn't the regular or honors kids who were having problems. It was the most advanced kids, the ones in their freshman and sophomore years who were taking college level science courses that would give them a college credit if they passed a different test at the end of the year. But the FCAT focused on science that is typically taught at the ninth and tenth grade level, so these students were being tested on subjects they hadn't dealt with since middle school or maybe not at all. These kids were getting college credit for physics, chemistry, or biology, but they hadn't had a physical science class since seventh grade and were failing the test. There is something wrong with a system that punishes kids for doing too well.

If the test is making classes change their focus, not teach the fundamentals of their subject matter, and sacrifice knowledge for test-taking skills, there is a problem with the test. This problem has existed ever since we have relied more and more on standardized tests to determine who is promoted to the next grade level and how well the school is doing as a whole. Since these tests need to be quickly and easily graded, they seldom evaluate higher-level thinking, and they always fail to capture creative or original thinking.

Because these are written tests, they're difficult for the kid who can defend a point verbally or the child who sees the bigger picture even as the small details trip them up, or the child who simply doesn't perform well on tests. These tests don't take into account multiple intelligences, learning styles, or the unique ways that students learn and express information.

For the past twenty-five years, I have watched the increase of standardized testing and the resultant teaching to the test. First with the FCAT then with the Common Core Curriculum there has been an acceleration of testing, and its impact on the classroom has been monumental. Having been a teacher during the start of this movement and before it, I can tell you there is less joy in teaching; less room for unique activities; less time for alternative assessments and in-depth projects; less time to engage and involve and interest kids; less time for hands-on activities; less time for kids to explore, and to find joy and value in what they learn. There is more reliance on textbooks and traditional teaching; more time on lecture; more time spent reading textbooks just to read textbooks, focusing on a skill as compared to understanding complex ideas, diagnosing text as compared to grasping it. All of this has turned off so many kids to school and especially to Social Studies.

But I would be remiss if I didn't mention that there were positive aspects of the Year of the D, just as there are of standardized testing in general.

When you are evaluated on something, suddenly it matters, and so the FCAT, or whatever test exists in your state, has put pressure on teachers to do a better job preparing kids to read, write, and do math. THAT IS A LARGE POSITIVE GOOD! The Year of the D made the school a better place because it made us focus on skills we had neglected. As a result, the school became a more academically solid place. We focus on skills we should have been focusing on from the beginning. We do a better job teaching reading, writing, and math.

But, it is what we lost that I regret to this day. We lost the ability to teach in the full scope of what teaching is meant to do: to challenge, to be creative, to make class the dynamic place it had been and always should be. The question is this: at what cost did we substitute the best of teaching to make sure we got the best school grade? I'm not sure we have the answers to that yet. Maybe we never will.

9/11/11

In the spring of 2011, I was sitting in my principal Pete's office. I don't remember why I was there, but it was likely concerning something I needed his permission to do.

Peter Bayer is the kind of guy who walks into a room and by the end of the event, has spoken to each person, knows their name, cracked more than a few jokes, and put the room at ease. I have known Pete for fifteen years, and it still amazes me that he knows every kid by name. I was once in the front office, and an alumnus who had graduated four or five years ago, a kid who had been in my class for a whole year, walked in. For the life of me, I couldn't remember his name. Pete not only knew his name, he knew his brother and sister, and he remembered specific stories about the kid and his time at PPCHS. I marvel at that skill. If you asked any kid who went to our school who was their favorite or best teacher, different kids would name different teachers, but ask them about Mr. Bayer, and even the most troubled kid will say only good things about him. How many schools, at graduation, give the loudest cheer for the principal? That's Pete.

As I sat in Pete's office that spring, we talked about many things; some had to do with what was going on at school, and some were not school related at all.

Near the end of the conversation, he mentioned that the coming fall would be the tenth anniversary of 9/11, and wouldn't it be good to do something to memorialize what had happened. He told me that two things had put this in his mind. First, the AP Senior English students were about to read a book about 9/11 and an event the local Jewish community center holds each year in remembrance of the Holocaust. High school students from all over the county gather at that event, and a series of presentations are done by Holocaust experts with videos and workshops. The most powerful part of the day takes place during lunch when students sit with a holocaust survivor at randomly assigned tables. This provides an opportunity for teenagers to interact with living history, people who were there and who can talk about the horrors of what the Nazis did because those horrors were done to them. Every kid we send to this yearly experience comes back changed.

And that's when Pete issued me the challenge of coming up with something to commemorate that day, 9/11/11. I left with my head buzzing with the possibility and the challenge.

I loved the idea of getting kids to interact with living history, but the question was whether we could find people in our community who had been in New York, Washington DC, or Pennsylvania on that day in 2001, and be able to speak with the kids about their experience. Even though we are a small high school by Broward County standards, we still had 1,600 kids. How could we possibly do this? Logistically having every kid at a table of ten kids meant we would have to find 160 people who were there on 9/11 and who would be willing to talk about their experiences. Even if we could do this, we had no space big enough to do this activity.

During our initial discussion, Mr. Bayer mentioned that the idea to do this came to him when the Advanced Placement Senior English teacher, Sarah Phelps, gave him a copy of a new book she was having students read called

Extremely Loud and Incredibly Close. So we considered having just the seniors in AP classes do this, but that would exclude about 1,500 kids. However, it would make it easier to find survivors and to organize everything.

In the years before this activity, I had begun to embrace activities that forced my students to take their learning outside of the four walls of my classroom. This had caused me to create a series of activities that made students speak and write and be in the world. It challenged them to see material as not some static thing that only mattered in my classroom.

As an example, for the year's culminating activity, the students in my law class read a previously argued Supreme Court case, examine cases that were precedents, read about and listen to the original oral argument, read the original legal briefs, absorb the majority and minority opinion of the court, synthesize all of this, and write a ten-minute legal argument. Following this legal argument, students are questioned for twenty minutes on their understanding of all the legal implications of their argument. The group asking the questions is a mock Supreme Court made up of lawyers, judges, the mayor, city council members, administrators, teachers, and alumni. This is still my favorite activity I have ever done. To me this activity includes everything we want kids to be able to do: to read complex writing, understand it, and then write a three- to five-page legal brief, and finally, to stand in front of a group and defend their ideas. What more could we possibly want from kids?

I had started a similar culminating activity in my government class, and I knew I wanted to incorporate these kinds of activities in whatever we did to commemorate 9/11.

The more I thought about it, the more my mind went in two different directions.

We could do something with a small group, such as a series of presentations from survivors or others who could talk about how the events impacted them personally. This would be done with an exclusive group of selected kids and span the entire school day.

Or we could come up with a series of activities that would take up the school day but would involve the entire school, every class, every kid, and every class period.

I developed activities for both proposals, and after several weeks, I met with Pete to go over them. Even as I spoke of each, I knew which one I hoped he'd pick. To me, this had to be a school-wide program. It would be harder, the logistics far more daunting, the organization more difficult, making sure every teacher understood what and why we were doing a challenge and getting 1,600 kids and about 100 professionals all working together toward a common goal. But this was the way to go.

The small group approach would certainly have the possibility of a very personal impact.

The whole school project would have an impact on more kids, even if it were less personal and less powerful.

In the end, even though it was the harder course for him and the administration, with a much bigger downside, many more problems, tons of logistics to consider making it much more difficult, Pete picked the school-wide approach.

Now suddenly I had to come up with activities to keep 1,600 teenagers interested and engaged for seven hours. Going forward it was decided that I would work alone to come up with a basic outline of the day; later we would have a committee of teachers and administrators work on the details. We also decided to keep the idea under wraps until we presented it to the department heads and later to the school as a whole.

The first challenge I ran up against was that 9/11 had been an ever-present part of the country's life for nearly ten years, but the students in the school were no older than seven or eight when the attack took place. The freshmen had been as young as four or five. The students' concept of 9/11 was remote; it wasn't personal; they saw it as just another historical event. So I had to make that day real, to put kids in that moment on that day. I recalled what I had told my students on 9/11 soon after the attacks happened: "When the school day ends, you need to be part of this. Go home, be with your families, watch this, be part of it. You will remember this day forever. It will likely change history and the world, and you need to be part of it. You are safe, no one is going to harm you, but as a human being, you need to be part of this. There are only a few times in your life when you will ever be part of something this big, and you need to share it with everyone else. It is very likely that you will be able to say, 'There was a world before these events happened, and a world after'.".

As I pondered how to approach this commemorative event ten years later, I knew that the students in our school in 2011, who had not experienced that traumatic day firsthand, had to connect to the events as if they were happening now. I knew that the best way to do that was to find the right video, and it had to be great because it would kick off the entire day. So began my month-long search for just the right piece that would do all the things I wanted the video to do. For weeks during my off periods, I watched 9/11 videos.

Again, no one outside of myself and the principal knew what I was up to, so as I watched video after video about 9/11, my fellow teachers began to wonder if I was okay because I seemed increasingly depressed. Watching these videos took an emotional and devastating toll on me. More than one colleague worried that something was seriously wrong. I spent many planning periods in tears watching the human, physical, and emotional destruction that was 9/11. I found lots of good videos, but one that stands out is *The Falling Man*, which attempted to identify the person who was photographed falling/jumping from the World Trade Center building. I watched many fine historical documentaries that detailed and evaluated the events of 9/11, but they didn't put kids in the moment, but rather kept them at a distance from the realities of that horrific day.

Finally, I stumbled upon *102 Minutes that Changed America*, and from the first frame of the video, I knew I had found it. If you have not seen it or if you know someone who wasn't alive on that horrible day, this is the video to recommend. It does not give background or history or talk about how the country was affected subsequent to the attack, but it does make you feel that day. It has this strange magical power that takes you right to the moment that the first plane hit the first World Trade Center building. What follows is entirely raw footage. There is no voice-over, no one giving context; instead, you see what happened in real time from the videos people took as it happened. The video is real and raw, and filmed by news crews as they ran down the street and people watching out the windows of their high-rise apartments in Manhattan using home video cameras. You can smell the smoke, taste the dust, and feel the horror of being in the streets of New York City that day.

The video takes you from the streets to the people inside the buildings, from people watching the plane slam into the building to police officers trying to bring order. Following the large plumes of debris and smoke when the buildings came down, you can see jumpers and those watching the jumpers as they try to figure out what is falling out of the buildings, and then the sheer horror as they realize what they are seeing.

The two most powerful moments of the video were a college student at NYU filming from the window of her dorm room and commenting on the building on fire, describing what is going on and hoping the people in the buildings will survive. Then, while one building burns, there is an explosion, and the woman screams as the second plane crashes into the second building. In that moment, she realizes, and we realize, this wasn't an accident; this was an act of war. The video goes back to the streets, and we see people running from the buildings, screaming, as now two buildings smolder, and as streams of people run for safety, the camera focuses on a line of fireman walking toward the building to do their job. You are never told but you can guess that some of these men and women did not make it out alive. Like much of the video, we are left with questions and our hearts breaking.

The movie makes every moment of that agonizing morning completely real.

Okay, so I had the movie to put students in the moment, to make them feel the real and powerful impact of that event. The movie is 102 minutes, the exact amount of time from the moment the first plane went into the first building to the collapse of the second building. My plan was to have all classes watch the movie during first and second periods then have a discussion. The teachers and I would need to develop questions for this discussion, including ones that would deal with the real and powerful emotions the kids were sure to feel.

Following this discussion, I wanted some type of creative activity that would allow the students to process the video and the discussion and to react to all they had seen and heard. After the discussion, we wanted to end the day with some kind of culminating activity.

I was worried that there were a lot of holes to fill, and it concerned me that I hadn't come up with everything and did not have a finished product to give the department heads. Regardless, as the 2011 school year drew to a close, I presented the plan to the administration and to the department heads. The idea was received very positively, and we went to summer with a plan and a commitment from all the departments. We all knew we would have a short time at the start of the school year to prepare for this day, as the anniversary of 9/11 would only be five weeks after we returned to school.

Throughout the summer, I continued working, writing questions, researching ideas, putting together a game plan for the day, and communicating with Pete.

When I returned to school, each department picked a representative to work on the committee that would fill in the holes of what was left to do.

This committee would create the single best experience of my entire teaching career. In that room were a committed group of people empowered to come up with an activity that would impact the students; the only mandate was that it be good and that it mattered to kids. We were given free rein to come up with the best day we could. From the very first meeting, each member was positive, each contributed amazing ideas, and everyone was receptive. No one owned an idea or kept firmly to some suggestion. Actually, the opposite happened; when a better idea came along, or if someone proposed something that added to an idea, it wasn't one person's idea — it was our idea. I kept looking around at the group of people and being blown away by how each person just wanted to make the best possible day for the kids. Throughout our discussion, we spoke about keeping in mind the emotional wellbeing of the teachers and kids. This day was not going to be a typical day. We knew we were stirring up all kinds of emotions, and so it was always in our thinking to make sure to not go over the line.

The head of the English department took on the challenge of creating the questions for the discussion. The discussion she created was as powerful as the video itself; it walked the fine line between talking about the video and allowing kids to react and speak openly about their feelings and emotions.

We discussed what creative response we wanted as a follow-up activity, and we agreed we wanted to do something to connect kids to the video and 9/11 but also to allow for expression and interaction with others. That's when someone suggested that the students each be given a slip of printer paper. On that paper, in whatever way they felt, they would communicate their emotions about 9/11, the video, the conversation. This could be done in a drawing, in writing, or in some combination of the two. We wanted each kid to react to what they had seen and felt in their own way. These slips of paper would then be connected as links in a chain. Then all the chains would be connected into one chain. We would end with 1,600 individual reactions connected as one school. Eventually these links spelled out UNITY and 9/11. This chain was left up for weeks to remind students of the event and what they had learned and felt on that day.

The last and most important part was to determine how to conclude the day's events. I had wracked my brain trying to come up with something, but I had nothing.

Once again, the power of a committed group working together as one voice brought about a solution. A teacher suggested we do a moment of silence together, but instead of moments of silence where everyone in separate classes bowed their heads, why not have the entire school come together. We could do it in the central quad, 1,600 kids all together bowing their heads in solidarity.

Simple. Powerful. Risky.

Would every kid join in? Would they be quiet? How could we get them to behave in a solemn and dignified manner? What if people were talking? How was this going to work? How would we signal them to be quiet? What if they wouldn't be quiet? What if some kids acted like typical teenagers, and disrespected the moment? This had the potential to be powerful or to ruin a wonderful, transformative day.

When the committee's work was done, I met with Pete to go over all of it. He listened and nodded his head, made a few suggestions here and there, but nodded his head in agreement. I was nervous about the culminating activity. This was an administrative nightmare, a whole school asked to come down to the quad and stand quietly — it was fraught with issues and concerns.

Pete listened to the suggestion and pondered it in silence, and then he surprised me. He said that after everyone went down to the quad, no one would tell the students what to do, when to be quiet, or how to act. We would simply ring the school bell ten times, and we would trust the kids to do the right thing.

I thought there was a really good chance this wouldn't work because I knew kids; I knew how rambunctious teenagers could be, but we were committed to the plan.

The moment of silence would be between the last two periods of the day. Students would go to their last class, and the responsibility would be on the teachers to come up with ideas of how they would address 9/11 in their individual subject area.

I can't say there was 100 percent buy-in from every department, but I will highlight what two departments did. In Social Studies, it was decided that for each of the 2,000+ people who died, the kids would research the person, find out who they were, then create images and write about each person on a piece of printer paper. The Social Studies building would be transformed into a memorial. This idea gave a human face to the people who died that day. The art department did a series of projects, but the most profound was based on Japanese culture, where the symbol of the dove represents the journey of life and death. A dove was made for each of the people who died on 9/11, and these were hung from the ceiling as a living art piece to commemorate them.

Ten days before the big day, I presented the committee's plan to the faculty. I began by thanking, congratulating, and giving credit to each member of the committee, making sure that any idea they had come up with was acknowledged. I then gave an overview of the day with a general description of each activity we would be doing.

I culminated the meeting by showing a preview of the video we had chosen.

To my shock, the reaction from the faculty was overwhelmingly negative. Teachers wondered why we would devote a day to this and take away academic time. Others feared how kids would react. Others worried that the kids might say or do something inappropriate during the day. How were kids going to just stand in the quad and be quiet? This video was scary; wouldn't it scare the kids? Teachers were frightened. I did my best to respond and put their fears to rest, but the reaction became so negative that Pete spoke up, pointing out that if any kids had an emotional reaction, we would have guidance counselors ready to help them. We would have a dedicated classroom where kids or teachers could go if they couldn't handle the emotional toll of participating in these events. And yes, it was very possible that the kids might react in a way that was inappropriate, but whatever happened would be a teaching moment. If a kid acted incorrectly, we would talk about it and direct their reaction and behavior.

By the end of the meeting, I worried that Pete would cancel the entire thing. Though I felt like this was going to be a great event, I understood the fears expressed. However, I did believe that kids being so emotionally moved that they identified and cared about those who died was a good thing. We want kids to care deeply about the loss of human life.

Luckily, if Pete had any fears, he never expressed them to me. We were going forward with the plan no matter what.

I was nervous that day. A committee had done much of the work, but I was the person who organized this activity. Was it going to work? How would the kids react? Would teachers handle things correctly? Would kids and teachers be overwhelmed emotionally?

At 7:15 a.m., Mr. Bayer's voice came over the loudspeaker, and in an even, relaxed but excited tone, he explained what the day was going to be about. He conceded that this was an emotional day, that the video we were going to watch and the other activities planned would challenge the students emotionally, but this was a safe place, and this would be a day they would never forget.

The video started, and for the next 102 minutes, throughout the school, no kid went to the restroom, no one was on their phone, no one fell asleep. Instead, the video did its purpose; those kids were there, on that morning, in that city, in the middle of the mayhem. This wasn't a Hollywood movie. It was real. They felt the realness.

When the movie ended, students in every classroom engaged in meaningful conversations, expressing their thoughts and feelings, sympathizing with those who had suffered on that day. They made it personal by talking about people they knew who had been there. They talked about things that had been told to them, what their parents had said, and they always came back to the video, connecting it to themselves and their families. Kids who had brothers or sisters in the military or law enforcement or the fire service burst with pride. Still others had personal stories of family members who had been in New York when it happened. Stories personal and real were shared.

After about two and a half hours, the students went on to their next class.

Here students created their paper link for the unity chain and continued their discussions.

Between classes, the hallways were unnaturally quiet. I could see the look in teachers' faces from the raw power of the video and the conversation that followed.

Students created and presented their links, their written expressions thoughtful, beautiful, and deep. This was the most human reaction, and even though some kids weren't artists, they created wonderful horrible beauty.

Throughout my time in class, through the video and conversations afterward, not one of my kids reacted with extreme emotion, but I did wonder how many kids and teachers had to go to our safe space.

It was only at some point later in the day that I would find out that not one kid or teacher had to visit the special room set aside to help them deal with the emotions of the day.

At lunch, kids were quiet and thoughtful; some openly hugged fellow students, and more than a few tears were shed.

Between the last two periods would be the moment of silence in the quad.

When it was time, Pete came on the loudspeaker to explain exactly what was about to happen. We would ring a bell ten times to commemorate the ten-year anniversary of 9/11.

The students were then invited to leave class and come down to the quad to stand together in silence to remember.

At that moment, 1,600 teenagers left class together and walked to the quad. No one told them to be quiet because there was no need; there was no talking, just silence.

Then the bell began to chime.

Sixteen hundred students, over a hundred adults, heads bowed, some crying, some hugging, American flags fluttering — the moment was sad, solemn seriousness. As the bell tolled, each ring was a reminder of how connected we were, how much we lost, and the value of community.

When the day ended, the kids had learned and felt a lot.

I had learned more.

Your classroom is not four walls. If it is, no matter how great a teacher you are, your teaching is confined.

Take chances — the best stuff happens when you take the risk of doing something different. Yes, it can fail miserably at times, but it can also change kids' lives!

When good people come together, you can change the hearts and souls of thousands.

Teenagers take seriously and care about whatever you take seriously and care about.

Throughout the next week, my class spent time looking at the causes of 9/11 and its impact on the ten years of history thereafter. I wanted students to know what led to 9/11, and I wanted students to have an idea of how the event changed the country.

The culminating activity in my class was for the students to create a video reacting to what they had seen, learned, and felt during the commemorative event and throughout our studies that week.

There were a lot of great videos done by my students, but I want to share one with you that shows you the power of these kinds of activities.

The video begins with a student walking through his house. He talks about all that he learned and felt, talks about his English and math and science classes and the things he learned in my class. As he walks and talks, he is holding a camera and talking directly into it. Eventually near the end of the video, he is in the dining room. He says to the camera, "Mr. Quigley, before we did these activities, I had an idea of what I wanted to do with my life." He sets the camera on a tripod, and for a moment he disappears, but he continues to talk. "But now I know for certain this is the right thing." The camera pulls back to show a dining room table, then it pulls in again to reveal two adults and then back to show someone in full dress military uniform. At that moment, the kid walks into the frame, and it's then we see the papers on the table. He looks up and says, "This is for all the things I saw during the last week, Mr. Quigley," and he signs the papers committing to serve in the US Navy.

School for Sale

For me it began at a dinner party on Wednesday, June 12, 2013, five days after the last day of school. I was laughing and relaxing when I received a text from a friend giving me a heads-up that something major was about to happen at PPCHS. I immediately returned the call, and when I heard what was about to go down, everything seemed to shift and go out of focus.

For the next seven days, every aspect of my work life was in flux.

I want to describe the series of events that happened, and honestly convey my feelings and fears, but I also want to be fair and admit that I only know what I know. And then I want to talk about how the events of those seven days changed my world and why it mattered to my journey and ultimately reinforced what I believe about teaching and kids.

On that evening, I learned that the city had decided to turn over the operation of the charter schools to a for-profit corporation.

If they did this, all of the teachers would be let go.

We would have to reapply for our jobs and hope to be rehired.

If this went through, the way the school would be run would change. Administrators would be retained, and they would continue to run the day-to-day operation of the schools, but the school would be run for profit. Control of the school would go to a corporation whose interest was making a profit and not necessarily providing kids with the best education.

The city published a contract with the company on their website the next day. They spelled out each of these changes. They placed this change of control on the agenda of the next city council meeting, which would take place the following week.

To give some background history, the city and the teachers' union had been unable to come to a decision about our contract. The union insisted that previously negotiated pay must be given to the teachers and that additional pay increases were warranted.

The city responded by claiming that the amount of money being given to the school through the state was not adequate to fund the negotiated pay increases, let alone cover additional expenses such as supplies and incidentals.

What was even more concerning is that the city's reserve funds to run the school were way too low. To give the teachers the previous or the newly negotiated pay increases, the city would have to dip into the reserve fund. If that fund went too low, the entire charter system would be in jeopardy of being insolvent, and if that happened, the entire system would fold up and close.

This dispute came a few years after the Great Recession of 2008, when money for education had begun to dry up.

The school claimed insolvency; the union claimed that the city was withholding funds that they had promised to teachers; and from the teachers' standpoint, this money was owed to us, period.

This decision had been in the works since the start of the school year, but these dire concerns had not been communicated to the teachers by the city or the union. The teachers had no inkling as to what was coming — thus my shock at receiving this text message five days after the end of the school year.

The city made its decision after the latest negotiations had failed to produce an agreement.

Since the issue was money, all contracts would be dissolved when the school's operation was turned over to the new owner. The union would not be able to represent teachers. Teachers' contracts would also go away. Teachers could apply for their jobs, but since this buyout was all about money, a new pay scale would be created, and teacher pay would be decreased.

It was generally expected that teachers with more years of experience were less likely to be rehired because they were the most expensive in terms of salaries.

On that Friday, the city issued a statement to the parents saying that the union was the cause of all the issues at the school along with the teachers who insisted on pay increases when the funds were not available. We were made to be the bad guys. Teachers were causing this. Teachers were the reason the school would be sold to a corporation, or so the narrative went.

Through the weekend, teachers were frantic that a nationally recognized school of excellence was about to alter how it was run, and that the entire faculty would be let go. We talked about what could be done. We reached out to each other to figure out our next best steps.

But there was also outreach to parents, students, and alumni, all of whom were made aware of the situation. The school they knew and loved would be changed by this decision.

On Monday, the union held a meeting with the teachers. The main point of discussion was that the union was willing to fight, to go to court even, to take on this cause. The union was certain the city had enough money to fund the school without selling it to a corporation. An armada of lawyers was ready to fight this decision if the city went through with it.

Then, the entire room erupted when it seemed like the union was willing to sacrifice teachers for the fight.

I attended this meeting and expressed concern that the union's position was going to destroy us. The teachers were as angry at the union as they were at the city.

Very quickly, the local TV stations and newspapers picked up the story and expressed what was on the minds of so many people: why was a successful independent charter system facing these daunting challenges? The system was working, so why change it?

Over the weekend and into the early part of the week, the wishes and concerns of the residents, the parents, the alumni, and the students were made known to the city council. In one unified voice, they did what they could to stop this.

The city and the union agreed to hold an open discussion on Tuesday, June 18. There was a glimmer of hope that maybe the school wouldn't be sold after all, but it seemed to the teachers that this was a done deal. We were certain the city would turn over control of the governing of the school to a for-profit company, the staff would be let go, the day-to-day running of the school would change, and the very character of the school would change, all in one vote.

The meeting room was filled to overflowing with teachers, students, parents, and alumni.

Local television news crews were present.

In the days leading up to this meeting, petitions, pleas, letters, and words of endorsement of what PPCHS meant to so many people were communicated to the city. I read many of these passionate letters. They were full of gratefulness for an education they felt was unique, an education they now felt was in jeopardy. All kinds of kids, all kinds of alumni, all kinds of parents wrote to the city pleading them to prevent this.

Whatever pressure those of us on the outside could bring to bear was brought.

You could feel the pressure inside that meeting room for the two sides to find a way through this.

At one point during the meeting, when all seemed lost, the two sides began to give way and talk, and really listen to each other. The city knew the jewel it had created, and the union knew the wishes of the faculty — to keep the school intact as it was.

There were moments when it seemed as though we'd had a breakthrough, and others when there was despair. Cheers and boos filed the audience, and at times attendees chided the city, but they also chided the union.

Teachers shouted for the city to agree and then shouted just as equally for the union to come around.

And then we reached an agreement.

The city would retain the running of the school. There would be no turning over of operations. The teachers would keep their jobs. The special environment at PPCHS would continue.

But there was a cost.

The agreed-upon bonuses from the previous year were given up, and the teacher pay scale was reduced and frozen. Teachers, depending on where they were on the pay scale, might lose a few hundred dollars or thousands. It was a difficult sacrifice, and teachers bore the brunt of it.

But it saved the school.

There was much joy and celebration and a lot of relieved people when the meeting finally adjourned. The city pledged to make sure that the school system would stay independent. Teachers, students, parents, and alumni were thrilled; this unique and special school had been preserved. The city, the union, the teachers, and those inside and outside of the building felt the joy of having saved something that was worth it.

It was only later, when teachers realized what they had given up, that negative feelings crept in.

Over the next few years, several experienced teachers left PPCHS.

Many of those who remained felt resentment at what they perceived as unfair treatment when they had done nothing but teach kids to the best of their ability. They felt that the city had waited intentionally until after the school year was over to threaten teachers with the destruction of the school they had worked so hard to make flourish.

People had always viewed the city as this powerful force for good. After all, they had created the charter system, built the buildings, and given us free rein in running the school, but now, many people saw the city as an outside force that didn't have the school's best interest at heart.

As the days and weeks passed that summer, a cloud of despondency formed over the school. At the start of the new school year, I wondered how we would ever come back together.

I will admit to having much of the anger that my fellow teachers shared. I looked upon what had happened with a jaundiced eye.

The first day back for teachers, we had our usual welcome back breakfast. The mood in the room felt depressed. Even being together with good friends and colleagues didn't help — if anything, that made it worse. This breakfast had always been a happy reunion full of excited chatter about what we had done during the summer vacation and what we hoped to achieve during the school year.

Not that year. It seemed the clouds had darkened.

Directly from this meeting, we went into our first faculty session of the year.

I was feeling a sense of despair as I walked across campus alone, but out of my despair, a phrase came to mind.

Over the next several years, whenever I felt resentment or anger from what had happened in the summer of 2013, I thought of this phrase. It became my mantra for all that the summer of 2013 had wrought:

REMEMBER YOUR JOY.

REMEMBER YOUR BLISS.

REMEMBER WHY YOU DO THIS!

I eventually shortened it and shared it with fellow teachers as simply JOY, BLISS, THIS!

I taught because kids mattered to me, my class mattered to me, making an impact on the world mattered to me. So I would go back to my classroom and try not to think about what had happened. I would remember my joy, remember my bliss, and remember why I did this.

It was the most sobering of ways to remember such a fundamental teaching lesson.

Now, several years later, I do believe the clouds have dissipated and our school has thrived. That's the thing about journeys: there will be dark clouds, and sometimes bad things will happen. They can infuse you with negativity if you let them, and they can destroy your class.

Or, you can . . .

REMEMBER YOUR JOY.

REMEMBER YOUR BLISS.

REMEMBER WHY YOU DO THIS!

JOY, BLISS, THIS!

Then go back and do your job!

Your Journey

"It is custom for adults to forget how hard and dull school is. The learning by memory all the basic things one must know is the most incredible and unending effort. Learning to read is probably the most difficult and revolutionary thing that happens to the human brain and if you don't believe that watch an illiterate adult try to do it. School is not so easy and it is not for the most part very fun, but then, if you are very lucky, you may find a teacher. Three real teachers in a lifetime is the very best of luck. I have come to believe that a great teacher is a great artist and that there are as few as there are any other great artists. Teaching might even be the greatest of the arts since the medium is the human mind and spirit. My three had these things in common. They all loved what they were doing. They did not tell-they catalyzed a burning desire to know. Under their influence, the horizons sprung wide and fear went away and the unknown became knowable. But most all the truth, that dangerous stuff became beautiful and precious."

~ John Steinbeck

"There is no word in the language I revere more than 'teacher.' My heart sings when a kid refers to me as his teacher, and it always has. I've honored myself and the entire family of man by becoming a teacher."

~ The Prince of Tides, **Pat Conroy**

So You Want to Be a Great Teacher

Two things compelled me to put in writing my thoughts and beliefs about teaching, which eventually led to this book. The first was a letter I wrote to a colleague after she mentioned that she wanted the kind of relationship with students that she noticed I had. The bulk of this chapter is a copy of that letter, which lays out the basics of how I approach teaching. Writing it also caused me to think deeply about the journey of teaching and the goal of excellence, something I had never pondered until then.

The second motivation for writing this book sprang from two conversations I had, one with a colleague, the other with two students. My colleague and I had discussed co-writing a book about teaching. Though this never happened, the idea of writing a book was planted in my mind. In the dedication of this book, I've acknowledged her, but I want to again thank Debbie Tabie for being an instigator of this book.

In 2007, I had two students in my World History class who several times brought up the idea that I should write a book so that other teachers would be inspired to teach like I do.

I thank all four of you for your encouragement. I am certain I would not have written any of this without your inspiration.

If you boil down all of the suggestions, they come to two basic ideas. First, you have to have **passion** for whatever subject you teach. You have to make this passion clear and obvious to every kid. You do this through your words and actions. Speak with love of the class; cradle in your arms like precious cargo the text you are teaching.

Secondly, you must have **compassion** for your kids. They must have a special, sacred place in your mind, in your words, in your deeds, in your actions, in your thoughts, and in your heart.

I have written this book in two parts. To understand the second part, I felt like I needed to write the first because I wanted the reader to understand my journey and every aspect of how long and hard it had been, the failure upon failure upon failure, and how I let myself and my kids down, and then through hard work how I had figured it out.

My journey has always headed in one direction: toward excellence, even if I have yet to reach that destination. I am not there yet. I am on that journey WITH YOU! I do not claim to have all the answers, nor do I claim that my way or my suggestions will work perfectly. But the knowledge shared in this letter is what I have come to realize about excellence, about the journey, and about the way to find the path forward.

I hope you will take the things that work for you and use them to guide you. In this letter, I offer you the signposts to excellence that I have found along the way. I hope they will help you strive for excellence and further your own journey!

Please feel free to share this with others.

Dear Teacher,

Ever since you mentioned your desire to be one of those teachers who other colleagues are impressed by, whom students call their best or favorite teacher, I have spent a lot of time reflecting and thinking about how that happens. How does someone get to the place where people think of you as one of the best? As you can see below, I do have a lot to say about this, as this is something I have spent a lot of time thinking about, not just over the last week but for years.

Understand this is my life's work.

I know what I am and am not good at. And the only thing that I will ever do that will really make a difference in this world is this job.

So, understand that I speak of the journey you say you want to embark on as someone who is on that exact same journey with you. I can point the way and tell you how I got as far as I have. But I can't get you there. In order for that to happen, someone wiser than me will have to take over.

So let us begin.

The way to greatness, to being a transcending teacher, is not easy or short. I am still on it and am not anywhere near it yet, but the rewards are great. Kids will think you are great, colleagues will respect you, teachers will seek you out, administrators will ask for your help, and the self-worth is tremendous, but there are lots of pitfalls and problems, and there is NO GUARANTEE OF SUCCESS. You also must understand that what I am telling you is my journey. It is not the only way; it may not even be the best way, but it is the only way I know. I bring this up because my first suggestion on how to get there may lead you to reject everything else I say. My first suggestion is the only one I know for sure is true. Everything else is — well, that's for you to decide.

Before I begin to talk of the journey, here are some caveats:

Are you sure you are willing to put in the time and money to attain excellence as a teacher? I don't just mean going to workshops. A lot of the work you have to do is internal, personal, and philosophical. You have to deconstruct everything you do. You are going to be spending a lot of time asking and re-asking yourself why you do things, assessing what isn't working and why, and asking yourself, *How do I fix it, fix me, fix my class?* And often, terribly, terribly, terribly often, the answer will not come to you immediately, and you will have to deal with that even as you continue to seek the answer. This is going to take years — not weeks, not months, but YEARS! Are you really willing to sacrifice time with your family, your partner, your friends, your enjoyment of TV shows and movies or other things that distract? Never, and I truly mean never is my class far from my thoughts. I am constantly thinking and rethinking what I've done in the classroom and trying to make it better.

This journey is an ego hit unlike anything you have ever felt professionally. Before you succeed, you are going to fail, and even when you do succeed, you will sometimes fail. From now on, you cannot ever again say that your class doesn't work because of the students. You are responsible for your class, and whatever goes on in there is your responsibility to fix. Getting a new group of kids is never the fix!

You must understand that you might not get there. I have personally known one teacher who got there — one!

This is a lonely pursuit. There are simply not many teachers who want what you want. People will put you down and make fun of your positivity. They'll say that kids like you because you're an easy teacher. People will be jealous. People will wonder why you have changed or whether you're just trying to show off. Others will find you odd.

Okay, if you are really sure this is what you want, here is what I think I know about how to become a great teacher:

You gotta know you

Until you know the kind of person you are, and truly understand what your strengths and weakness are, and until you bring that into your classroom in a POSITIVE WAY, you will never succeed at becoming a great teacher. Ultimately you are you in that classroom, and until you let yourself be you in that classroom, then you will be fighting yourself, fighting your greatness. Maybe the best lesson I ever learned as a teacher was taught to me by a student. When I first started teaching, I tried to be the strict disciplinarian. I had rules. I enforced them. I was strict, tough, no nonsense. I was fighting myself, and my classes suffered because of it. This is not who I am. But it was what I thought I should be. I didn't know any better. And for three years I had discipline problem after discipline problem.

One day, following a really bad class, one of my students stopped me in the hall and said, "Why are you trying to be tough, Mr. Quigley? You know you can't do it." This was said with complete kindness. And at that moment, it dawned on me. He was right. I'm not that tough guy. I never will be.

So I spent the next few years trying to figure out how I could bring what I believe into the classroom. This is how I created my discipline system; this completely changed the focus of my class, of me, of what I do and why I do it. I realized that every year I would be teaching new kids, maybe a new subject, and maybe even in a new school, but I was the one constant. I had to work on myself.

You have to think about who you are and how to bring yourself to the classroom. Stop thinking about your classroom as four walls and desks and chairs, and start seeing what you do in your classroom as an extension of you. The moment you become comfortable with yourself and bring yourself into that room is the moment you take your first step. Think of who you are and the roles in your life: mother, father, daughter, son, friend, coach, team player, wife, husband, partner, and then think which of these roles are YOU! Then, figure out how you bring this to life with your kids. How do you see yourself? How can you translate that to your classroom? Think about this and then build your classroom around it.

For example, you have known teachers who are mothers; they act like mothers with their students , and this is how the kids see them. The relationship they build with kids is mother-child. They run their classroom as though they were trying to get a three-year-old to pick up their blocks, one moment cajoling and the next giving them a slap on the rump, but always done with the demeanor of a mother.

I am not suggesting this is you. Who and what you are has to come from you. This is what took me the greatest amount of time and work to get right. The question is how you are going to relate to these kids. As I said earlier, this is the only thing I am going to say to you that I can truly feel and say with any kind of certainty because it is true.

You gotta teach with heart

You don't teach history; you teach kids! If you are not here for them, then why the hell are you here? If it is to teach a subject, quit, go back, get a master's degree, and teach college because you love history, not kids. At a college or university, it matters how much you know about a subject. Here in high school, it is all about the kids. Time and time again teachers say they are here for kids, but they never once stop to ask HOW they demonstrate that. How are you here for kids? Forget every academic thing you do, forget the projects, the assignments, the homework

— forget all of that and ask what you do for them. How do you try to reach them? How are you here for them? If you are drawing a blank, then that's the problem. How do you reach out your hand to help them beyond academics? How do you talk to them? How do you draw them to you, and not just the cool fun nice kids, the ones that are easy to like and be there for, but the ones who are the least lovable, and God knows they are the ones who need it the most. How do they know you care? And the fact is that *saying* it does not equal *being* it. What do you *do* to show them you care? Again, this should cause you to rethink everything you do. If it doesn't, then I don't think greatness is what you want!

You gotta impart, not just teach

Teaching is the dissemination of knowledge, and it is what we do. When I say we I mean any teacher. We must teach a subject, a grade level, a set of standards, but ultimately very little of that is what we impart. What do we really give our kids? What do we share with them beyond the text? Much of the factoids we teach kids can be found online in a matter of minutes. What do we impart to help them understand themselves, the world, their place in it, what they can do, what they can be, how they can be, why they can be, why it matters, why they matter, why what you have put them through is going to matter.

Teachers teach, but great teachers impart. We impart to our kids a greater sense of — well, that's for you to figure out. So you need to ask yourself some questions: What are the goals of your class? What do you want kids to leave your class knowing about themselves, the world, and their place in it? MOST IMPORTANTLY: What are you honestly doing to help them make these discoveries? This to me is the dividing line between good and great. Good teachers know the information, know how to teach the information, and their students learn and enjoy the class. But that's where it ends.

If I were to ask you the goals of your class, how many of those goals can kids use anywhere else and truly benefit beyond the four walls of your classroom? There isn't a kid who has left my class who doesn't understand how to shake hands with another person. It seems like a silly little thing, but do you know how that hooks them? They know that I cared enough to want to teach them something they can use in the real world to connect with others and to make a good first impression.

What use is your class? What are you imparting to them that will have a lasting impact?

You gotta be original

What makes you and your class stand out from all the others? What makes kids happy to walk into your class every single day? What project makes kids in your class better? How are you using your curriculum to help them see themselves and the world in a different way? How are you engaging students, making them think, making them reason and write, pressing them to interact with the material? Other than a grade, why should kids care? In other words, you gotta work on the work. If you are not doing this, then why should any kid engage in you, your class, and what you are trying to teach them? Where is the joy? Where is the play? The fun? How do you structure your class to breed creativity and originality? How do you shake things up? Is today like yesterday like last week and next week? Why aren't you daring to take a chance?

When I was in the Keys, my principal every year gave every teacher a Get Out of Mistake free card. She gave this when a teacher took a chance and failed miserably. When was the last time you were in your class and scared, not because of discipline but because you were trying something that you didn't know would work, but you were doing it because you wanted to push them, challenge them, and by so doing make everything different, for them, for you, for the class. If you are not tense, scared, and wondering if something you are doing is going to work because it's so unique and unusual, then you are not doing your job! I can tell you from experience the very best things I have ever done were the ones that five minutes before I did them I was scared to death they were going to blow up in my face.

So it really comes down to three things:

You gotta work on yourself.

You gotta work on your class.

You gotta work on the work.

And in everything you do, you gotta look at what does not support what you want your class to be: Are you giving homework just to give homework? Does that test serve a purpose? Is the assignment something of value, or are you doing it because you haven't entered a grade in a week? If there is no purpose to what you're doing, get rid of it. Some will criticize this, scoff at this, question this, but you know what you are doing and why.

So the question you might be asking yourself is how the heck do I do these things?

Ah, now that is the rub, isn't it? How?

It has to begin by you looking at your class, looking at what you do, looking at who you are, and then plunging in. Tear down the things that don't work, that don't support what you want, and throw them away; no matter what they are, they will prevent you from getting to where you want to go. Start over. It isn't going to be easy. I told you that you are going to fail. Stuff is not going to work. You are going to try things, and you will have to rethink them. Things will evolve and change, and you will add and subtract things that just don't work. But its gotta start now. Now is the time, when you have the hours and no school to go to, in the summer, between naps, when you are in bed, think, reflect, write about your class, figure out what goals you have and who you are. Realize the kind of person you are and what makes you special and unique — and God knows you are special and unique — and decide how you can bring you into your classroom.

Think of the first day of school, think of the way you set up your classroom. Think of what you have on your walls. Think of the way you address the students and how they address you. Think of how you communicate and miscommunicate the person you are and the type of classroom you maintain. You know you want to do something more than just teach the subject, and you want to know how to do that now. But how can you communicate everything about you, your class, and what really matters in one day? Think of the teams you were on, the coaches you had, the friends you know; could you truly understand them in one or two 50-minute periods? Everything you do in your class either supports what you are trying to do, or it muddies or directly goes against what you are doing. To whatever degree you can, get rid of the stuff that contradicts who you are, and try to figure out why you are muddying the message you are hoping to send.

All of this is daunting and overwhelming, and I will caution you not to bite off more than you can chew right now. To give you an idea, it took five years of teaching before I brought my true self into my classroom, another five years to get my classroom to the place it should be, and the last nine years to figure out what works.

Practical steps to help you achieve greatness

You need to seek out and attend education workshops in the county and outside of the county. This is the sacrifice I was talking about earlier, because this might mean spending money that you would rather spend on a vacation or going out to dinner, shopping, and a movie.

You need to seek out people who know, and spend hours listening to them describe what they are doing that works. Go to your administrators and tell them what you need. Listen to their advice. You will be shocked at how readily people will help you once you let them know why you are seeking their advice.

Look to teachers you respect, go to their classes, watch them teach, talk to them, get them to talk about teaching, and it doesn't have to be people who teach the same grade level or subject you teach. Seek out outstanding teachers and sit in their classrooms for a day.

Look to your kids for subtle hints as to what they need, and listen to them. Have them evaluate and review you and what you do. Be very sensitive to the mood and atmosphere in your classroom. If your lessons are dragging or boring, or if kids are tuning you out, you've gotta change things. Part of this is keeping your own excitement and engagement level up.

You need to read the words I have written and then think, reflect, talk to someone you truly trust, and then after all of that, you are ready.

It's time to get to work!

Work on Yourself

Being the Best YOU

S everal years ago, I was preparing a presentation for the faculty at the high school where I work. The workshop was entitled How to Engage, Inspire, and Involve Every Kid. I wanted the participants to get an idea of how a teacher can do each of these things regardless of the subject. If the teachers enacted my suggestions, they would experience a paradigm shift in how they saw their role as a teacher and how they interacted with their kids. I wanted this presentation to apply to any subject, so it had to be entirely student centered.

I have always believed that one of the best ways to get an idea of what great teaching is and is not is to ask your students. On the day of the workshop, I was struggling to come up with an introduction, and I wanted my students' input, so I challenged them to think about and then to explain to me what great, excellent, amazing, engaging teaching is. To answer the question, I allowed students to work alone, in pairs, in groups, or as an entire class. I didn't care how they came up with the answer as long as they were able to explain it, and they conveyed their ideas in writing and in a visual image. I gave them twenty minutes to prepare both. They would present their answers to the class in any way they wanted. They could act out their ideas in a skit, sing a song, recite a poem, or give a brief lecture, as long as they answered the question and did something visual. I got a lot of great answers, but one stood out above the others:

A great teacher should be like the main characters in *The Wizard of Oz*.

Like the scarecrow, you should have a brain; you need to understand, be passionate about, and teach the material.

Like the lion, you need to have courage to try different things and not teach like every other teacher.

Like the tin woodsman, you need to have a heart and let kids know you care about them.

And like Dorothy, you need to make kids feel like they are at home in your classroom.

When this group got done, I was blown away. This said it all. In the following pages, I hope you will realize that you have to teach with a heart, a brain, and with lots of courage to make your class your students' home.

To understand teaching, kids, and education, and to achieve excellence as a teacher, there are three areas you must focus on:

Work on yourself.

Work on your class.

Work on the work.

As you read on, think of these three aspects of excellence, and let them be your guide on the yellow brick road of your teaching journey.

But before we talk about the journey to excellence, we must first reject a preconceived notion and ingrained idea about teaching that will never lead you to excellence.

Whether your classroom is "good" or "bad" does not depend on the kids. You are the only constant in your classroom. Because of this, you must reject the most common excuse a teacher uses to explain away their responsibility, their failure, and the failure of their classes: "bad" kids. But it is never ever about the kids. Your class is yours; you are the captain of that ship, and you must stop blaming the kids. If you have a tough class, a tough kid, a tough year, the easy thing to say is the kids are the reason. The moment you allow this thinking is the moment you stop striving for excellence.

It is not about them; it is about you! The surest, quickest way to never finding excellence is to believe that with a change of kids everything will be okay. It is about you. You can do something different, you can reach the kids, you can do more; if things don't work, it is not their fault. The solution to YOUR issues is not found in them, in a new class, in a new year, in a different school — it's in you.

I know this is hard, but you must take responsibility for what happens in your class, even when it feels like it's not your fault. I am not so naïve that I believe that every kid is willing to learn and wants to be reached. That's not what I'm trying to convey here. The idea is that you must always endeavor to figure out a way to reach the most unreachable kids, and if you do, you'll reach the reachable kids too. If you don't, you can't throw your hands up and give up. That only leads to failure. Oh, and the fact is you are going to fail. I fail every year. I don't reach every kid, but I will not make the excuse that it is their fault. It is all on me. I control me, and I will do whatever I can to make my class be the best it can for every kid.

Find YOURSELF!

I have a simple and profound question for you: at your best, who are you? What kind of person are you? What are your best, most positive, most honorable attributes? What positive role do you play in your family and with your friends? What makes you unique? Dynamic? Different?

Your answers to these questions will reveal the most important thing that will change you and ultimately your classroom. The answers I get when I ask myself these questions lead me to the most important suggestion I can give you to find your way on your journey as a teacher.

You must be your best self, the best of what you are, in the classroom. You have to be you! Anything else is a lie, which makes everything you do in your class a reflection of that lie.

YOU ARE A UNIQUE AND SPECIAL PERSON, AND YOUR KIDS DESERVE THE BEST OF YOU IN THEIR CLASSROOM!

You are you, and to deny that in your classroom means you will spend the rest of your teaching career fighting yourself. I did that and it led to disaster. For over three years I played the role I thought I was supposed to play. I was the teacher I thought I was supposed to be. I thought teachers were tough and focused on discipline as a way to gain control, so that's what I did. That wasn't me! I don't know you, but if you are not you in your classroom, it won't ever be as great as it could be. Stop fighting yourself. Stop pretending to be the teacher you thought you were supposed to be. Stop trying to be the teacher you loved in high school. Stop being your mentor. Stop being what you thought a teacher was supposed to be. Stop it!

If you try to be anyone else in your class, you are lying to yourself and your kids. Maybe it will work to a certain extent, but you will always be a fake in class, and kids can spot a fake a mile away. To truly teach, to truly impact lives, to truly be excellent, we must be ourselves. And if we are not being ourselves, then by definition we can never be our all. You will either become your best self in the classroom or some pale imitation of someone else. And you will never be happy, your kids will not learn as well or as much as they should be able to, and you will never achieve the excellence you seek.

Worksheet: Being the Best YOU!

The first thing you must do to become the best you in your class is to read the following questions and jot down the answers that come to you. Think on these things. Let them roll around in your thoughts, then forget them and come back to them later. Thinking time is one of the most important ways to allow you to answer the really tough questions:

1. At your best, who are you?

2. What kind of person are you?

3. What are your best, most positive, most honorable attributes?

4. What positive role do you play in your family and with your friends?

5. What makes you unique? Dynamic? Different?

After you have thought about and reflected on these questions, brainstorm some ways to bring your best authentic self into the classroom. That is going to require lots of internal rummaging and thinking and creating.

This is the hardest of hard parts. But it is also the only way you will ever attain excellence in your classroom. I can't necessarily say how you will do this. I will provide some guiding questions to help you find a way through this, but a lot is going to be trial and error and figuring out what works and what doesn't.

Whatever answers you gave to the questions above, you now have to bring that best, most dynamic, most true version of yourself into the classroom. Let's say the answer to the first question was any one of the following: mother, father, brother, sister, leader, coach, artist, the person who is there for their family and friends, adventurous, loving, kind, scientific, actor, party animal, athletic, hard worker, smart, nerd, singer, musician, lover, open, thoughtful, and so on.

Whatever your answer, you have to bring that to your classroom. You are you, and your best self is yours, not mine. My journey was to figure this out for me. It took me five years to find and implement my best self in my classroom. It took failure first because I denied myself for far too long, and then, once I figured out who I was at my best, I had to do the work to bring this alive in my class. It wasn't easy. I had to throw out everything I had relied on as the way to "do" teaching — my discipline plan, the way I talked to kids, the way I taught lessons, the assignments I gave — everything had to be thrown out and redone.

YOU are the author of YOUR class, the creator of the atmosphere of growth and achievement that prevails in your classroom. YOU are the maker of what happens. YOU create the theme of your class. YOU SET the time signature. YOU are the lyrics and the music. YOU make the pattern. YOU make kids feel the mood and tone of your class, whether it is open and accepting or closed and rigid.

If, for example, you answered that you are a mom, how do you bring being a mom to your class? If you're a coach, how does your class become your team? If you're an artist, how do you paint the kind of class you want? If you are a brother or a sister, how are you a big brother or sister to your class? If you're a musician or actor, how do you make your class your greatest performance? You must take the best of you, the thing that most defines you, and make THAT your class. Your class is an extension of you. The sooner you realize this, the sooner excellence will be within reach!

Maybe you are resisting all of this. Maybe your mind is saying, *My class is a middle school English class. That's what it is, period, exclamation point! ALL of this bringing myself into my class is folly. I'm there to teach English!*

That's fine, but understand that you might be a great teacher, and you might reach excellence in how you teach English, but when all is said and done, what kids will remember about your class is that it was a middle school English class and only that. You will not have transcended your subject. You will not have made the greatest kind of impact you can. And if that's enough for you, then that is fine, but it will limit you.

So now, you have some homework to do, the homework of a lifetime, the homework that will make your class the amazing and dynamic place it can and should be.

Be you. Only by being and finding the best in you and bringing that into your classroom can you ever hope to find the path to excellence.

The following page contains the next part of your homework.

Worksheet: Bringing the Best YOU into Your Class

1. After having thought and reflected on yourself, what have you decided is your truest best self?

2. How can you bring that self into your classroom?

3. How can you make it part of your discipline plan?

4. How can you make it part of the instruction, assignments, and activities you do?

5. How can you make it part of the ways you interact with your students?

6. How can you make it part of the atmosphere of your class?

7. What other ways can you bring your best self to the design, setup, and even the décor of your classroom?

Find Others to Help

No teacher is an island! You are not a rock. You don't have all the answers. You are going to get lost, things will happen, and you won't know what to do. You are going to need help, and other teachers who have been there before can help you.

Ironically enough, the two groups of people who need this the most are the two that are the least likely to seek guidance.

The first are new teachers, who are often too scared to ask for help, don't know they need help, or even what to ask for when it comes to help. The second group are the teachers who have been teaching for years, who know what they are doing but are stagnant, trapped, caught in a rut, and either don't know where to go next, or worse, things have become so easy that changing the way they do things doesn't have the appeal it should.

No matter who you are, seek mentors, seek people to help and guide you along the way, people who have more experience, more knowledge, and are willing to share. You may be assigned a mentor when you start teaching; if so, use this person. Don't just ask for advice; go to their classroom to watch what they do, and invite them into yours. Be open, be willing to listen, and be challenged.

In teaching there are only three ways to get better: do it, see others do it, or go to experts who know how to do it.

There are people in your school right now who do aspects of teaching better than you do. Seek them out. Ask them for help and advice. This includes your department head, your principal and assistant principal, the curriculum specialist, and others. Find out who has won Teacher of the Year in the past, and go talk to them. And remember, it doesn't matter if they teach what you teach! Yes there are specific pedagogical aspects to teaching one grade level versus another, one subject versus another, but good teaching is good teaching is good teaching.

Some of the best things that have enabled me to teach high school seniors is what I learned teaching fifth graders. What an elementary teacher has to say about good teaching can help a middle or high school teacher and vice versa. Like everything else, you need to sift the information; go over what you see and what is shared with you. What works for someone else won't necessarily work for you. Often simply talking through what you want to do with an experienced teacher will help you see things from a different point of view. Sitting in an expert teacher's class will help you see your own class in a different way. I have had the luck over the years to be able to sit in many teachers' classrooms, and some of the best stuff I got was not from Social Studies teachers.

When meeting with these mentors, these excellent teachers, it's so important to talk about process. It's great to hear what a teacher does, but it's far more important for teachers to explain HOW they work their class. This is why it's so important to observe other teachers teaching, and then afterward, to talk about the process that she or he uses. It's wonderful for a new teacher to see a well-run class, but just seeing it isn't enough; the follow-up conversation of how a teacher got the class to that point is key. Actually, the process question is the most important.

To make an analogy, suppose you have a brand new high school football coach, and to teach him excellence, you only show him the game from the previous year's Super Bowl. This would be instructive, but far more important and useful to the new coach would be to watch practice, talk to other coaches about how they teach plays, observe how they interact with players, and learn how the culture of the team was created. This is true for teaching. Just observing an excellent classroom is not enough. Talk about the process the teacher uses to achieve that excellence.

And don't limit yourself to subject/grade level, don't limit yourself to the number of teachers you talk to and observe, don't limit yourself to the number of years they have taught, because the moment you limit yourself is the moment you stop seeking out those who have been successful on their journey and can help you navigate yours.

You must surround yourself with people who are positive about you and teaching and kids. Surround yourself with people who will challenge you. Your best self will not come out until you realize that in order for you to be the best, you must engage and be around the best, and reject those who negatively affect you. There is an easy way to gauge this. Listen to how the people around you speak about teaching and kids. If they are negative, then they are not doing anything to help you on your journey. Think about it like this: If you told these people what you were seeking, that excellence is what you want in the classroom, would you fear that they would put you down or make fun of you? If the answer is yes, then you already know what you need to do.

Reflect

When I first started teaching, I kept a journal about my classroom and wrote in it frequently, usually on a daily basis. It is important to be reflective to see what is not working, to figure out why, and to be willing to reject it if it's not. I taught World History for eight years. Every one of those years, I hated the way I taught Rome. Every year, I threw out the way I had taught it the previous year and tried it a different way. I hated having to do this every year. Some years the way I taught it was okay, but I knew it wasn't good enough. So I threw it away and started again. I wanted my students to really understand what is arguably the most important world civilization BCE. So I kept trying to find a different way to teach it.

You have to be willing to do this about everything in your class — to constantly be reflective about what is and is not working, and to keep trying different approaches, throwing out what doesn't work, keeping what does. If you're an excellence-minded teacher, you will chase this goal for the rest of your career. The easy thing would be to say, well, I do all of these other things great; what's the problem with only one okay/good/average/meh aspect of what I do? If excellence is what you seek, the only way to get there is by embracing the idea that you have to work on the areas where you are failing as well as the areas where your teaching method is okay/good enough/fine.

To do this you MUST examine yourself in the harsh light of honesty and DO THE FOLLOWING:

- Admit when it isn't working!
- Reject what isn't working and come up with a plan for what will work.
- Seek out others to help you.

- Try a new way.
- Assess whether this new way worked. Was it completely bad, or does it just need a few tweaks here and there?
- If it didn't work, be willing to start again.

A good teacher is always reflective about what is and is not working in class, every class, every day, every kid. When you see failure (yours or theirs), you have to be willing to make the changes that might bring about what you want. There is no guarantee, but you have to be willing to plunge in and just do it.

To help me with this, as the year goes on, I keep a running list of the issues and problems I have. At the end of the year, I look back at this list and try to find solutions to these areas. Sometimes, no immediate answer comes, but that's okay. Seek mentors. Seek guides. Go online. Give yourself time. Continue to reflect. Try something new. Be open enough to accept that the answer may come from a person you didn't expect and in a situation or at a time you didn't expect. Be open to the new; try the unknown; take a chance. Good is never good enough when excellence is the goal.

As an experienced teacher, this means you share, you guide, and you help those who are new to teaching. Paint a realistic picture of how you got to the place you are. Put yourself in the shoes of those starting down the road of teaching, and remember what it was like to be new, clueless, and terrified.

But it is more than that. Your journey should also be shared with your kids.

Now, I will caution here that we are dealing with kids, so all aspects of your journey are not appropriate to share with them. You must be smart about the group you teach and the appropriateness of what you share.

In my room, there is an entire wall of pictures, of writings, of things given to me over the years, and all of it is important to me. At the center of this wall is a picture of every year I have been a teacher. There are images of my family and friends. There are images kids have given me, pictures of projects and classes. There are pictures students have drawn of me, some of them going back to my very first year as a teacher. There are pictures of me on trips and in silly outfits, of receiving awards and being ridiculous, and there are also special items given to me by kids, each with a separate special story connected to it. Above it all is a photo of my mother and father.

I encourage students to look at this wall and to ask me questions about what they find there. When I do this, I am inviting students into my life, and by doing that, I am inviting them to know me. This serves two functions: it allows kids to identify and connect with me, and it motivates kids to be inspired about my class in a way they aren't with teachers who maintain a cold, professional distance between themselves and their students.

Throughout my room are all kinds of mementoes, on my desk and decorating my walls, that reflect special parts of who I am and my journey. I want kids to be part of that, so I invite them to ask and engage me about these special items.

Very early in the year, usually the third or fourth day, I introduce them to Mr. Quigley, the monkey. I tell them there is a special story behind him. I also tell them I do not like monkeys or stuffed animals, but that he is by far my most valuable and important possession. I explain that I am willing to tell them the personal story about him if they are willing to ask for the story. I will not tell them in a day or a week or even a month what that story is because they must ask daily and weekly to hear it. Making kids ask me for a long period of time creates a bond between us because they want to know the story. The anticipation brings the class closer together, and it makes me far more than just a teacher. I become a teller of secrets just for them.

It is amazing what kids will do to hear this story. Again, by doing this, I am inviting my students into me, into my class, and into the story of Mr. Quigley, and the important role he played in my life when my mother passed away.

You have a story to tell, and your kids want to know it. How you tell it, how much you tell of it, when you tell it is up to you. But you want kids to care about your class, to care about you, so tell them, and invite them into you. You will be amazed at how kids respond and how they will care about you and your class.

Once you know what you want your class to be about, your job is to focus everything around that idea, theme, and concept, because that is an extension of you. The way you discipline, the way you run class, the rules you have, the way you assign work, the way you teach, the way you interact with kids, the way students present their work, how you design your class, all of it should be an extension of you and the kind of teacher you are. This means that you need to throw out anything that doesn't work! Anything that doesn't meet your theme, the extension of who you are, has to go.

The thing that defines me is the concept of **respect**. This is me through and through, and everything in my class reflects this concept. I have eliminated anything that does not reinforce this idea because it undergirds everything I do. In your classroom, as in mine, the kids are the variables and you are the constant. Your class is an extension of you, how you view kids, how you view teaching. Students want to feel like they are home, that you have the courage to take chances and the heart to care for them. How better to do that than to make your class a reflection of your best self. This will make your class the kind of place they want to be.

In the presentation I mentioned earlier on How to Engage, Inspire, and Involve Every Kid, I had teachers introduce themselves to the group in a unique way. Instead of having all the teachers introduce themselves at the beginning of the presentation, I asked two or three teachers at a time to say their name and tell the group what they taught. Some of them named the subject they taught. Some answered a grade level. Some answered a specific class: Biology, Ceramics, American History, Algebra II. Still others answered a level of teaching: honors, regular, gifted, AP, and so on. And many answered a combination of these: AP Environmental Science to primarily eleventh and twelfth graders, regular and honors English, sixth grade English Lit, etc. After a few people had introduced themselves, I continued on to the next technique in the presentation.

When I came to the end of the presentation, after all the others had introduced themselves, I introduced myself:

"Hi, I'm William Quigley, but everyone calls me Liam, and I teach kids."

I paused.

"I don't teach Social Studies. I don't teach a grade level. I don't teach a subject. I teach kids."

Now this might seem small or subtle, or the idea may even be lost on you, but of anything in this section of the book, if you understand and embrace what this means, it will have the greatest impact upon your classroom. Above all else, you are a teacher of kids. The subject or the grade level or anything else doesn't matter. You should first see yourself as a teacher of kids because they are the reason you do this. In everything you do, the kids come first. The way I see them, how I run my class, how they feel about it, how I feel about them, SHOULD NOT CHANGE no matter what class I am in front of. The way I treat my class, my students, my approach, my way of dealing with them, has been the same whether I have taught a middle school elective, a core high school course, or a class that earns them college credit. What matters to me is them. Why I teach is them. What I do is to give them a better idea of them. I involve them. I engage them. I inspire them.

If this is hitting close to home, and you are feeling defensive about who and what you are as a teacher, let me encourage you that when you make this paradigm shift, teaching will feel more alive and vibrant and exciting than it probably has been for a long time. On the other hand, if you see yourself as a teacher of a subject or a grade level or a particular class, this is causing a disconnect between you and your kids. When you think like that, you're not teaching them or putting their needs first, but rather, you're putting the subject matter first. Doing that makes your class less impactful than it could and should be. You need to say to your kids, you matter far more to me than any grade you will get; you matter far more to me than anything I will teach; you have more importance than any test, any homework, any assignment, any lesson, or anything I have you do in this class.

I currently teach an Advanced Placement course, and if my students pass an exam created by the College Board (those wonderful people who gave us the SAT, LSAT, MCAT, and Common Core exams), they will get college credit. I am judged by that score, and yet I let my students know from the very first day that they matter more to me than any number you can attach to them.

You teach kids.

Anything else makes them less important, and they know that, they feel it. Love what you teach, teach with passion that literally drips from you, use all of your skill and all your love to teach your subject as though it were the only other thing that matters. But remember: the kids come first. ALWAYS!

Work on the Class

Transcending Mediocrity

Teaching is a mystical experience. It is art. It is theater. It is athletic. When done right, it engages a child on many levels. It allows expression. It is hard, challenging, difficult, and demanding. There are things about it that you can never quantify. There are teachers with the best of intentions who can't make their classroom rise above anything but dull or average. At its best, teaching makes life better. It elevates and gives joy, knowledge, and passion. It lets kids glimpse their best selves, their creative soul, and their possibilities. At its worse, it is horrific, pointless, mind numbing, soul draining drudgery. See it done right and you will ask how; see it done wrong and you will ask why.

Teaching is an experience we all share because we've all been students.

You may marry or not, have kids or not, go to college or not, travel or not, go to museums or not, love sports or not, but we all have sat in a classroom and seen teaching done. Each of you reading this right now can remember that good great amazing teacher, remember their name, the class, the time, the feeling; you can describe what you learned and what you loved about that teacher, that class. People thirty, forty, fifty years later can still recall that class, that teacher. Now think of the opposite, that teacher, that horrible teacher, in that horrible class teaching in that horrible way that horrible subject you could not stand. You remember their voice and the demeaning way they treated you and your fellow students. You hated it, resented it, and to this day, the thought of that class makes you angry.

So, hopefully you have rethought the kind of teacher you want to be in your room and the kind of class you want to create, and now it is time to teach in a way that will positively impact your kids forever.

Kids want to be comfortable and feel good about themselves, and when they don't, they want someone to help them. They need to be encouraged when they fail. When they fall, they need someone willing to show them how to pick themselves up. And when they fear that they are not good enough, smart enough, likeable enough, or normal enough, they need reassurance. All of this they need from you. Kids sometimes loudly but often in quiet despair need to be seen and heard, noticed as unique individuals worthy of your consideration. The harder it is, the tougher things get, the less "cool" they are, the more they need to know that you will love them, even at the most unlovable moments of their life. It is your job to find the balance between teaching academics and caring for them on a personal level. This is part of what you must do, and if you don't, they learn less, care less, do less, and become less.

From the first moment you speak in class, you create a relationship with your students. That relationship exists. That relationship is defined by you in the ways you teach and how you treat your kids, the way you speak to them and reach out or don't reach out to them. You may not like it, but for many of the kids you teach, you are the most stable person in their life. You very well may be the only person who is kind to them. You may be the only person who asks how they're doing. You may be the only person who really knows who they are and how they feel. Or you can be the opposite, a person who adds to their burden, just another person who doesn't care about who they are or the struggles they face.

Do you really want to spend a whole year with fellow human beings, interacting with them every day and not caring who they are? Would you do this with your coworkers? Would you want someone to do this to you? Precious few of us are trained to be counselors, but that shouldn't preclude you from caring. Besides, if what you do is important to you, and if being a great teacher matters, then this must matter as well.

There is also a selfish reason to want to connect with your kids. When you do, they do better. They try harder. They achieve more. They care more.

I have kids who sleep in every class but mine. I have kids who come to school sick just because they don't want to miss my class. When you reach out, every aspect of your class gets better.

So here are some things I do to bridge the gap and welcome kids into my class and my heart.

We are our stories

As much as I can, I make myself a story in my class. I really believe it is so important to guide kids with my story. Many, not all, of the stories that I tell are the ones in this book. I try to get kids to see that life is a journey, and you are going to fail, but you can glean so much from everything that happens to you. I tell them about my experiences in college and how I became a teacher. I tell them about William and Mary and how I ended up at Saint Leo College. They know the story of my mom and Mr. Quigley, the monkey, and why he matters. I tell them about my successes and failures, and what I learned from each of those events in my life. I tell the kids about almost being fired and what an awful teacher I was.

There are three reasons I tell these stories: to teach my students some important lesson about life; to teach them something about the curriculum; and the last reason, which is often the most important, is to bond with them, to show them I'm real and fallible and human, just like they are, and to make the story of me and my life matter, because when that matters, I matter. And when I matter to them, they work harder and care more.

But kids also use these stories to help them figure things out, to make what's happened to them understandable, to help them reconcile how to get through disaster or sadness. I had a student a few years ago who kept pestering me for stories from my past, and I told her lots of silly stupid things from my life. It was only at the end of the year, in an essay she wrote, that I learned how awful certain aspects of her life had been. She told me later that my stories had helped her realize that she could make it through whatever had happened to her. You as the teacher need to decide when to tell these stories, which ones to tell, and which details to edit out that shouldn't be shared with your kids.

If you want to bond with your kids, tell them a story. You'll be shocked at how much your truth matters to them.

Think Piece

I mentioned this one earlier in a story I told of my first year when I was trying to get to know my kids. Around the end of the first quarter, about two or three months into the year, I give a writing assignment in which students are to write to me about who they are.

As with a lot of the things that I ask my students to do, I begin by telling them a story. In this case, I describe what I went through during my thirteen years of being a kid in school, and how I believed that no one cared about who I was. I tell them that when I decided to become a teacher, I vowed to be a teacher who cared about his kids. I explain that the intent of the assignment is for me to get to know them because I want them to know I care about them, and that none of them can leave school thinking no one cares, because I do!

How this assignment works is unlike anything else I assign.

First, students can write as much or as little as they want to in their essays, which are actually letters to me. I always hope they'll write a lot because I really do want to know my students, but some students are not willing to reach out to me. I tell my students they can write about anything they want and tell me anything they want, or tell me nothing if that's their preference. They can write about their childhood ten years ago or what happened ten minutes ago or both. Consequently, I have gotten essays that were one word and some that were twenty pages. Either one is worth the same grade. I have actually stopped giving a grade because this is not about teaching something; instead, it's about reaching someone.

These essays are often very personal statements about these kids' lives. Knowing this is asking a lot of a kid, I give my kids several days to think and to write. I tell them to go someplace quiet and safe, and in the safety of that place, I ask them to think about their life and the degree to which they want to share with me the good and bad of it, and then to write what they want to write. To help set their minds at ease, I make two promises:

1. No matter what they write, I will not treat them any differently than before I gained this new understanding of them. If they are willing to tell me their truth, I have no right to change the way I treat them or think of them. This also applies whether they write little or nothing. It is not my right to hold it against my kids no matter what they tell me.
2. No matter what they say, with one exception, what they write to me stays between them and me. I

always tell them the story of the girl at Redland Christian Academy whose mom found out about this letter and wanted to see it. I tell them how I refused to do so, how the principal asked if I would give it to the girl's mother, and when I explained why I wouldn't, he told me he backed me. And then, as I was leaving his office, he asked me what I would do if he had insisted I give it to the girl's mother. I tell them I said it would take me an hour to clean out my desk. I tell them that if anyone asks to see their letter, I will say the same thing, and if I need to, I will quit my job before anyone sees the letter. I always explain that there is one exception to this rule. If in the letter they say someone has abused them sexually or physically, or that they are sexually or physically abusing someone else, then I must, by law, by punishment of losing my teaching degree and going to jail, report this to my administrators.

I give them the following writing prompt to start their letter:

MY LIFE RIGHT NOW IS . . .

What they write after that is up to them. Whether they write me pages or a word, they can talk about their childhood or their dreams of the future, the joys and sorrows of their life, the events and people who have defined them, as long as they write, express themselves, and help me to know them in real and special ways or not. All of it is okay.

This assignment takes me twenty minutes to explain, and those are often the best spent twenty minutes of the year. In one assignment, I have said everything a kid needs to know about me and how I feel about them.

And oh, the things you will learn. I honestly feel bad for my colleagues who have no idea of the dynamic and deep and amazing people who sit in their classes every single day waiting and wanting to bond with them.

But I know, because of a letter.

A handshake is everything

I stand at my open classroom door, put my hand out, take their hand in mine, and shake it. That's how I begin every class, for every kid, every single day of the year.

As I shake each kid's hand, I invite him or her into my class with a smile on my face, my words full of welcome. As we shake, we share a moment of hello, we crack a joke, they tell me what happened over the weekend, whether they won the game, how they did on that test, what's new with them; sometimes I am silly, sometimes serious.

You will relate to your kids whether you like it or not. It happens every day, in every interaction. How you do that defines your class. I choose to define it at the very first moment of every day by being at my door and welcoming them into my classroom.

My kids have bad days. They make mistakes. They get in trouble. They do dumb kid stuff. When that happens, it is even more important that I be at my door to greet them. Whatever happened yesterday happened yesterday. What happened in the past has to be left there, by me and by the kid. When I was developing my discipline philosophy, and there were issues concerning discipline in my class, I would take the kid aside before class began and clear up what happened. We would talk it out. I would tell them how the incident felt from my point of view. I would always give the kid a chance to tell me whatever they wanted to share. If there were any lingering concerns, I would deal with it. If I didn't, if you don't, the kid carries that with them. At the end, I would shake hands and let the kid know that what happened was done.

Kids are going to mess up. There is no question about that, but will you hold that over their head for the rest of the year? No matter what transpires between a kid and me, I know how I will act.

The next day, I am at the door, shaking hands, smiling and welcoming the kid into my class.

Here is why I do handshakes. For the rest of my students' lives, they will be judged by the way they shake someone's hand. They will be judged positively or negatively, but either way they will be judged. Knowing this, and knowing that few of my kids know how to do it or even how important it is, I teach my kids how to shake hands properly.

I follow the same method of teaching them to do this as I do everything else in my class. I explain why it's important. I explain how to do it. We then practice it. Then over the next few weeks, I correct students when I greet them each day.

And often, out of all the lessons, all the work I give kids, when the year ends or even before the end of the year, this one small thing is something kids are most grateful for. Hardly a month goes by that some kid, even a kid who hasn't been in my class for years, comes back with a handshake story.

For example, one of my former students was up for a full scholarship in softball. PPCHS has one of the best softball programs in the country, and the scholarship was at one of the best college softball programs in the country. The coach had come down to scout her. After the game, the coach walked in, they shook hands, and they had a conversation. When the conversation ended, the coach offered her a full scholarship and told her that she had known before they met that she was a great player, but when they met and shook hands, she knew in that moment everything about what kind of person this girl was.

Over the years, kids have come back to tell me about jobs, internships, scholarships, or ways they've impressed people by shaking someone's hand correctly. Shaking hands matters, but kids don't know how to do it, so we need to teach them. You will create an amazing relationship with a kid just from this one simple but meaningful gesture. Oh, and you might change their life!

Respect is the KEY!

I have already gone into detail about my discipline plan and how it has eliminated the issue of disrespect in my class. I don't have to discipline so much anymore. I teach. But another effect of how I run my class has nothing to do with discipline. It has also changed my relationship with my kids. They see me less as a teacher and more as a friend, a mentor, a coach, someone who has their back and is on their side. As this has happened, I have been able to teach more. The less I acted like their superior, handing down knowledge from on high, the higher the students have held me in esteem as their teacher.

My wall, the Think Piece letters, and handshakes are big things I do to make kids feel welcome in my class, but there are small gestures that often mean as much if not more.

- Touch matters: a pat on the back, a high five, an arm on the shoulder, a hug; it matters to kids, that moment of real contact.
- Celebrate moments of, "Yes, you did it!" through words of congratulations, a name on the board, a round of applause, a smile and a nod, a sign on your wall, anything that says hey, you accomplished it. Celebrate success. Have a wall for the best-behaved kids, the ones who had the best test grade, the coolest project, who did something unique. Judge yourself as a teacher based on how much they care to get on that wall and how many different kids make it.

- Go to your kids' events — band concerts, sporting events, plays, musical performances, art shows. Take your kids on field trips, attend graduation ceremonies, the prom; any event that is bigger than your class matters in ways that you may never know.

- Acknowledge when you see a kid down even if it is just letting a kid know that you're aware something is going on with them, and if they need someone to talk to, you are there for them. They may never tell you what is bothering them or why they are down, but letting them know you care will help them not feel so alone.

- When you really push kids hard, recognize their efforts, and understand that they need a break, a few moments to do something silly or just to pause.

- If a kid misses a few days of school, let them know they were missed.

- Just be aware that your kids are going through things. KNOW YOUR KIDS. Know when something is going well or not well. This is why you build relationships with your kids. I think often of a friend who told me the story of how her mom died her senior year, and she went from an A student to almost failing. No one at her school knew, or cared, or bothered to find out why. This is your job and your challenge. Love them and let them know that even if they fight you, hate you, disrespect you, disregard you, they matter to you.

Give yourself a Get Out of a Mistake Free card

My first year at KLS, a card appeared in my mailbox at school. It was modeled after the yellow Monopoly Get Out of Jail Free card. This card sent an exciting message. The card had the same escaping bird flying free from its cage, but the words had been altered. It said in bold letters **Get**

Out of a Mistake Free Card, and in smaller letters at the bottom were the words *I took a chance and it didn't work.*

My principal, Mrs. St. James, put a new card in every teacher's box at the beginning of every new school year. The idea was that when you took a chance and it didn't work, you were to sign the back of the card and give it to her.

Mrs. St. James was only upset with you when she HAD NOT gotten a card with your name on it by the end of the year. If you didn't give back the card, it meant you had not taken enough risks in your class.

I loved her for this because it allowed me to teach with complete freedom, to be able to take risks knowing I had a safety net below me.

I cannot tell you how many times since then I have been in my class thinking *why am I doing this?* I have thought this so frequently as I've stood in front of a group of kids, created some assignment or activity that I thought would be amazing, come up with an idea, or supervised a school-wide presentation, or started whatever scary new thing I was attempting. At some point, I would think of that yellow card. It would be easier not to take chances, to just stay quiet in my classroom and teach without inducing all this anxiety of failure, and that might mean. But what that card said, and what every scary experience has taught me, is that you've gotta take chances!

Fundamental life-changing growth only happens when a teacher takes a leap and that leap causes a child to jump with you, and even more when you can get a school to take the same plunge into the scary. The most terrifying moments of my teaching career have happened when I've had no idea of the outcome of what I'm about to do.

But the rewards for you, for your kids, and for your school only happen when you do something that makes you ask *why am I doing this?* in the midst of it because you have no idea what is about to happen.

In the days, weeks, hours, and moments before the leap, that's when the fear happens; then, after the activity, every time, all I feel is how the leap into the unknown was so worth it. That does not mean that everything I have ever tried has worked. Yes, far more times than not, it has, but even when something has crashed and burned spectacularly, I've sent a signal to my kids that it's okay to try and fail. Failure won't defeat you, failure won't define you, and taking a leap has value in itself.

The enemy of that mentality is one phrase above all others that I despise: "you don't have to reinvent the wheel." Teachers often say this to justify doing the same old thing as they prep for their class. The easiest thing to do is to just take what someone else has already done, do a little modification, and boom, you haven't had to do any work, and your kids are going to produce for you the product every other kid before them has produced.

But is that what we really want as brilliant, creative teachers? No! I want a kid to reinvent the wheel! I am a teacher of history. I know what wheels used to be like and what they used to be able to do. If we had not reinvented the wheel, then we would have no cars or planes. If we had not reinvented the wheel, our phones would look like they did a hundred years ago. If we hadn't reinvented the wheel, our lives would be poorer for it. It is through reinvention that we create the new.

The greatest lesson any kid can learn is that WE WANT THEM TO REINVENT THE WHEEL, and we will give them the skills to do that! I push my students to see the world from different points of view, to think, to write, to read, to create, to show, to present, to interact with ideas, and hopefully, to internalize all of it and be able to live their own authentic life. But they can't do that if they don't take chances, if they don't take a leap, if they can't see the world in a new way.

And this growth, this leap, this reinvention of you, your class, your kids, only happens when you take a chance, when you stand on a precipice and have no idea what's going to happen next.

If during a school year you don't do at least four leaping-reinventing-taking-a-chance things, you are not doing your job.

Think of the leaps you've taken in your life: going to that college, starting up a conversation with that person, asking someone out or saying yes when asked, moving to that city, taking that job, buying that house, marrying that person, leaving that job, having a child. All of these were leaps, all of them defined your life, some of them were bad, but it was in the leaping that growth happened.

What leaps have you taken in your classroom? If the answer is none, don't you think it is time to make your class everything it could be?

What will cause the most regret? That you took the leap and failed, or you stood on the edge then stepped back and just went quietly back to teaching? Either will send a message. What will yours be?

Come on, do something original. After all, you've got a Get Out of Mistake Free card. It's time to use it!

The play's the thing

Being a teacher is a sacred calling and a sacred act.

Teaching, that's a different story. Your class is your stage.

Just as you would not sit through some droning, dull, lifeless performance, day after horrific day, you can't expect good reviews (or grades or learning) if your performance is sleep inducing. A teacher must fill the room with awe and laughter and silence and engagement.

How?

Think what an actor does to engage — movement, movement, movement.

You need to be in constant motion in and around your class. This keeps kids involved. This allows you to be where you see issues growing. Look the kids in the eye. Teach an entire class from the back of the room. Watch your patterns of where you stand and who you teach to. Make sure you talk to and walk to every part of your class every day! Look every kid in the eye.

Teaching is a performance. Yell. Whisper. Raise your voice. Jump up, jump around, be bold! You're on stage. You're a performer. Engage kids. Be active. Change what you say and how you say it. Speed up, make noise, slow down, scream, be completely silent, cry, laugh, be a verbal acrobat. If you are not interesting in the way you present information, why should a kid be interested in listening to you? Your class is a space; use it, change it, move the desks, get rid of the desks, teach while standing on a desk, teach using an accent, tell a joke, do something ridiculous, be the clown, wear silly hats, wear silly clothes, be silly. All the classroom is a stage, and if you want a long successful award-winning career, you will up the performance and leave them wanting more! If you read all that and it didn't make you want to run, skip, scream, and go a little crazy in your classroom, you read it wrong or I wrote it wrong — either way, DO IT! It's time to teach with bravado and take some bows for a stellar performance.

Extend the walls of your classroom

How far does your classroom extend? Where does your class exist? When are students required to interact with and use the information you teach other than in your classroom? Is your class comprised of only four walls? Do you ever challenge your kids to use the information, the content, and the ideas, and apply them beyond your class? If not, then you have segregated the things you teach, the ideas you want your kids to know, to four walls and one hour per day. You need to extend your class beyond the walls of your room. You need to extend your class to the rest of the school, your community, your city, your state, and beyond. Today, with access to the internet, your classroom should extend to the world. It is a profound, powerful life-changing thing to see your kids' newfound knowledge become part of the universe of ideas; to see your kids go out into the world armed with knowledge and use that knowledge to have something to say. The more we get kids beyond our four walls, the more the ideas matter, and the more value the kids see in what they are doing.

For our state-mandated study of the Constitution, students stand in every hallway in the school, between every building, anywhere and everywhere, all day, before and after school, between each class, using soap boxes and bullhorns, and read the Constitution aloud. By the end of the day, the entire Constitution has been read in full, and every kid in every class has heard the original text of the document. As students move between classes, they hear the words of the founding document of our nation. And of course, my students have taken this and run with it. They dress up like George Washington, wave flags, create banners, and gather in large groups as they proudly read the Constitution.

Between classes, once a week, in a central area of the school, students stand up and give a speech on any topic that matters to them about government, law, politics, and current events. This "U speak zone" (U because the building it takes place in is the "U" building) gets kids to stand up, speak out, give an opinion, and inform their fellow students. And yes, students have had controversial opinions and said controversial things. And when they do stand up for what they believe, I feel nothing but pride because they took a chance, a leap into the scary unknown.

Every year, to end the study of the Constitution in my law class, my students participate in an after-school debate concerning some constitutional issue. We have debated the death penalty, the Iraq War, gay marriage, gun control, immigration reform, and prayer in school, to name a few. Students take what they have learned about the Constitution, and with the entire school invited to watch, they defend an issue. Their understanding of the topic is challenged, questioned, and put up for scrutiny.

To conclude the semester of government that I teach, students must pick a local, state, or national law, a school rule, or a constitutional amendment that they would like to see changed. They have to research the history of the law and write a research paper, write an argument for the change, and figure out how they would deal with arguments against their change. But this is only a third of this activity.

Students then have to go into the world and advocate for the change. They have to contact government officials, write letters to news media, make and post videos about their issues, create and post in public places posters for their change, write petitions, get legal petitions signed, organize meetings on the issue, go to meetings where their issue can be dealt with, find existing groups who are for their change. All of the work, the research, the arguments, and the advocacy goes on a website they create.

The assignment concludes with them presenting to a panel of elected officials, members of the community, teachers, administrators, and alumni. These panels question and challenge my students to see if they really understand the law, what it would mean to change it, how much it would cost, why it should be done. My students also present pamphlets they have designed, show their websites, and defend their legal changes, and they do so dressed in professional attire. What a joy it is to see your kids talking to some local official about changing the world.

Teach with rigor, not rigor mortis

There is a growing emphasis in education on rigor, on challenging kids to do complex work. For so many teachers, this means just giving more work. The science teacher assigns five worksheets instead of one, the English teacher assigns a five-page essay instead of a three-pager, and the

Social Studies teacher has the students answer twenty questions from the end of each chapter instead of four or five.

This isn't rigor. More isn't necessarily rigorous. It's time consuming, and it's more work, but it isn't challenging the way we want kids to be challenged. We want kids to think critically, to read and understand complex text, to interact with ideas and show original thinking.

The following is an assignment I did in my World History class that's an example of the kind of authentic rigor we want.

When we were studying the Renaissance and the Protestant Reformation, one of the last assignments I gave asked them two questions. I told the students that whatever conclusion they came to at the end was fine, but what I wanted to know was how they got from the question to the answer. They had to show me the thinking that led to the conclusion. They could write this in the form of a dialogue with me. They could do this as an essay. They could create a formula. They could write this as a series of statements or as a poem. They could come up with their own unique way of doing this.

This kind of metacognitive assignment meant that they had to thoroughly understand the Renaissance and the Protestant Reformation.

The assignment was deceptively simple yet one of the most complex things I have ever asked my kids to do.

When I presented this assignment, the look of sheer panic on their faces was palpable.

As always, I gave them a full class period to plan, think, and talk — to each other, as a class, and to me.

My conversation with the kids, and their conversations with each other, was one of the richest experiences of my teaching career. It was the embodiment of transforming information into the world of ideas to reach a unique conclusion.

I gave them several days at home to work on this assignment. This was the entirety of their homework during this time.

Daily I asked if anyone had any questions so I could make sure they weren't having difficulties with this assignment.

Here were the two questions:

1. Was the Protestant Reformation a reform?
2. Was the Renaissance a rebirth or something else?

My only requirement was that the kids had to have an answer, and they had to show how their thinking led from question to answer. What I got from them was incredible. Some kids drew cartoons, some created videos of them talking their way through the process, some wrote stream-of-consciousness poetry, other students held group chats during which they discussed the answer then turned to their textbook to support their reasoning. I saw thought, insight, frustration, rethinking, dead ends, and starting over. The diversity of conclusions and processes, and the individuality of how students demonstrated their thinking amazed me.

I responded to each student in writing, pointing out where their conclusion and thinking did not align. This sparked incredible conversations between us. I encouraged this. It was a moment of pride to sit after school with my kids and talk about their ideas as they hashed out their thinking and came to new conclusions.

This assignment is instructive of how we need to think of rigor in terms of getting kids to think, interact with complexity, and express their ideas — not in terms of more work.

As you prepare to step into the task of teaching with rigor, ask yourself to what extent you are challenging students to interact with complex ideas. In what ways are you asking students to show their understanding of those ideas? To what extent are you prescribing the thinking and conclusion for them instead of letting them do their own original thinking and arrive at their own conclusions? To what extent are you prescribing how they must show that complex learning and thinking? Are you expecting rigor or just more work? How often are you asking students to analyze, synthesize, and evaluate the subject matter you are teaching them?

If you feel lost and overwhelmed just reading about this kind of teaching, I want to encourage you to seek out people who are willing and able to guide you. It will change your outlook on this exhilarating but very demanding career we've chosen. These could be mentors, advisors, administrators, or fellow teachers. Each of these people can share their journey, what worked for them and what didn't, and help you when you feel stuck.

I encourage you to look beyond the walls of the school for guidance. Workshops, the internet, trainings — these can give you insight into how to effectively teach the curriculum and manage other aspects of teaching.

These are the obvious places to look for help, but there is another untapped source, an entire treasure chest of help that just needs to be opened. When it is, the rewards will be great. This group really wants your class to be better. These people are experts in good and bad teaching, and what's more, they are willing to help. And their help is free! It doesn't require you to miss school or lose days of your summer break or even to leave your class.

Just ask your kids.

In your class right now is an amazing and career-changing resource. I know what you might be thinking. The moment I say to ask kids, hope drains out of teachers' faces, and is replaced by incredulity or fear. Neither is the reaction you should have, because this group will make you a better teacher.

Sure, right, the kids? What do they know about teaching? How could they possibly help me? Won't they just say terrible things about me?

Let me begin at the end: if you are worried about your kids saying terrible things about you, doesn't that tell you everything you need to know about the effectiveness of the job you are doing? If you think the kids are going to unload on you and tell you all the ways you are a failure, doesn't that tell you something? Remember, I was there once, failing miserably. When I started asking kids for feedback, did some kids dump on me and the things I did? Oh, yeah. And it hurt. And then I got over it. Kids don't want to dump on you. They want you to be a good teacher because they need you. And if they do dump on you, you need to hear those things anyway, so hear them.

As to what kids can possibly teach a college-educated professional with a teaching certificate — they can teach you how to make your class better. What more do you want? Remember, these kids have years of school experience. They have had good teachers and bad teachers, and even a few great teachers. They can give you insight into your teaching. They are in your class every day.

Some of the things my students love best about me and my class can be attributed to former students in the form of suggestions and ideas for how to make things more challenging and exciting.

So, let me explain how I do this.

For the better part of ten years, I had students evaluate my class. After each quarter, students were asked what they liked about the class, the way the class was taught, and yes, what they thought of me as a teacher. They were asked what they would change about the class and the way it was taught. Finally, I asked them to grade the class, A-F. Whenever I did this, I always emphasized why I was doing it. I told them how much I desired to improve. I wanted the kids to know that my goal was to be the best teacher possible for them, and that I really wanted their opinion and needed it to help me be the best teacher possible.

This evaluation was done in writing, with three questions:

1. What do you like about the class, the teacher, and how it is taught? Be specific in three to five sentences.
2. What would you change about the class, the teacher, and how it is taught? Be specific in three to five sentences.
3. What grade would you give the class, the teacher, and how it is taught, A-F?

I compiled their responses and grades, and created my own report card.

As I went over the report card, I explained how I would make changes *because of what they said.* I'd go through specific changes I was willing to make because of their suggestions. These were solemn promises, and to help me keep them, I posted the report card on my wall.

Sometimes kids made suggestions for changes that I could not realistically make. I would explain why that was true and why I would keep doing some particular thing. For example, students were always critical of having to do projects in my class. I explained to them that it was important for kids to be able to show learning in various ways and that projects weren't for everyone. I knew that. But it was good teaching to do a variety of activities. Having said that, their criticism of projects made me more sensitive to how I formed groups, how I graded projects and group activities, how I made kids responsible for their part of a project, the time I gave them to complete a project, and the way I graded it. Their suggestions really made the projects so much better, and I am forever indebted to those kids.

The best example of how I changed because of my students was the number one area students were critical of when I started asking them to evaluate me: they said I lectured too long and too often. After hearing this repeatedly, I knew I had to do something about this. So I made the following promises: first, I would never give notes for more than twenty minutes; the kids could time me to make sure I didn't go over the time limit, and at the end of twenty minutes, I had to stop. If at the end of twenty minutes, I needed no more than five minutes to finish, I could take that time, but only if I asked their permission and they gave it. If they said no, then the lecture was done.

My kids loved it! They knew that if I was giving notes, there was a limited time I could talk. It empowered them. But I also noticed that when I was teaching with a deadline, my lectures became clearer and better organized. Gone was the repetitive information or going off on tangents that had nothing to do with the focus of the lesson. I became a better teacher.

When I started these evaluations, lectures and note taking were the two areas the kids dinged me on the most. Today when kids evaluate me, these are my strongest areas. Kids love my lectures; they take notes and are always focused. Why? Because I asked for their feedback, and I put their suggestions into practice.

It will make you a better teacher if you are willing to listen to your kids, but there is another reason these evaluations matter. When you do them, you are telling kids that their opinion matters to you. You are taking into account how they feel and what they want. This validation engages them more deeply in you and your class. Their opinion has value to you. Everything you do is for their benefit.

Lastly, when doing these evaluations, students often make comments about something that has happened in class. They may have been bothered by something you did or said. This gives you the chance to deal with a problem you didn't know existed. You can take that kid aside and talk about how to make the situation better. If I didn't do this evaluation, a kid could be upset with me the entire year, coming into class every day bothered by something I had said or done, and unable to focus as a result.

Having your students evaluate you is a win for everyone. You become a better teacher, and they care more about you and your class. Isn't that what you most want?

Work on the Work

The Right Tools for the Job

If you were to ask a doctor to describe all the tools used to diagnose and cure whatever disease or illness a patient has, the number would be in the hundreds if not the thousands. Ask a carpenter to list all the tools necessary to build kitchen cabinets, and the list will be long and varied. Ask an artist to describe everything that goes into creating a painting, from the medium used to all their artistic influences, and you will get a novel-length response.

The tools we use to do our jobs and the experiences we have had that influence how we do that work inform and make us the people we are. But ask a teacher what tools we use to teach, to construct a lesson, to make our classes come alive, and you will often get a blank stare or a limited answer. They might point to a textbook or talk about lecture or maybe give you the list of work they ask students to do.

But the conversation dies quickly because teachers seldom approach teaching the way a builder does a house. A builder doesn't look at a saw, a screwdriver, a hammer, and say, okay, what kind of house can I build? They consider the challenge of building a house and say, what tools will I need? And so it should be with teaching. The job of the teacher is to acquire tools for building the best classroom and the best kids, and to make that job easier and better.

Just as a carpenter would not use a hammer for every task, a teacher cannot use the same tool for every lesson. This begins by asking what other tools are out there, and to look at what they do and how they are doing it and realize that sure, this tool is working fine, but is there another tool that would work better?

As a teacher, you need to consider everything a teaching tool.

Textbooks are tools. Lectures are a tool. Homework is a tool. Tests are a tool. Group work is a tool. Notes are a tool. Projects are a tool. Discussions are a tool. Pairing students up is a tool. Games are a tool. Independent work is a tool. Questions and worksheets are a tool. Technology is a tool. Coaching is a tool. Praise is a tool. Presentations are tools. Group discussions are tools. Hands-on experiential learning is a tool. Guided reading is a tool. Summarizing work is a tool. Answering the questions at the end of the chapter is a tool. Everything you do in class to teach a lesson is a tool.

The next question can only be answered by you. Thinking about the previous month in your classroom, how many different tools did you use? Which tools did you use most often? Did these tools work? Did those tools lead to a good outcome of learning for your kids? Do you think another tool would have worked better?

The truth is that the vast majority of teachers use one or two tools repeatedly. Day after boring day, we go to our toolbox and pull out the same tool and teach the lesson in the same way we've taught it so many times that we could teach it in our sleep. We do this out of ease, out of convenience, out of not knowing better, or of knowing better but not having other tools to approach a job, or thinking that the one or two tools we use are the ones that are ALWAYS the best for the job.

Or, maybe you are a new teacher, and you just aren't experienced enough to know how to use a variety of tools. I want to look at each of these possibilities.

For those of you who understand and know that there are lots of tools to use but instead you use the same tool over and over, STOP IT! You are building an inadequate house. Your patient is sick but you won't use the tools you know exist to make them better. Your kids are losing and suffering. Yes, I know those other tools take a lot of work on your part, take more preparation, and require you to spend lots of time on a particular lesson. As teachers we want our kids to spend a lot of time learning, considering, studying, working, preparing for our classes. How can we ask any less of ourselves? Yes, group work takes a risk on our part. Yes, discussions will fail. Yes, a project means lots of prep beforehand and lots of grading afterward. But you are failing kids when you do only what is easiest for you, what is best for you; furthermore, kids who could grasp difficult concepts if taught in a more cohesive, thorough way will not learn as much and will not do as well. This is on you.

If you're an experienced teacher, take a moment to list the tools you have. List everything you know how to do to teach your subject matter. Then, begin using these tools. What actually might surprise someone who has been teaching five or ten or more years is that you don't have as many tools as you think you have. Or, you may know of a tool, but the truth is you've never really learned how to use it. For example, we all understand at some basic level what group work is. But do you really know the best way to form groups for any given kind of work? The different ways you can form groups? The way groups work best together? How best to monitor groups as they work? The best way to grade the individual work and the group work? Do you really know when group work is the best method for teaching a particular lesson?

The only thing worse than a person who knows how to use a tool and knows that it should be used but doesn't use it is a person who knows about a tool but doesn't really know how to use it and then uses it in correctly. Then of course the lesson doesn't work, and you dismiss that tool as having failed. The tool was fine, but the way you used it was the problem.

So this brings us to our second group of people when it comes to tools: those who don't know which tools exist.

When I address new educators, I always tell them their first three to five years of teaching, in regards to pedagogue, is about acquiring tools.

So how do you get more tools?

Go to every workshop you can. You will learn from experts who have tools that they are willing to give away, shiny bright new things that you can look at, learn about, and bring to your classroom. And that's the other thing about these new tools. It is not enough to learn them and put them in your toolbox. Pull them out and use them. When you do this, don't be surprised if you fail at first. You are going to use that wrench, and it is not going to work. That doesn't mean the wrench is bad; it means you have not learned how to use it correctly, or it was the wrong tool for that lesson. Try again. Learn. Figure out which tool works best to accomplish the learning objective.

Go to the people who teach what you teach and ask how they will teach an upcoming subject. Hear their ideas; bounce them around with others. Talk about alternative ways they know how to teach. Ask anyone you know. Email the department head and ask for whatever they know works best. Go to the teacher of the year from last year and ask what their best tool is and how they use it. Go to your curriculum specialist and tell them what you are teaching and ask them the best way to teach it. Have a conversation with your assistant principal and tell them you want to try a different way of teaching, then ask who they would suggest you talk to. Look to the people around you as guides. Avoid anyone who discourages your quest to find new and different tools.

Go online and scour the internet for ideas. There are tons of great websites, programs, and organizations dedicated to providing innovative ways to approach whatever subject you teach. The internet is a great place to get lost when you want to teach something different. If you are sick and tired of notes and lecture and bookwork, go find other ways to do this job. If you always know exactly what you are going to teach and the exact way you will be teaching it tomorrow, next week, next month, then you are creating a repetitious, boring classroom. What are you doing? If the students know your usual pattern — first you do some opening work, then you give a lecture, then you assign some bookwork — you are losing your kids. I love it when kids come into my class wondering what we are going to do because they legitimately have no clue. It makes me happy as a teacher to say that they never know what the day is going to bring.

Part of the idea of acquiring new tools is to realize that as helpful as school, fellow teachers, workshops, and websites can be, you must realize that tools are all around us.

I am sitting here at IHOP eating breakfast as I type this. The manager came by to talk to me about how my breakfast was going. I had just ordered and noticed the breakfast I had picked was $8.47. I asked why the odd price, and he started explaining price points, how they price certain menu items at a loss knowing that people are willing to pay more for other items. He explained how they can get ingredients at wholesale, which makes the food relatively inexpensive to purchase, but what makes certain menu items more expensive to the customer is how labor intensive they are to prepare.

I had no intention of going in for breakfast and getting an amazing lesson on economics that I could teach to my class. It inspired me to come up with a project to look at menus and figure out what it would cost to make a particular favorite restaurant meal at home. It was amazing for the kids to see how the economy works, and to learn, for example, that a restaurant doesn't make much profit on a steak dinner, but they do make a huge profit on the soft drinks they sell.

My classroom is never far from my thinking, never far from my consciousness, never far from my life. I constantly filter the world through the lens of how it could affect my class. Every trip I take, interaction I have, conversation or experience, good or bad, I try to see if there is a lesson for my students in it. Some of the best lessons I have taught intersected with what was happening in my life at the time.

You have to be open. The worst teachers will go to a workshop and dismiss whatever is said as something that could never work in their class. Good teachers take educational activities and think openly about how to modify lessons to their class. Great teachers know that the classroom of teaching is life, the world, and everyone and everything in it.

The tools for great teaching are all around us. Seek them out and watch the kind of kids you will build.

You need to know your strengths. Which of these tools are your strengths?

Are you a great lecturer? Are you fantastic at group work? Do you excel at projects and alternative forms of assessment? Is writing your gift? Do student interactions bring out the best, most vibrant side of you?

If you had to list your top three strengths when it comes to teaching your class, what would they be?

Take a moment to ponder these. Now, whatever you have as number one, you need to teach against that strength. If you are great at lecture, awesome, and when you do lecture, your kids get the benefit of your excellence. However, if all you do is lecture, you are making sure to lose 50 percent or more of your class. You are certain to have a bunch of bored kids, kids who are getting very little out of your class because they do not learn best by listening to a teacher lecture. Maybe they learn by doing. Maybe they are visual learners, the most prominent type of learning style among people everywhere. One of the best lecturers I ever heard was an AP American History teacher who could tell such great stories about our history. I loved sitting in this teacher's class, loved the information, loved the depth of the teacher's knowledge and instruction, and I am not too proud to admit that I took some of the information and used it in my class. But all this teacher did was lecture. There was no other variety of instruction, no discussions, no projects, no writing, and in the end, only a small percentage of students in that class passed the AP exam.

As a teacher, you must be aware that to have a good class, a varied class, a class that allows kids' strengths and the way they learn to shine, you have to do a variety of activities. Day to day, week to week, unit to unit, your kids must be given the chance to demonstrate their knowledge in a number of different ways.

I know that even good teachers might claim they don't know how or don't like to do certain types of teaching strategies because those don't work for them. If you don't know how to do something, you need to learn. If you don't believe that teaching techniques work, do the research, and you will find that you are mistaken. Does group work fail? Well yes, sometimes, but that just means you need to find a way to make it succeed. Do projects and alternative assessments work for every kid in every situation? Nope. That doesn't make the technique suspect.

The techniques that teachers most often dispute are projects, group work, and discussions. Before you dismiss the validity of these techniques and their importance to your class, you better have qualified answers to the following questions. Have you been trained in these techniques? Did you spend a considerable amount of time researching them before you implemented them? Did you monitor them as they were happening? Did you have a clear idea of what you wanted kids to get out of them when you were making them and when you used them in the classroom? Did you communicate and explain what you wanted from your students and how to get there? When the students completed the assignment and you graded it, did you talk to your students about why the activity did or did not work?

If you answered yes to all of these questions and feel like the activity really didn't work, then you need to ask if the activity you chose was the best for whatever you were teaching. Often we want to attack the technique when in truth the problem was our own inability or the content itself. There is a reason why these techniques have been well established and are widely recognized as what the best teachers use for optimal learning.

To use myself as an example, I am a natural lecturer and storyteller.

But if you could ask my students, they would tell you that I love projects and student-centered activities. It always makes me so happy at the end of the year when students say they wish I had lectured more or told more stories. Earlier in this narrative, I described how my students were bored and listless because all I did was lecture. What changed wasn't that I suddenly became better at lecture. I learned that when I mixed the tools I used, when I used a variety of teaching techniques, students were more engaged and willing to do the work. They knew I wasn't talking just to fill time or giving notes just to make them write something or assigning bookwork just to keep them busy. They knew I was doing these things because these were the best methods to help them learn a particular concept. Everything I did took on greater importance because I taught against my strength.

Imagine if you, as an adult, had to sit in the same classroom doing the same thing day after day, hour after hour, chapter after chapter. You would be so bored that you would eventually tune out what was being taught. That's what we do to kids. Now imagine a class where every day you walked in you had no idea how you were going to learn. The teacher might not use a technique you like, but you know the next day will be different, and each day you will be challenged. That's the kind of class you want as a student. Shouldn't it also be the class you want as a teacher?

I was working with a new educator who decided to be bold and creative, and try his first group activity. When the day ended, he came into my room and literally fell into a chair. He told me what a disaster it had been. He went on and on about how the kids just weren't capable of group work, how they took forever to get into groups, when they got into groups they wouldn't listen, and when they finally got to work, they did it wrong and didn't accomplish what he expected.

I listened as he listed all the failures that had taken place and how the kids had failed to do any part of the activity the way he had hoped they would. When he ended his rant, I had one simple question for him: "Did you explain to them how you wanted them to do those things?" I went further and asked, "Did you teach them how to get into groups, meaning how to physically move their desks and chairs? Did you explain what they were to do when they got into their groups? Did you explain how they were supposed to do the group activity? After you explained it, did you practice it with them before setting them loose? And finally, did you make sure every kid understood what you wanted them to do throughout every part of the activity?" I paused and smiled, because I understood his frustration. Then I said, "Or did you just tell them, 'Okay, everyone get into groups and do this activity.'"

I knew by his expression that was exactly what had happened. He looked at me like none of the things I asked had ever occurred to him. Then he and I talked about one of the biggest problems that so many teachers have. We expect students to do something in an exact way that we have in our minds, but we do so without telling them. We expect without explaining, and we expect without teaching and practicing.

How can we expect kids to do what we want, the way we want it, without ever telling them what to do, how to do it, and then practicing it? So many teachers act like the basketball coach who is teaching a group of kids for the first time how to play the game. He looks at his team and says, "Basketball is the game." He rolls the ball to the center of the court then steps back and wonders why no one knows what to do. No coach who is worthy of the name would do that. The coach would break the game down, explain it, demonstrate it with a few skilled players, and then have the kids practice: here is how you dribble, here is how you pass, here is how you defend, here is how you block, and here is how you shoot. It's point by point. And when there is a mistake, the first thing a coach does is break the mistake down and reteach the skill.

Why don't we teachers ever see that this is our job too? When I want a group of kids to get into a group to do group work, I explain what we are going to do it, and as I explain it, I have them practice how to do it. We go through how to get into groups, how to position their desks, how to form groups, what they are to do when they get into groups, the responsibility of each group member, and so on. If anything goes wrong, we practice it again.

But this doesn't apply just to group work; it applies to everything we do in class.

You have to explain to kids what to do in any given situation.

You have to practice it.

You have to let kids fail and then reteach it to them until they understand what you want.

The following are just a few of the things I go over and practice with my kids. These will seem like basic classroom skills, but you'd be surprised at how frequently these need to be reinforced at every grade level:

- Going to the bathroom
- Turning in papers
- Raising their hand
- Asking questions
- Asking for help
- Taking a test
- What to do at the start and end of the class period
- How to get a textbook
- How to put away a textbook
- What to do when they get their work done early
- Where they sit
- Where to put their name on the paper

Anything that you expect kids to do, you must follow this pattern: teach it, practice it, do it. Repeat as necessary.

If you sit with a group of teachers long enough, one of them will start talking about their class, and they'll make a comment something like this: "I can't believe that these kids don't know_____. Those teachers last year/last school/last subject didn't do their job and teach them how to do_____." Other teachers will nod their head in agreement with a look of disdain and remark that they're shocked a kid doesn't know something they "should" know by this age or grade.

I always look at them and tell them how lucky they are. I get this look of surprise. I smile and say, "You're lucky because your kids are telling you what they need you to teach them. You now know the job ahead of you."

"But it's not my job to teach them stuff they should've learned already," they say.

Again, I smile and say, "It's your job to teach them what they need to know, and if that means you have to go back and reteach them, okay, then go back. Anything else is punishing a kid for not knowing something. We are teachers. If a kid is missing something, it is our job to teach them."

If you expect without teaching, expect without practicing, and expect when kids don't have the knowledge to reach those expectations, then you know what your challenge is as a teacher. You MUST DO whatever it takes to make your class function successfully and to help your kids learn. Anything else is an abdication of your responsibilities!

Teaching Is More than Testing

C onsider this scenario: You are a diligent, hard-working, caring, loving teacher. You're sitting in your classroom after school grading tests, shaking your head with despair and frustration as yet another kid does even worse than you thought s/he would do. It hurts and bothers you that so many kids are not doing as well as you would like them to do and know that they are capable of doing. As you get more and more upset, your friendly principal or assistant principal walks into the room, and the following conversation starts.

"I am so glad to see you working so hard. It does my heart good to see how much you care. I just wanted to see how you were doing. I wanted to see how successful you and your class have been so far this year. As you have demonstrated and seem to know so well, the best way to evaluate anything is by taking a test, so here, I want to find out how good a teacher you are by having you take this test."

You sit there confused. "But wouldn't it be better if I were to have the kids do something in writing? Maybe you could have a discussion with the kids. Or, I could show you their grades on their most recent unit test, or maybe you could come in and see me teach. How does me taking a test on teaching have anything to do with good teaching?" You sit perplexed waiting for an explanation.

The principal smiles, nods, and says, "That's a good question, that's a fair question, that's the right question. I have another one for you. If you know good teaching isn't about a test, then why are you evaluating their learning by giving them tests?"

Tests are not real world. Where do tests exist outside of school?

When we look at whether people are doing their jobs well, we evaluate them on a series of rubrics. Do they get the job done? Do they treat their coworkers with respect? Are they competent at their job? Do they complete their assigned tasks on time? In the real world, the answer to all of these is almost never determined by a test. We create a product. We have something to show for what we have done. It doesn't matter if the product is customer service, growing food, fixing a car, making someone healthy and well, managing finances, managing a business, preaching a sermon, driving a truck, installing a roof, putting in plumbing, repairing an AC unit, running a restaurant, hitting a baseball, dancing across a stage in pointe shoes, acting in a movie, OR TEACHING KIDS. Our job is to create a product. Only in teaching do we feel that this product can only be evaluated and determined by giving a test. If you believe that's the way it should be, please go into your general practitioner's office and give them a test to see if they can do their job.

This is the unfortunate truth about education today, but not everything we teach needs to be on a test.

For many teachers, here is the most common teacher equation:

L + BW + HW + CW = T and **GT**

Got a solution?

Let me solve this equation for you:

Lecture plus **Bookwork** plus **Homework** plus **Classwork** equals **Tests** and **Good Teaching**.

Many who are reading this might believe this is the mathematical formula for a good class.

I don't.

Here is the twenty-five years of truth I have learned:

A test is not right for everything you do.

A test isn't always the best way to assess student knowledge.

A test punishes students who could show mastery of the subject in another way.

A test, even for those who get As, is not always the best way for students to demonstrate what they've learned.

A test is not always the best way for kids to keep information in their long-term memory.

So here is my equation:

V of **T (L + P + AA + BW + HW + CW + SD + W + R + T) + BA** to **AGS/U/SM** = the **B** of **T!**

Got it? No worries. Thankfully, don't need to memorize this for a test! Here's the answer:

Variety of **Techniques (Lecture** plus **Projects** plus **Authentic Assessment** plus **Bookwork** plus **Homework** plus **Classwork** plus **Student Discussion** plus **Writing** plus **Reflection** plus **Tests)** plus **Best Approach** to **Any Given Subject/Unit/Subject Matter** equals the **Best** of **Teaching!**

Let's take a closer look at some creative ways you can go beyond testing and merely teaching to the test to bring creativity to your classroom and make it a vibrant atmosphere where true learning takes place.

The brilliance of alternative assessments

We labor under the delusion that the only way for students to express their understanding of what they have learned is to make them sit and answer questions. It's true that for certain types of knowledge, the best way to access whether your students have learned is through a test. And it is true that for some kids, the very best way to demonstrate their understanding is by taking a test. But for as many kids, it isn't. It is not that these kids can't learn, but rather, the method you have chosen as a way for them to show their understanding goes against their unique form of intelligence. And to remind you that tests are not life, what *is* life is that we learn something and then prove our mastery by using that knowledge. I am judged as a teacher by how I teach, a plumber is judged by how they do plumbing, a doctor by doctoring, and a nurse by nursing. We expect that these people have learned. Sure, they took tests along the way, but we want them to do something with the things they learned. Why don't we expect the same out of teaching and kids?

When I realized this, I had some of the best moments of my teaching career, the "a-ha!" moment, the moment I realized what my job should be.

And this only happened when I let go and let the kids *show me what they could do*.

So here is what you've got to do to really let your kids shine.

First, acknowledge and let go of the idea that everything must be on a test.

Second, teach the kids whatever you need to teach them.

Then let them choose what comes next.

This last part is the hard part! So to help, I have included a form I always give to my World History students when we're going to do this kind of activity. This can be used for almost any unit of study. It has a simple premise: I have taught you (your students) a bunch of info; now show me you understand it! How? Well, that's up to you.

Here is the assignment:

You (the student) need to show that you have grasped the information we have covered in class by manipulating it in such a way that you demonstrate understanding. How you do this is up to your own creative intelligence. The only thing not acceptable is for you to turn the information in as is. Generally the more creative you are the less writing you have to do. Conversely, the less creative you are, the more writing you have to do to cover the information. For example, if we've covered 30 important facts in class, and you choose to do this assessment by creating a test, I would expect a test with 30 to 50 questions. However, if you choose to do the assignment by drawing images, you could complete this assignment in as few as three to seven images depending on the content of the images.

Remember, in this assessment, you must convince me that you understand what we have been studying.

Given below are some *possible assignments* to show you how you can do this

However, I want to challenge you to use your individual strengths, abilities, and intelligences to come up with *a completely unique way to do this assignment.*

Do not feel like you must pick one of these and do it the same way. *Take a chance and try something different!* Remember, I reward kids who take chances!

The following are in order from least to most creative depending on how you do them:

- Make a test
- PowerPoint presentation

- A-Z Graphic Organizer
- Website
- Create a book (there are various kinds you could do: comic, recipe, coloring, pop-up, children's book)
- Mobile
- Poems
- Story/Song
- Pictures (collages, comic strips, 3-D model, paintings)

REMEMBER: The key is to make your own assessment using your own rules. Be you!

After I give out the assignment and go over it, I step back and watch the magic happen. Now it's time for you to try this.

Watch kids do what they do best.

Watch kids use their strengths to create something.

Watch kids use their unique creativity.

Watch kids use their own unique ways of seeing and doing things.

Watch kids see themselves, their passions, and their abilities in a new and different way.

Not surprisingly, kids often became overwhelmed. I was not telling them what product I wanted, how it should look, how it was to be done, how they would turn it in, or what the finished product would looked like. I could see the panic in their eyes as they desperately tried to figure out what to do. Knowing this would be their initial reaction, I always set aside at least one class period for thinking time so the students could formulate a plan. My job was to walk around and talk with each kid as they worked. For the ones who knew exactly what they wanted to do, I'd flesh out their idea, see if it would work for the challenge, and guide them through conversation to add to or improve their idea. For the kids who had no idea what to do, the conversation was even more fun. I'd always prepare ahead four or five ideas of how to do the assignment. I purposely wouldn't bring these up when presenting the activity because I really wanted them to come up with their own idea, so when I talked with a kid who was struggling, I'd always start by asking questions about what their strengths were, what school subject was their favorite. I wanted to know something they loved to do and felt competent doing even if it had nothing to do with school.

I then used their answers to connect their strengths to the assignment in front of them, and I watched kids click with the most incredible ideas.

One student said what he loved most was Disney. He loved Disney World, the park, the rides, all of it, so we talked about how he could change the activity into a theme park. He thought about it, and you could see this flame of understanding. Suddenly, I had a student plotting out a Roman-based theme park with plebian and patrician restaurants. The plebian restaurant had simple basic foods while the patrician restaurant had rich, expensive foods. There was the Rise and Fall of Rome rollercoaster, and the parking lot areas were named after famous Romans. There was a Julius Caesar theater where you could watch a reenactment of the famous stabbing, a Romulus and Remus lazy river, and so much more. He sketched out the park with detailed descriptions of each section, and when it was finished, he had designed his own theme park, but he had also demonstrated his understanding of the Roman Empire.

His idea was so amazing that the next year I used it when we studied the Middle Ages. I don't know who had more fun, the kids who created the projects or me grading them.

One young lady loved drama, she lived for drama, so she wrote and created a screenplay based on the French Revolution. She created puppets to represent the various significant characters from the history of that period, designed backdrops such as the storming of the Bastille and the Tennis Court Oath, and then recorded it all and turned in the finished film as her assignment.

Students have created books of poems, children's coloring books, board games, mobiles, newspapers, recipe books, reenactments, written a CD full of songs, made multiple choice tests, and many more creative ways to express their learning that I can't list them all.

One student was very good at mathematics and he loved math, but Social Studies was something he was only marginally interested in. So I said okay, how can we take your abilities in math and connect them to this assignment? We spent a long time talking, and then I walked away to let him ruminate. He knew his challenge, but I had no clue how he was going to connect math and the unit on the Enlightenment. The Enlightenment produced some notable mathematicians, but that period of history is primarily known for some of the world's greatest artists, writers, and thinkers. I had no idea how my student was going to do this, but he crafted one of the singularly most creative and unique projects I have ever seen in my years of teaching.

What did he do? Well, he took all the historical data he had learned from the Enlightenment and turned it into mathematical equations.

I can remember flipping through his Enlightenment Math Book. How did he come up with this? I would never have thought of this. It was incredibly unique. It showed deep understanding. It was learning in its purest form.

Other teachers often wondered why kids always turned in really great projects, why they always did so well on my tests, and why they always seemed to try so hard. It was because my students knew that if I wanted them to do something, it wasn't just to keep them busy or make me feel like I'd done my job as a teacher. The assignment mattered because of the impact it would have on their sense of accomplishment and thus their life. I always explained why it mattered, and I demonstrated that the work I asked them to do had value to their learning.

A way to understand this is to consider the usual scenario. If you give ten tests per quarter, you are in essence telling your students that each individual test is not really important. If you assign thirty worksheets for homework just to go over stuff you already taught, you are teaching the kids that either your teaching doesn't matter or those worksheets are just homework for homework's sake — a waste of everyone's time. If after every chapter the kids answer the questions at the end of the chapter, you send the message that what matters is doing the questions, not learning the material.

I have a simple rule: for every test I give, I must use some other way to assess the students' learning. This could be some kind of writing, a project, a presentation, or some other authentic assessment. If you are not doing this, you are merely teaching for your convenience. You are not doing what is in the best interest of kids.

Homework is not a substitute teacher

Most of the homework given in schools today is a valueless waste of time. Most homework is given by teachers who believe one of the jobs of being a teacher is to give homework. They had homework when they were a kid, so they think they are supposed to give it. That's what teachers do, right?

There has been a ton of research about homework, its value, and whether it is effective. Here is what I know: homework that is given to teach new concepts that you have not gone over or will not teach in class is a waste of time. It is our job to use our skills, tools, and abilities to teach new information. If you are relying on a kid to go home and learn what you will not teach, then you are setting kids up for failure.

Even when we don't fall into that trap, teachers often give excessive amounts of work that has no value but lots of burden. In a math class, it is typical for teachers to assign twenty or more problems to solve for homework. If a kid struggles to solve the first few problems, s/he will fail at the rest, so the rest is just a waste of time and effort. Slogging through eighteen more problems and getting them all wrong breeds a feeling of inadequacy, which is partly why so many kids think they're bad at math. It also sets you up for the unpleasant scenario of having to undo incorrect learning, because the repetition of solving problem after problem incorrectly teaches the students the wrong way to do it. On the other hand, if a kid can solve problems one and two, the rest is just excess work without value.

In my class, homework is for review of major concepts that have already been taught, or for major assignments.

This is one of the reasons when kids do projects for my class or take tests they seem to do really well. If I am asking them to do something significant at home, it is a vital part of what we are doing in class. My kids seldom get homework, but when they do, it's of major importance, which is why they're far more likely to do it.

In general, as you prepare to give kids work, ask yourself these questions: How does this assignment fit into the unit of study? Why am I giving this particular assignment? If my students do not complete this assignment, will there be a negative effect on their learning? Am I doing a variety of assignments and activities in this unit and during this grading period? When was the last time I allowed students to take hold of their own learning? Do students understand the value of this assignment in relation to what I am teaching in this unit, this quarter, this class? Am I assigning this for my needs or theirs? Is there a better more effective way for kids to learn than this assignment?

Every assignment needs to exist for a purpose. That purpose needs to be clearly defined as to its value to your kids' grades and their learning.

I grade everything that requires work my students must do. This is one of the reasons I make sure all the work I give has a specific purpose and value to my students' learning. If not, they are doing BS work, and I am being forced to grade BS. I don't mind being buried in grading assignments that have value, but I don't want to be buried in grading BS. I'm sure you feel the same way. But that's what you are doing when you give too much homework and too many busywork assignments. You are burying your students and you in TONS AND TONS AND TONS OF BS.

To give you an example of what I mean by valuing learning, when it comes to something like notes, an activity teachers often complain about students not doing, I want my kids to take notes because I value it as part of their learning. So, for each unit that I give notes, I collect and grade those notes. I want them to do the notes, so I reward their work with a grade. If I am giving notes for a test, a test that will primarily come from their notes, I will often make the grade for the notes nearly equal to the test. It is amazing to watch the kids scramble to write things down when they know how valuable the work is, not just to their grade but to the learning they have to do. This has three positive aspects: every kid has to take notes; note taking helps them do better on the test; and when it comes time to study, they have all the information they need to do well.

It is important for kids to know that what you are assigning them is valuable to their learning, that you will grade the work they do, and that the grading you do is not a steaming pile of "work for work's sake" BS.

And that brings us back to the topic of giving tests for no reason other than thinking that's what you're supposed to do. I remember walking into a new teacher's class who was trying to think of the best way to test the unit she was about to start. "Not everything needs to be tested," I commented. You should have seen the look of pure joy and happiness on her face. It was like I had set her free and given her permission to do so much more. It unleashed her creativity to teach the class and to guide her students' understanding.

When you take this approach, the subject matter, not the test, becomes the driving force of your class.

The question to ask yourself when you prepare to teach is not *How do I test something?* but rather *What is the best way for me to know if kids have learned whatever it is I want them to learn?* Sometimes the answer will be to give a test, but a test is usually NOT the best method!

If not, what is? The answer is limitless.

Going back to the student who demonstrated his learning through mathematical equations, it would never occur to me to do this. Never. My mind doesn't work that way. Thankfully, it did for one of my students. To create a class of excellence, you must teach against your strength and embrace that a test is not the end all or be all of education or of life.

I am finishing the writing of this section at that same IHOP. My waitress was great. She did her job. Did it well. Brought what I needed, was attentive, and cared about my needs. I evaluated and learned all of this without ever giving her a test. That's the real world. When is teaching going to catch up?

Learning Styles as Unique as Kids Are

To be a teacher of excellence, you must create a classroom environment where a variety of teaching tools and techniques are present, but you must also be aware of the various learning styles represented by all those faces looking at you. Learning styles are not to be confused with multiple intelligences. Learning styles are the various ways that a person takes in information. Multiple intelligences are the various ways we express that knowledge using our unique abilities.

I go to great lengths to allow students to use their individual strengths to express knowledge, but when it comes to teaching my students, nothing impacts my instruction more than an awareness of learning styles.

The concept of learning styles dates back to the 1960s when educators, scientists, psychologists, and researchers set out to determine why people of the same intelligence, motivation, and skill level can go into a classroom and learn varying amounts of information. The conclusions reached by those who studied this should have a profound effect on your classroom, as it has had on mine.

As I often tell my students, the first conclusion reached by these researchers was not surprising at all, but the second was shocking.

The first conclusion was that there are **three types of learning styles**, or ways that people learn:

- Visual learning
- Auditory learning
- Tactile-kinesthetic learning

Visual learners are those who learn by seeing things. These are the people who will read every word of this book, underline passages, highlight sections, and make notes. If you're a visual learner, you are the doodler, the learner who loves written material and PowerPoint presentations. (Admit it, you just got excited about the idea of this being in a PowerPoint!) Most likely, you were a good student and did well in school. Much of what is taught through most of the thirteen years of elementary and secondary education is visual. Around 30 to 40 percent of students are visual learners.

The second is **auditory learners**, those who learn best by hearing. If this describes you, you're probably wishing this were an audiobook. You are most likely listening to music or you have some other sound playing right now, such as recorded nature sounds, or you make your own sounds. You know the auditory kids in your class because that is exactly what they do. This is the kid who, when the class is reading quietly, will raise his hand or turn to his neighbor and ask questions such as, "What page are we on? How much are we supposed to read? Where do we stop reading? Do we answer the questions? What do we do when we are done?" This is the child who dreads PowerPoints but loves lectures. The auditory kid doesn't like taking notes but tends to create mnemonic devices. These kids talk to themselves when solving math problems. They make up 30 to 40 percent of learners, and they do well in school, but not as well as the visual learners.

Then there are the kids who are often the problem children of your class, and not because they aren't bright;

they just learn in a different way. These are the **tactile-kinesthetic learners**. They are the doers. They are the ones who don't want to read or hear about it. They want to do it! They love things hands-on. They are not strong readers, don't see the use of a PowerPoint, but give them a problem to solve and they will do it. Not surprisingly, considering that most of what is done in school is either visual or auditory, they have the greatest difficulty in a typical classroom setting. These are often the kids who get in trouble because they want to move, to do, to get their hands into something, and when asked to sit quietly and do work, they will find a way to make things hands-on. These kids make up 20 to 40 percent of the kids in your class.

This idea that there are three types of learners likely does not surprise you, and you've probably learned it at some point in your teaching career, but it's vital to allow your understanding of learning styles to guide what you do in your classroom. When we teach, no matter what we teach, it is incumbent on us to make things as inclusive in our class as possible.

You have a particular learning style, and that is almost always reflected in your strength. If you learn in a particular way, then most likely that is the way you will teach. Auditory teachers lecture, visual teachers assign reading, and tactile teachers have their kids up and moving. But no matter how strong you are, 60 to 80 percent of the kids in your class have a learning style that is NOT THE SAME AS YOURS. If you let your learning style drive your class, then you are losing your class. This is the reason behind teaching against your strength. If not, no matter how good you are, you are losing so many of your kids! And maybe even more important, your kids are not learning as much or as easily as they could if your lessons incorporated all three learning styles.

When we use a variety of activities and tools, and teach against our own strength and learning style, every aspect of our class will improve.

Those who researched learning styles came to a second conclusion, and as much as the first conclusion should impact your classroom, the second should have an even greater effect.

Their conclusion: there are factors in the environment that make learning easier or harder. As teachers, we want to make learning as easy as possible for our kids. This means we need to adapt the environment in which kids learn. Some things are constrained by being in a classroom, and schools/counties have rules that govern some of what can be done in class. But within these constraints, we should change our classes to reflect these scientific conclusions.

Those who study learning styles identify seven factors that affect learning either positively or negatively:

- Lighting
- Sound
- Seating
- Intake (food and drink)
- Peers
- Time of day
- Room temperature

With these in mind, we can manipulate the environment in our classrooms to improve learning. Let's examine each of these in detail.

The first and most important factor that impacts learning is lighting. If we simply change the lighting that students learn under, they will learn more and do better.

Those studying learning have said there are three basic kinds of lighting: natural, low, and bright. Of the three, by far, the best for learning is natural lighting. If you can primarily light your room with natural light that filters in through windows or skylights, you have won half the battle. If you can't, the next best alternative is low lighting.

Most people learn best in an environment with low lighting. Having said that, there are people who want and need bright light. If you were to come into my classroom, you would see a room primarily lit by natural light, with several lamps to make areas of the room brighter, but the overall lighting in the room is low.

The more you can do to reduce the brightness of the lighting in your room, the better the students will learn. You will also notice something else happen: as the lighting is reduced, student behavior changes. Students are generally calmer and less likely to act out. Those who study learning have also determined the worst kind of lighting possible. When I go over this with my kids in class, they loudly and immediately say florescent lighting. Kids know. They know what it does to them and just how bad it is. This type of light is pollution to learning. Everything you can do to get the fluorescent lights off in your class, the better your kids will do!

The second factor that impacts learning is sound. Some kids cannot focus very well in a classroom with all sorts of extraneous sounds. On the contrary, some kids in your class will not be able to focus very well in a quiet room. It's always easy to see the extremes and know who is who. The ones who don't want sound will cover their ears when people are talking, will move away from sound if they can, and will raise their hand to say when a kid is making an annoying sound. To these students, noise and random, unnecessary sounds completely distract them.

The kids who need sound in their environment are also easy to find. I will give you one of my former students as an example. Kevin was a kind-hearted boy and a great student. But ask him to do a quiet activity and he would start drumming. He would be working away, reading or writing or doing whatever, all while drumming. I would walk over and simply touch his hands to make him stop. He would always look up at me shocked, as if he had no idea what he was doing, no idea he was making loud noises. I would walk away and he would go back to work, quietly, but you could almost see his body fighting him, and within a few moments he would be back to drumming. Kevin needed sound to help him focus.

Because I know this about sound, in my class there is a simple rule. If we are doing an assignment that does not require them to listen to me or to each other, the kids who need sound can listen to music through earphones. This keeps the class quiet for the kids who need quiet and filled with sound for those who need sound.

The third factor that affects learning is seating. Where a kid sits, and even the kind of seating has a huge impact on a child's ability to focus and learn. There are two kinds of seating: formal and informal. Formal seating involves desks, tables, chairs, and sitting upright. Informal seating is everything else: a bed, couch, beanbag, hammock, or sitting on the floor. In my class, I have a variety of places for kids to sit. I honestly don't care where a kid sits in my class as long as they can focus. When it comes to seating, I have three simple rules: you have to learn, you can't distract yourself (sleep), and you can't distract other people (lay on the floor with your friends and ignore my teaching). I have tables, and I have had kids live underneath the tables. I have had kids sit on top of my bookcase. I have had kids who paced the back of the room, and kids who made nests of beanbags.

The best story I can tell you as an example of how much seating matters happened a few years ago. I was explaining this to a group of parents, and I could see by the look on a father's face that something was dawning on him. So I called on him to explain what he was realizing. He said his daughter had just graduated from a local high school, and was valedictorian of her class. He said he finally understood her. Starting at some point in late elementary school, she would come home from school, lay on the couch, put her feet up on the back of the couch, and tip her head over the edge. That was how she studied, read books, took notes — whatever involved concentration and focus. He said he had wanted to stop her, but she was a great student and got great grades, so he said nothing. As I explained to him, if he had made her stop, I would not say she wouldn't have been valedictorian, but he would have made learning more difficult for her.

And that's what this comes down to: if we allow kids to learn in a way that is innate to them, learning will be easier for them. This is why I always caution parents to be careful not to impose their learning styles on their kids. My first year teaching high school, I had finished going through these things the first week of school. Near the end of the week, my phone rang just after the final bell rang. I answered, and before I could say anything beyond hello, a man shouted at me through the phone.

"NO ONE CAN LEARN WHILE LYING ON A BED!"

I said, "But sir...."

"NO, NO, NO! NO ONE CAN LEARN WHILE LYING ON A BED."

"Sir."

"NO!"

It went on like that for a while. I had told his daughter that it was okay to lie on a bed while doing her homework if that helped her focus. When I heard her father's extreme reaction, I knew he was really saying that *he* could not learn while lying on a bed.

As parents and teachers, we need to be very careful about imposing the way we learn on our kids. If we do, we will hinder their ability to learn.

The fourth factor that impacts learning is intake. We intake two things into our bodies that affect our ability to learn: food and water. For some of us, having something to eat and drink helps us focus; for others, it does not. In my class, my students are allowed to eat and drink as long as they clean up after themselves.

The fifth factor that affects learning is peers. For some students, having someone to study with helps them focus, but for others, having someone around keeps them from focusing. Teachers need to realize who these students are, because those who need peers will make their own, which can cause behavioral issues.

The sixth factor that affects learning is the time of day. Unfortunately, you can't really do anything about this because your class is at a particular time, but it's helpful to keep in mind that some kids do their best work in the morning; for some it's the afternoon; and for others, it's in the evening. Your first period class probably has kids who are still half asleep and others who are raring to go. The same is probably true of the last two class periods of the day: some kids are nodding off because they've used up the bulk of their energy, and others are just hitting high gear.

The seventh factor that impacts learning is temperature. This is the least important for most of us, but for the few it matters to, it is by far the most important. Some people are always hot, and some are always cold. These are the people who wear long sleeves in the middle of summer because they just can't get warm enough, even with the air conditioning on full blast, or in the middle of winter, they don't even wear a jacket because the cold doesn't bother them. If there are certain spots in your classroom where the temperature tends to be very warm or cold, let your kids sit where they will feel most comfortable and therefore be more able to learn.

All of these factors matter greatly to the kids you teach. If you take each of these into consideration and adjust the environment of your classroom accordingly, your kids will learn more and do better.

There is another reason why this matters. If you explain that your room is set up to help all of your kids learn, this sends the powerful message that each kid in your class is a unique individual, and you want all of them to learn at their best in a classroom with a supportive environment. What a wonderful message to get kids to work harder for you than they have ever worked for anyone!

Often teachers wonder how you know what kind of learner a particular kid is. There are tons of online surveys that you can have your kids take, but I do something simpler. Before I teach anything about learning styles, I hold up a book and say, "We are going to pretend that in order for you to graduate from this school, you have to read this difficult and complex novel and then take a test. Assuming that is true, describe the perfect place for you to read this book and really learn what it's about, the place where you would have one hundred percent focus. Where is that place? What would be in that place? What would not be there? What would help you focus? What would distract you? Describe this perfect place to learn."

I am always amazed at what they write. Almost every kid mentions lighting, seating, and sound. Kids say things like a hammock at the beach with something to eat but no one around, which includes five of the seven environmental factors we've discussed. Some will say in their bedroom with a single lamp on their bed listening to low music. Some will say sitting in a stuffed chair in a coffeehouse with people around and low background sound. Some even say in a bathroom, in the middle of the night, alone. Kids are always so afraid to admit this one, but in doing so, they're describing the perfect time of day, with no sound, no peers around, and bright light. Some people say in a car, in the middle of the day, with no one around and the AC on. Others will say in a room, completely alone, with no sound, sitting at a desk. The variety of settings is as unique as kids are.

When the kids are done describing their favorite way to learn, I explain all seven environmental factors. It's such a cool thing as a teacher to see the "aha!" moment in your kids' eyes when they realize that the way they want to learn is fine, and they are not alone in being like this!

For you as a teacher, having a deep understanding of learning styles and how to create an atmosphere that's conducive to learning will help your kids learn, make them feel at home in your room, help them accept and understand themselves better, and make your class the cool class that every kid wants to be in.

Our Journey as Teachers

W hen Terry Bradshaw, the four-time Super Bowl-winning quarterback for the Pittsburgh Steelers was inducted into the Hall of Fame, in one part of his speech he talked about how he would give anything to be under center one more time, to take the ball, to drive it down the field, to score the winning touchdown.

I know how he feels.

There is no better feeling than when you're in a classroom, and the kids are following your every word, and you know that through the magic of teaching you've got 'em hooked. It's a kid's laughter, the joy of discovery, the feeling of accomplishment, the explaining of a complex idea, and the revelation of a new thought, the moment when a kid gets it, and they see the world differently.

Being around teenagers means being around kids at a time when everything about them is changing; every part of them is in transition. They are finding themselves, discovering their talents, becoming who they are. If you are open with your kids, you get to play such a huge role in that process. You begin to realize that as much as you are a teacher, you are a mentor, someone to listen, to comfort, and yes, to confront. Part of what you do is to challenge your kids when they need it. But just as often, you need to have your hand out for a hug, a handshake, or to offer help.

Just give me a class, give me a kid to teach and the freedom to run the class, then step back and watch. It's all I want, and nothing in my life feels better.

My twenty-fifth year as a teacher will also be my fifteenth year at PPCHS. A lot has happened. But what I remember most are the kids.

Of the thousands of kids I've taught, I want to share some of what they've given me.

If you ask me to define kindness, I will tell you about the standing ovation an autistic student got at graduation.

"I didn't know I was so popular," he said as he passed by me.

If you ask me about intelligence, I will describe to you the students who stood in front of Harvard-educated lawyers and made such cogent arguments that the lawyers said, "This was better than what we did in law school."

Bring up perseverance and I will introduce you to one of my students who spent two years living in a car; just making it to school every day was a victory. He graduated with honors and went on to college.

Say the word dedication and I will tell you about a kid from Afghanistan who had the luck to be taught in the United States but who dedicated his time to raising money to make life better for people in his home country.

Speak of diversity and I'll show you the group of friends in my law class arguing, disagreeing, fighting, speaking, and then standing up and walking off to lunch together: the blonde girl, the Jewish guy, the Indian kid, the black girl, and the Latino all friends walking off together.

In my time at PPCHS, I have seen goodness in the form of student helping student and student sticking up for student.

Mention creativity and original thinking, and I will point to the kid who took the principles of mathematics and applied them to expressing his understanding of the Enlightenment.

Speak of bravery and I will introduce you to the kid who told me their coming-out story, the first adult they ever told their story to, a kid who trusted me with that information knowing that if it got back to their parents, they would be shut out and shut off. I have heard about other kids whose parents did throw them out of their house and of the kindness of their friends and their friends' families who took them in.

I've seen kids crushed by bullying, torn by abuse, destroyed by a future they did not know how to make, and yet they kept trying, kept pushing forward, no matter the burden they had to bear.

I've seen kids enter high school uncertain, never the star of anything, just a kid in class, loaded down with learning difficulties, labeled as "one of those kids." One student in particular always told me, "Mr. Quigley, I'm going to make it big." Through four years, I checked in with him as he struggled, barely passing his classes, and he always smiled and renewed his promise that he would make it big. Several years after he graduated, I got a large envelope in the mail with a letter inside and a poster of a drag-race car. The letter explained how the student had just been named a mechanic on one of the top drag-race teams in the world. On the poster was his signature and the words "I made it big."

And then one day there was a knock on my door, and there stood a former student in full dress Marine blues. I barely recognized the face of the boy I knew as he saluted me and handed me a picture of him graduating from boot camp. I invited him in and got the story of his life. He told me about the night when he was walking point, it was raining, and he glanced down and saw himself reflected in a puddle of water, his body hardened from weeks of training, in uniform, and he gulped and thought, *I really did it.* And then he thanked me for helping him become the man he had seen in that reflection.

I will never forget the kids who come back to tell me their stories, so many of success, some of failure, but the ones that make me happiest are the ones of redemption, of kids finding themselves, of failing and getting back up, of mistakes made and lessons learned: the kid who got into drugs but made it out; the student arrested in college for making fake IDs who had just finished his graduate degree; the young men and women who left PPCHS to become nurses and doctors but also chefs and police officers.

The kids I teach are from fourteen to eighteen years of age, but some of them have been burdened and beaten down by life. They have had to endure things that would break the strongest adult, and yet they persevere — kids who walked across the stage at graduation who had no business even getting that far; the kid who suffered years of awful physical abuse; the girl with cancer who everyone said wouldn't make it; the boy who lost his mom and nearly lost himself but found a path forward.

I have seen my share of anger. I will never forget during my first week at PPCHS, one of my students came into class looking like he was ready to explode. When you have taught as long as I have, you learn the signs of someone going through something, and I could see he was dealing with something major. The rest of the class had begun whatever opening work I had on the board, everyone, that is, but him, so I quietly walked over and asked him to get to work. He didn't. I again walked over, tapped on his desk, and whispered for him to get to work. After five more minutes, he still had done nothing. So I approached him again, and he flipped the desk over and walked out of the room saying, "Fuck this."

Now, if I had been a younger less experienced teacher, I would have taken this personally and reacted with anger, but instead I quietly wrote the student up, knowing that whatever just happened had nothing to do with me or the class. Later I learned that his parents had thrown him out of their house because he had come home several hours after curfew, so he had slept in his car. That day, when he had gotten to school, his girlfriend had broken up with him. In the class before mine, he had a major assignment due, which of course he hadn't done because he had stayed out late then spent the night in his car. So my asking him to get to work was the tipping point of a really bad day.

I have watched kids get beaten down by life, succumb to drugs and drinking or sexual promiscuity and failure; seen kids led astray by bad influences, and allowing themselves to fail. These were good kids who lost their way despite the adults in their lives reaching out to help them. I have seen others go down this same path, stumble and fall, and figure it out. I think of one kid who became addicted to painkillers and failed out of school, letting his parents, his teachers, his friends, and worse, himself down. I have seen that kid make something of his life and become the kid anyone would be proud of.

I have had the greatest luck to teach great kids. I will never forget two classes in particular, one that I became so close to that they created a religion based around me called Quigleism. This actually says more about them than me, as I am far from anyone's idea of a deity. Instead, it shows how creative and original these kids were. They created an entire history of the religion, how it started and evolved. They went so far as to write a Wikipedia page about it, though rightly, the website rejected it.

Another class I taught was a group of seniors who were the perfect balance any teacher would desire: funny, thoughtful, silly, creative, hard-working, and willing to do whatever I placed in front of them. The seniors at PPCHS finish several weeks before the underclassmen. So it was with shock that a week after the seniors had graduated, nearly the entire class showed up in my room at their regular class time just to spend the period with me reminiscing and laughing and talking about their future. The only thing more surprising was that they did the same thing for the next two weeks.

I remember the young lady who I could do no wrong with. She loved me. She loved the class. She loved the atmosphere. She responded to me and to my personality. But she didn't do the work to the level she was capable of. So as the end of the year approached, I could not in good conscience recommend her for the highest course she could take as a junior, which was a college level Advanced Placement course. When I informed her of this, she stopped speaking to me and refused the rest of the year to say a word to me.

I had another student a few years later who I also could not recommend for the same AP class. She told me that she would show me. And she did. Nearly a year later she brought in her report card and showed me an A in the AP class. From then on, when I had to tell a student I could not recommend them, I would say, "If you decide you want the class anyway, your parents can get you in, and I hope a year from now you come back and put it in my face."

I had another student who did beautiful work and got straight As in my class, who turned in a project and I gave her a B for it. She asked me why, and I told her it was because it was not as good as she was capable of. She looked at me shocked and took the grade. At the end of the year, she told me how grateful she was that I had said that because I was right; she so often skated by on good enough when she was capable of so much more.

I have failed kids, kids who I couldn't get to open up, kids who no matter how hard I tried or what I tried I couldn't reach them. It would tear me up, day after day to see a kid not work, not care, not succeed, and to know that no matter how hard I taught or how much I cared, I couldn't help them. Every hour of every day that they were my students, I was drenched in that failure, and it humbled me.

Then there was the kid who came into my class and worked harder for me than for any other teacher. I would sit in conferences where the parent wanted to meet with all of their kid's teachers, and listened to teacher after teacher talk about a kid I didn't recognize. Troublemaker? Lazy? Failing? Disrespectful? Didn't turn in work? Missed class? None of that was my experience with this kid!

I'll never forget an all-night field trip. I was just starting to fall asleep when a kid interrupted me and told me he had just found out, at age eighteen, that he was going to be a dad. For the four-hour drive, through the middle of the night and early morning, I talked to this young man about his fears of having a child and whether he could be the kind of man and dad he wanted to be.

I had a kid who from the first day of my law class made it clear he could not and would not be able to speak in class. My law class was based on student discussion, and throughout the year, he did not speak; in fact, he did not even make eye contact. This is a common behavior of many high functioning autistic students. As we approached the end of the year, students would have their most challenging activity. Working in pairs students had to take an existing Supreme Court case, research it and all its precedents, create a ten-minute legal argument, give this speech as a team, and then have twenty minutes of a mock Supreme Court.

From the outset, the student said he would not give the speech. He did the research, he wrote the speech, but he insisted that his partner would give the speech and answer the questions. On the day of his competition, his partner did not show up, so he had to give the speech and answer the questions afterward. Never was I more proud than when he stood up, gave a brilliant speech, and answered every question. It was one of the best things I have ever been a part of. I remember literally shaking with excitement in the ESE director's office, pacing and recounting what he had done. A few years later, that kid entered law school.

I have sat at the funeral home for the memorial service of a student, one of the nicest, happiest, sweetest kids I've ever met, a true decent and kind gentleman, whose life ended way too soon. He had done nothing wrong but drive his new car a little too fast. I can only feel the loss of what could have been with a life destined for so much possibility.

I have had the experience of two of my students getting caught putting swastikas on walls in the school. One was because he liked the way they looked and had no idea what they meant. The other kid, when asked why he did it, said, "Fuck them all." I don't think he even knew who he was referring to, and I have had kids like that, kids whose issues are far deeper, darker, and more terrible than any teacher can reach. These are the kids I hope and pray somehow get the help they desperately need.

I have a commemorative coin from the Tower to Tunnel Run in Chicago that was given to me by a student I had spent a lot of time talking to, mentoring, guiding, helping, and just being there for him whenever he needed someone to listen. So much of the job of teaching is not stuff that is contained in a book or the things you teach from the curriculum; it's what happens when you extend your hand and heart to a child and let them know you are there for them. And so I was for this boy, watching him go from this shy child, who admitted to me his biggest fear was that no girl would ever want him, to become a proud graduate who went off to college in Chicago. He came back to see me after his sophomore year and presented me with the commemorative coin he was given when he finished the race.

He told me, "When I felt like quitting, I just kept remembering what you always told me to do, and I kept going." It is one of my prized possessions, and when I look at it, I remember to never give up on a kid.

If I could pick one kid from my time at PPCHS that represents what I have tried to accomplish as a teacher, it would be Chris. Chris was not my strongest student or my best, but he was a hard-working good kid. I had had Chris as a junior in law and a year later as a senior in AP Government. The year was going on as years do. He was the kind of kid I loved goofing with because he could take a joke, and he often had a great comeback.

In late December, I got an email from Chris that he wasn't going to be in class because he had been in a car accident. It wasn't anything serious, a little concussion, but over the weekend he had not been feeling right, so he was going in for an MRI.

The next day, I got another email. They had found something in the MRI, a dark mass that the doctors were so alarmed about that they were going to do emergency surgery. I was very concerned and sent him a pic of Mr. Quigley (the monkey) to let him know we were thinking of him.

As homeroom began, my closest friend on staff came running into the room. She said that Chris had been trying to call me. He wanted and needed to talk to me before he went into surgery. She handed me the phone. I took the phone and went outside of my classroom to talk to him.

What was I supposed to say to this kid? I am no parent. I am no counselor. In my mind, two things directed me. First, it was likely that he knew the worst of what could happen, and he had lots of people telling him how fine he would be, that this was nothing. So I decided I was just going to tell him the truth: this was going to be hard, it was going to be long, but I knew that he would make it, and he had lots and lots of people who loved him, and lots and lots of experts who would give him the best care. And besides, I told him, all of this was messing with him getting ready for my AP class; this missing of class time was clearly unacceptable. The other thing I knew was that this kid wanted to hear my voice for some reason, so I just talked to him and let him know I was with him in this ordeal.

I stood there with my head against the wall trying not to cry as my best friend Carrie tried to comfort me.

Those moments with Chris tell you everything I believe about teaching. You can teach kids and legitimately call yourself a teacher in the barebones sense of the word. Or you can teach them AND be there for them when they need support. That conversation was hard, but I am glad that I was there for him before the most significant moment of his entire young life. It meant I had done my job.

As of this writing, Chris is fine and will be headed off to college soon.

Most of all, at PPCHS I have had the luck to know hundreds and hundreds of kids. I have known their stories, their fears, and their hopes. I have laughed with them and cried with them. I have sat for hours and heard the good, the bad, and the ugly of life but also the joyful, the hopeful, and the plans and futures they were just starting to make real. For most of these kids, I don't know where life has taken them, or if they've gotten from this world all they hoped for. But I feel incredibly lucky that for a few special moments, I got to walk with them.

In each student's yearbook, I always write two things. The first is the Gene Roddenberry quote on the opening page of this book; the second is the Stephen King quote. I hope that both great writers would be okay with how I use and even slightly change their words.

Here is how I conclude whatever else I write:

I feel thankful that I have gotten to walk with you for a few moments on your journey to become the person you were meant to be. As you journey on, just remember:

Be true.

Be brave.

Seek love.

STAND!

All the rest is darkness.

And, in the end, it is still true that teaching was never a journey I expected to take. When I started down this road, I never could have imagined the mistakes, the joys, the triumphs, the failures, and the rewards of my life's work.

I know that excellence is possible even if I have yet to get there.

And I know it can be yours too.

Yes, it's hard, it takes work, sacrifice, and dedication, but we can make it.

I hope when I reach it, I'll see you there. Till then, I gotta get to work. It's a long path, and I have miles to go before I am done.

Blessings on your journey!

About the Author

When he is not hanging around with his plush monkey collection or screaming his head off for his beloved Miami Hurricanes, William Quigley, or Liam to his friends, loves traveling, visiting art galleries, hiking, camping, and being in nature. He has a particular fondness for photography, and when he's done shooting images of the beauty of the world, he makes his photos available on his website, www.quigleyphotography.zenfolio.com. His classroom is where he finds his true calling, fulfilling the purpose of his life: the dedication to the art and craft of teaching and making the impact he can make on kids' lives. Since 1992, at five different schools, in three South Florida counties and at all levels from fifth through twelfth grade, he has been on a journey which he shares with you here, in his first published book, *Joy Bliss This*.

The author will donate 10 percent of the sale of each copy of this book to a general fund that he established at his school to help students pursue their passions.

If you enjoyed reading this book and believe that it has positively impacted your life and inspired you to reach the goal of excellence in your career — whether teaching or any other walk in life — the author and I would be very appreciative of a great review on Amazon.

Thank you so much. ☺

Janet Angelo
Editor and Publisher
IndieGo Publishing

Think Indie. Go Create. Publish.
www.indiegopublishing.com

Made in the USA
Columbia, SC
20 May 2020